Forecasting High-Frequency Volatility Shocks

Holger Kömm

Forecasting High-Frequency Volatility Shocks

An Analytical Real-Time Monitoring System

Springer Gabler

Holger Kömm
Ingolstadt, Germany

Catholic University Eichstätt-Ingolstadt, 2015

First Supervisor: Prof. Dr. Küsters
Second Supervisor: Prof. Dr. Wilde
Date of disputation: April 29th, 2015

ISBN 978-3-658-12595-0 ISBN 978-3-658-12596-7 (eBook)
DOI 10.1007/978-3-658-12596-7

Library of Congress Control Number: 2015960928

Springer Gabler

Printed on acid-free paper

Springer Gabler is a brand of Springer Fachmedien Wiesbaden
Springer Fachmedien Wiesbaden is part of Springer Science+Business Media
(www.springer.com)

Dedicated to my parents
and my priceless wife

Abstract

The effect of public observable but unexpected incidents on financial market volatility is of primary interest, both for tradespeople willing to take a risk as well as for risk regulators, willing to bypass potential imponderables. Therefore, this thesis presents a new strategy that unites qualitative and quantitative mass data in form of text news and tick-by-tick asset prices to forecast the risk of upcoming shocks. The proposed strategy is embedded in a monitoring system, using

1. a sequence of competing estimators to compute the unobservable volatility,
2. a new two-state Markov switching mixture model for autoregressive and zero-inflated time-series to identify structural breaks in a latent data generation process and
3. a selection of competing pattern recognition algorithms to classify the potential information embedded in unexpected, but public observable text data in shock and non-shock information.

The monitor is trained, tested, and evaluated on a two year survey on the prime standard assets listed in the indices DAX, MDAX, SDAX and TecDAX.

Acknowledgements

It is a genuine pleasure to express my deep sense of thanks and gratitude to my mentor and guide, Prof. Ulrich Küsters, holder of the Chair of Statistics and Quantitative Methods at the Department of Economics & Business, Catholic University Eichstätt-Ingolstadt. His dedication and keen interest above all his overwhelming attitude to help his students had been solely and mainly responsible for completing my work. His timely advise, meticulous scrutiny, scholarly advice and scientific approach have helped me to a very great extent to accomplish this task.

I owe further a deep sense of gratitude to Janko Thyson, Jan Speckenbach, Ekaterina Nieberle (formerly Kokotchikova), Alexander März, and Alexandar Pramov for their keen interest on me at every stage of my research. Their prompt inspirations, timely suggestions with kindness, enthusiasm and dynamism have enabled me to complete my thesis.

Herzogenaurach, 2015
Holger Kömm

Contents

List of Figures

List of Tables

Abbreviations

AIC	Akaike Information Criteria
AICc	Corrected Akaike Information Criteria
API	Application Programming Interface
ARCH	Autoregressive Conditional Heteroscedasticity
ARIMA	Autoregressive Integrated Moving Average
AUC	Area Under Curve
a.m.	Forenoon (ante meridiem, *Latin*)
a.s.	Almost surely
BaFin	Federal Financial Supervisory Authority (Bundesanstalt für Finanzdienstleistungsaufsicht, *German*)
BGG	Bagging
BIC	Bayesian Information Criteria
BOO	Boosting
BPV	Bipower Variation
Càdlàg	Right continuous with left limits (Continue à droite, limite à gauche, *French*)
CQV	Conditional Quadratic Variation
CRAN	Comprehensive R Archive Network
C++	ISO Normed Programming Language
DAX	German Large-Cap Stock Index (Deutscher Aktien Index, *German*)
DGAP	German Society for ad-hoc-publicity (Deutsche Gesellschaft für Ad-hoc-Publizität mbH, *German*)
DGP	Data Generation Process

DOW	Dow Jones Industrial Average
DT	Decision Tree
etc.	And so forth (et cetera, *Latin*)
FN	False Negative
FP	False Positive
FSE	Frankfurt Stock Exchange
FWER	Family-wise Error Rate
GARCH	Generalized Autoregressive Conditional Heteroscedasticity
GMT	Greenwich Mean Time
HQC	Hannan-Quinn Information Criteria
ISIN	International Securities Identification Number
ISO	International Organization for Standardization
IV	Integrated Volatility
i.i.d.	Independent and identically distributed
k-NN	k-Nearest Neighbours
LDA	Linear Discriminant Analysis
LRZ	Leibniz Supercomputing Centre (Leibniz Rechenzentrum, *German*)
MDAX	Mid-Cap-DAX, non-technology sectors
ML	Maximum Likelihood
MNR	Multinomial Regression
MSE	Mean Squared Error
NN	Neural Network
OHLC	Open, High, Low, Close
OLS	Ordinary Least Squares
OTC	Over The Counter

PCA	Principal Component Analysis
POSIX	Portable Operation System Interface
p.m.	Afternoon (post meridiem, *Latin*)
QV	Quadratic Variation
R	The R Project for Statistical Computing
RF	Random Forest
RMNR	Regularized Multinomial Regression
ROC	Receiver Operating Characteristic
RTSRV	Robust Two-Time-Scales Realized Volatility
RV	Realized Volatility
SDAX	Small-Cap-DAX, non-technology sectors
SLDA	Stabilized Linear Discriminant Analysis
SV	Stochastic Volatility
SVD	Singular Value Decomposition
SVM	Support Vector Machine
TecDAX	Mid-Cap-DAX, technology sector
TML	Truncated Maximum Likelihood
TN	True Negative
TP	True Positive
TSRV	Two-Time-Scales Realized Volatility
UTC	Universal Time Coordinated
vs.	Against (versus, *Latin*)
WpHG	Securities trading act (Wertpapierhandelsgesetz, *German*)
XML	Extensible Markup Language

Symbols

$\xrightarrow{D}$	Convergence in distribution
$\xrightarrow{P}$	Convergence in probability
a_{ij}	Term i of document j in the term-document-matrix A
A	Term-document-matrix A
A^c	The complementary set of a set A, that is $\Omega \backslash A$
$\mathcal{A}$	A σ-algebra, that is a set of countable subsets of Ω
α	Significance level of the applied Wald test
α_i	Non-negative vector of parameters
B	Ensemble of base classifiers B_m building the boosting algorithm
B_m	Base classifiers $B_1, \dots, B_m$ of the boosting algorithm
B_t	Brownian motion or Wiener process
β	(1) Factor declaring volatility clusters, or (2) factor declaring the importance of recall and precision in the F-measure
c	Constant in the Markov switching mixture model with c the pre-incident and c^* the post-incident measure
C	Part of the Walsh test statistic
C_α	Critical values of Grubbs' two-sided test
χ^2_r	Chi-squared distribution with r degrees of freedom
$df(i)$	Number of documents in which term i occurs
δ	Vector of restricted parameters to test for volatility shocks
Δ	Sampling frequency, $1/\Delta$ gives the number of observations
Δ_i	Parameter to test for outliers in Grubbs' outlier test
$E(X)$	Expectation value of the random variable X

ε_i	Vector of error term considering window i
ε_t	(1) Stochastic process of error terms which are return residuals with respect to the mean process $x_t\beta$, or (2) microstructure noise process
$\varepsilon_{t,i}$	Observation i in period t of the microstructure noise process ε_t
$\widehat{\text{error}}_i$	Estimated error of fold i in a cross-validation setting
η_t	First difference of the stochastic process of microstructure noise
$\eta_{t,i}$	First difference of the noise process $\varepsilon_{t,i}$
$f_{i,\Delta}$	Interday periodicity factor of window i using data sampled at frequency Δ
f_i^{wn}	For the purpose of outlier correction weighted variant of the non-parametric interday periodicity estimator
F_{n-r}	Empirical distribution of the sample of size n minus the r lowest or highest observations
$gf(i)$	Total number of term i occurrences
$g_l(i)$	Global weighting function g_l for $l = 1, \ldots, 4$ where i gives the term in the term-document-matrix
G	Test statistic of the two-sided Grubbs test
$\mathcal{G}$	Full grid
$\mathcal{G}^{(k)}$	Sub-grid k of the full grid $\mathcal{G}$
h_i	Hypotheses i applied on incident r_{ij} to predict the label of the supervised learning algorithm
h_t	Stochastic process describing the variance of y_t by the error terms ε_t
i	Observation index in different uses
I	Indicator function returning the value 0 or 1
I_t	Information set available at time t
$\mathcal{I}(\vartheta)$	Fisher-information-matrix of the vector of parameters ϑ
J	Total number of sub-grids of the fast time scale $\mathcal{G}^{(j)}$
J_t	Jump intensity of a finite counting Poisson process

k	(1) Grid index, (2) number of parameters in a model, (3) corresponding class $k \in K$ in a classification context, or (4) the number of folds used for cross-validation
K	(1) Total number of sub-grids of the slow time scale $\mathcal{G}^{(k)}$, (2) total number of restricted parameters in the Markov switching mixture model, or (3) number of classes in a classification context
K_1	Number of parameters, restricted by the logit transformation
K_2	Number of parameters, restricted by the inequality transformation
κ_t	Jump size in the jump-diffusion-process
l	Number of labels in a classification
$l_k(i,j)$	Local weighting function l_k for $k = 1,2,3$ where i gives the term and j the document in the term-document-matrix
λ	Test statistic of the likelihood-ratio-test
$\lambda(t)$	Intensity function of the jump process J_t
ℓ_{ij}	Log-likelihoods for $i,j \in \{0,1\}$, corresponding to the four transition states of the Markov switching mixture model
L	Loss function used to evaluate the costs of wrong predictions
L_R	Likelihood value of the restricted model
L_U	Likelihood value of the unrestricted model
m	(1) Number of iterations, (2) number of hypothesis in the Bonferroni correction, or (3) grade of dependency in a TSRV setting
m_i	Bootstrap prediction for $i = 1,\dots,B$, with B the number of samples of size n
μ	Unconditional mean
n	Sample size and number of observations
n'	Reduced sample size
n_i	Total number of observations within fold i
n_k	Integer to find the last element in sub-grid $\mathcal{G}^{(k)}$

n_t	Total number of observations in period t
$\bar{n}_K$	Average number of elements over all sub-grids $\mathcal{G}^{(k)}$
M	Number of elements in a sample
N_i	Index set of indices, that belong to the identical time as index i
$\mathbb{N}$	Index set natural numbers, $\mathbb{N}_0$ includes the 0
∇	(1) First difference operator, or (2) gradient of the absolute continuous differentiable function $h(\cdot)$
$N(\mu, \sigma^2)$	Normal distribution with expectation value μ and variance σ^2
ν	Random variable declaring the shocks, usually assumed to be i.i.d.
ω	Constant in a regression model
ω_{01}	Transition probability of the Markov switching mixture model to change from state zero in a non-zero state with ω_{01} the pre-incident and ω_{01}^* the post-incident measure
ω_{11}	Transition probability of the Markov switching mixture model to remain in a non-zero state with ω_{11} the pre-incident and ω_{11}^* the post-incident measure
ω_{i1}	Either ω_{01} or ω_{11}
Ω	Set of all possible outcomes of a random experiment
$p(i,j)$	Ratio of term i occurring in document j to the overall frequency of term i
P	Function assigning events to probabilities
P_ϑ	Population of probability distributions, depending on the unknown parameter vector ϑ
Φ	Density of a normal distribution
ψ_t	Information set available at time t
r	The return process
r_i	Returns within window i
r_{ij}	Incident j in fold i

$\bar{r}_i$	Standardized high-frequency returns r_i
$r_{t,\Delta}$	Discrete with period Δ sampled returns
$r_{t,i}$	First difference of the observed log price $Y_{t,i}$
$r^*_{t,i}$	First difference of the true log price $X_{t,i}$
$\mathbb{R}$	Index set of real numbers, $\mathbb{R}_+$ denotes the positive sub-set of $\mathbb{R}$
R_i	Rank of the ordered differences in the Wilcoxon sign rank test
$\hat{R}_{CV}$	Estimated k-fold cross-validation error
$R(\vartheta)$	Restriction function of ϑ
ρ	Autocorrelation of order one in the Markov switching mixture model
s, t, u	Time indexes in different uses
s_i	Periodically adjusted volatility estimate of the returns r_i
s_{ij}	True label of incident j which is element of fold i
S	Set of labels
S'	Set of potential predictions in form of labels
S_t	Stochastic process of the asset prices
$S_{t,i}$	Observation i in period t of the stochastic process of the asset prices S_t
σ	Sample standard deviation
σ^2	Natural variation and variance in the Markov switching mixture model
$\sigma^2_{x_1-x_2}$	Variance of the difference of the cross-validation errors of supervised learning algorithm 1 with the corresponding errors of algorithm 2
σ_i	Integrated volatility of window i
σ_t	Non-negative stochastic process
Σ^{-1}_{ϑ}	Inverse of the asymptotic non-singular variance-covariance matrix of the maximum likelihood estimation
$tf(i,j)$	Term frequency of term i in document j

T_1	Test statistic of the one-sided Grubbs test to test for the lowest observation
T_n	Test statistic of the one-sided Grubbs test to test for the highest observation
t_{paired}	Test statistic of the dependent t-test for paired samples
T_α	Critical values of the one-sided Grubbs test
$t_{\alpha;n}$	α quantile of the t-distribution with n degrees of freedom
τ	Truncation parameter in the Markov switching mixture model with τ the pre-incident and τ^* the post-incident measure
θ	Parameter vector
ϑ	Vector of estimates in the multivariate δ-method with ϑ the pre-incident and ϑ^* the post-incident measure
ϑ_0	Theoretical post-incident Wald test vector
ϑ_i	Restricted parameter, this can be any one of the parameters in the Markov switching mixture model
w_{ij}	Term i of document j in the weighted term-document-matrix A
W_0	Wald test statistic
W_1	Applied Wald test statistic
W_+	Test statistic of positive differences in the Wilcoxon sign rank test
W_-	Test statistic of negative differences in the Wilcoxon sign rank test
W	Test statistic of the Wilcoxon sign rank test
W_{min}	Test statistic of the one-sided Walsh test to test for the lowest observations
W_{max}	Test statistic of the one-sided Walsh test to test for the highest observations
x_i	(1) Sample observation i, (2) vector of variables considering window i, or (3) cross-validation errors of supervised algorithms i
$\overline{x}$	Arithmetic mean of the sample

$x_{1,i}$	Cross-validation errors of supervised learning algorithm 1
$x_{2,i}$	Cross-validation errors of supervised learning algorithm 2
$\bar{x}_1$	Mean of x_1
$\bar{x}_2$	Mean of x_2
X_i	Input layer $X_1, \dots, X_p$ in a neutral network
X_t	Logarithm of the stochastic process of the asset prices S_t
$X_{t,i}$	Observation i in period t of the stochastic process of the logarithmic asset prices X_t
x_t	Stochastic process, used to declare the mean of y_t by $x_t\beta$
$[X, X]$	Quadratic variation of the latent true process $X_t = \log S_t$ without microstructure noise
$\langle X, X \rangle$	Conditional quadratic variation or integrated volatility of the latent true process $X_t = \log S_t$ without microstructure noise
Y_i	Output layer $Y_1, \dots, Y_k$ in a neutral network
Y_t	Stochastic process of the observed asset prices
$Y_{t,i}$	Observation i in period t of the observed asset prices
$[Y, Y]$	Quadratic variation of the observed process $Y_t = X_t + \varepsilon_t$ including microstructure noise
y_t	Stochastic process to be explained
z	Continuity corrected and z-score transformed normal approximation of the Wilcoxon test statistic W
$z_{1-\alpha}$	1-α quantile of the standard normal distribution
Z_i	Hidden layer $Z_1, \dots, Z_m$ in a neutral network
z_t	Stochastic process assumed to be i.i.d. with zero mean and unit variance, or first difference of the estimated integrated volatility, that is $z_t = \nabla\widehat{IV}_t$
z_t^*	Latent value of the first difference of the estimated integrated volatility, reported as observable if z_t^* is inside $[-\tau, \tau]$, and reported as zero if z_t^* is outside $[-\tau, \tau]$

1 Introduction

The principle of forecasting is to extrapolate identified structure to the future. Hence, the process of forecasting starts with the identification and splitting of the latent process structure from the remaining random variation. The extrapolation of the identified process structure to the future gives the subsequent forecast, where the random variation gives the uncertainty of the forecast.

This fundamental approach of forecasting is usually based on the analysis of time series, or generally speaking on the exclusive analysis of quantitative data in form of numbers. The sole use of quantitative data, however, lacks the ability to uncover fundamental changes caused by qualitative information conveyed in text form. This thesis proposes a framework to forecast the potential of shocks in high-frequency volatility estimates. Shocks, that need not to have been observed in prior time series under analysis, but that have been observed in at least one other time series under consideration. For this purpose, this thesis unites elements of quantitative time series forecasting with elements of qualitative text prediction.

The following introduction to the thesis is structured as follows: Section 1.1 motivates the thesis by illuminating historical events and initiates the demand for shock forecasting systems. Section 1.2 considers the economic relevance of the proposed monitoring system. In contrast, Section 1.3 considers the scientific relevance of the applied theories. Section 1.4 carves out the gap to present literature. Finally, Section 1.5 reflects upon the content.

1.1 Motivation

> *"The advantage of knowing about risk is that we can change our behaviour to avoid them."*[1]

Substituting the term *risk* with *volatility* tailors this central statement of Engle to a more concrete terminology in finance.

At the beginning of the 1990s most financial market players preferred the concept of volatility to be a concept of an established risk measure and therefore an ingredient of risk controlling. But in the mid 1990s, a new asset class appeared and volatility suddenly became much more than a univariate risk measure. Volatility evolved to an asset class, tradeable, and at any time available. This

1 Excerpt from the commemorative speech of Robert Engle on the Nobel prize ceremony on December 8th, 2003, see Engle (2004, p.405).

is the asset class of volatility swaps, which is a forward contract on the future volatility where the underlying asset as well as the details on the estimation of the latent volatility of the asset are regulated in the contract, e. g. Demeterfi et al. (1999).

With the beginning of the millennia, further advancements in volatility swap theory emerged with the new class of volatility derivatives, see e. g. Carr and Lee (2009). First proceedings in semantic analysis in combination with volatility derivatives and machine readable economic news emerged further to new high frequency trading strategies. Trading platforms accelerated the development with new, user-friendly products and simplified the access to this new, technically complex industry. A famous example of the trading platforms is AlphaFlash®, the ultra-fast Algo-News provider developed and distributed by the German Stock Exchange, see Petring and Bayer (September 9th, 2011).

The beginning of the financial crisis in 2007/2008, however, changed the public awareness about financial markets and algorithmic high frequency trading and formed the new willing to narrow the risk of uncontrollable market destabilizations, e. g. initiated by misplaced rating reviews and unconfirmed and disadvantageous news.

The consequences of disadvantageous news is exemplarily illuminated in Section 1.2. The connection of asset returns to the corresponding volatility estimates is illustrated in Figure 1.1 on the next page. Please note, that the object under analysis are the volatility estimates as illustrated in Figure 1.1b, where the volatility is exemplarily estimated by the area adjusted TSRV estimator, which is discussed in Section 3.2.5.

1.2 Economic Relevance

The economic relevance of information is illustrated by two scenarios of disadvantageous news:

The first scenario demonstrates the potential consequences of publishing new ratings: Rather than delivering a sustained assessment of the market, the rating agencies tightened the Euro crisis with their painful, unsolicited, and not approved "opinions". In consequence, the European Commission obligated the rating agencies thereupon to publish yearly three official news publishing days for each of the rated EU countries. News about ratings as well as changes in ratings should in future be exclusively published during the official publishing days, see Eder (January 17th, 2013).

The second scenario demonstrates the potential consequences of misplaced news: This example is based on an event from April 23rd, 2013. On this day unknown hackers gained unauthorized access to the Twitter account of Associated Press. The hackers released the hoax of a bomb explosion in the White

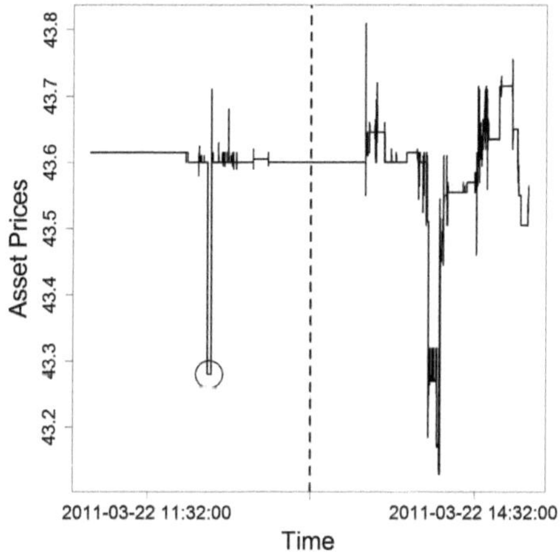

(a) Bid quotes of Biotest AG

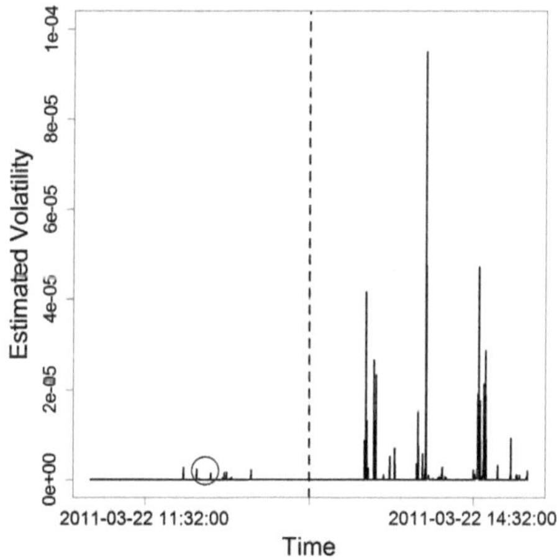

(b) Estimated volatility of Biotest AG

Figure 1.1: Asset prices and corresponding volatility estimates of Biotest AG on March 22nd, 2011. The vertical line through both plots marks 1:02:00 p.m. GMT. At that time, an ad-hoc disclosure (to be discussed in Section 5.2.1) about a growth in sales of Biotest was published on dpa-AFX. The plots show the bid asset prices (Figure 1.1a, to be discussed in Section 2.3.2) of Biotest as well as the corresponding volatility estimates (Figure 1.1b, to be discussed in Section 3.2) two hours before as well as two hours after the ad-hoc disclosure. The circle shows that a significant but single price change in the underlying asset is estimated with a negligible response in volatility. Sequences of non-zero price changes, however, induce significant estimates in volatility. This is the case on the right side of the vertical line.

House, USA on Twitter. Within the following minute the Dow Jones Industrial Average (DOW) lost about 1% as a reaction to the news, see Dowideit and Ertinger (April 24th, 2013). The automatic processing of textual news in combination with algorithmic high-frequency trading surely holds a share of the blame of this excessive response.

Both examples demonstrate the danger of the methodological and analytical eclecticism common in financial markets, and the associated influence of few press articles on the stock markets volatility. It generally applies, that applications of high-frequency forecasts depend considerably on shocks triggered by unexpected text news. Risk regulators and tradespeople interested in high-frequency volatility forecasts should therefore account for unexpected text news to forecast potential fluctuations, given the fluctuations are in a forecastable way. The forecastability of volatility, however, varies with the forecast horizon, see Christoffersen and Diebold (2000). What is forecastable on one-minute intervals is not necessarily forecastable on daily intervals.

The proposed engineering approach in this thesis is to forecast the potential of shocks in real-time, or near real-time. The forecast horizons are minutes and hours, but not days. In the following, the used data granularity is tick-data of assets, which is discussed in Section 2.3.1, and unexpected text news about these assets, which is discussed in Section 5.1.1. The forecast is a binary decision about the expectation of a shock within the forecast horizon of two hours. Note, that in this thesis, a shock is understood as a structural change, not as a single jump. Hence, a shock is a sequence of jumps rather than a single jump in a pre-defined time window.

The field of applications surrounds two background scenarios. Both scenarios differ in respect to (1) the actors involved, (2) the actors risk profiles, (3) the decision processes, and (4) the decision consequences:

A. The first scenario is the trading application: The actor, hereinafter referred to as trader, is in the position to invest, holding actually no position in the considered asset. The trader is willing to take risk and the decision process is mainly build on the error of falsely forecasting a volatility shock. The consequence is, that the trader tries to be very confident in the investment decision to bet on an upcoming volatility shock. The hereinafter proposed engineering approach provides the monitor to signal the trader with individual confidence potential shocks in the volatility of each monitored asset. The higher the confidence the less shocks will be forecasted.

B. The second scenario is the risk-managing application: The actor, hereinafter referred to as risk-controller, is in the position to control an already existing investment. The risk-controller is interested in hedging the potential risk of upcoming volatility shocks. Therefore, the decision process is mainly built on the error of missing to forecast a volatility shock. The consequence is, that the risk-manager tries to hedge as many volatility shocks as possible. The forecast of potential shocks gives the risk-controller the opportunity to hedge the position before the shock will cause given contractual obligations. This case holds, the higher the confidence the more shocks will be forecasted.

1.3 Scientific Relevance

The scientific relevance results directly from the economic relevance to engineer a monitor to model and to forecast the risk of high-frequency volatility shocks. A corresponding approach to engineer the required monitor has not been exhaustively investigated yet. The gap between the current literature on volatility forecasting and high-frequency forecasting is discussed in Section 1.4.

Tools to account for forecasting approaches are common in time series analysis. The list of established techniques includes alongside naive models also sophisticated models such as exponential smoothing, ARIMA models and the computing intensive neural networks. More modern developments provide even further tools, e. g. the forecast of wavelet transformations.

However, all of these tools have in common that the forecast is only based on the extrapolation of the estimated model. Classical time series models have hence less power to forecast the effect of rare events causing a shock in the observed series and thereby a structural break in the underlying data generation process (DGP). Real-time investigations of the latent process volatility, however, make it necessary to investigate structural breaks in high-frequent DGPs.

Unfortunately, in this case a clear clarification of the terminologies "high-frequency" and "ultra-high-frequency" is missing. The hereinafter used logic is high-frequency, whenever the time granularity is in minutes, and ultra-high-frequency, whenever the time granularity is in seconds and milliseconds.

The scientific challenge of real-time high-frequency volatility shock forecasts is, to engineer an approach that combines the information embedded in quantitative ultra-high-frequency data with the information embedded in qualitative text data. The dimension of the quantitative data is up to some millions of transactions per asset and month. The dimension of the qualitative data is some hundred words per news with a few news per asset and month.

Please note, that adding a jump component to the theoretical DGP will condition the jump component to the DGP in distribution. In contrast, the hereinafter proposed engineering approach is designed to condition on exogenous information using additional qualitative information.

1.4 Literature Gap

The central gap is the hitherto (except the here presented engineering approach) non-existing system to monitor the risk of upcoming high-frequency volatility shocks. The gap to the current literature is, beside this central aspect, threefold and thematically subject to

1. volatility estimators,
2. zero-inflation models, and
3. algorithmic text forecasting.

The first gap is addressed to volatility estimators, which is discussed in Section 3.2. A core topic of volatility estimation is the initial selection of the most appropriate estimator. The systematic analysis of the effects of the considered estimators in this monitoring approach can make a decisive contribution to this field.

Furthermore, the sampling scheme, which is discussed in Section 2.3.2, is of direct importance for volatility estimates and noise. The effects of noise are omnipresent in financial markets and not negligible, see e. g. Black (1986). The systematic analysis of the effects of the different volatility estimators is therefore also an analysis of the effects of noise on volatility estimates.

The second gap is addressed to zero-inflated models. A considerable part of the financial market forecasting literature is on daily data in the sense, that the 1-day-ahead forecast is a single number. Even though the corresponding literature makes often use of data sampled in 15, 5, or 1 minute frequencies, the used terminology of high-frequency corresponds to the data used to generate the forecast, not to the forecast itself. Nowadays, the increasing availability of ultra-high-frequency data shifts large parts of the research efforts from daily to high-frequency forecasts, although most of the ultra-high-frequency data is still non-public. A special feature of ultra-high-frequency data is the unavoidable zero-inflation, caused by the frequency of measurement.

Zero-inflation in time series is not unknown and already common in microeconomics and intermittent demand forecasting. Kömm and Küsters (2015) developed recently a new model, that combines the elements of zero-inflation with the elements of traditional ARIMA-GARCH models. This thesis provides the application of the proposed model on ultra-high-frequent sampled asset prices.

The third gap is addressed to the algorithmic text forecasting embedded in financial text forecasting systems. Early approaches of text mining systems to predict the market response to news mainly aimed to predict the trend of prices, see e. g. Mittermayer and Knolmayer (2007), not to forecast volatilities or volatility shocks. Recent approaches on text mining systems to predict the market response to news miss, in delimitation to the approach of this thesis, one of the following subjects:

1. *The proposed system does not forecast volatility shocks.*

   The system makes use of machine learning algorithms to forecast volatilities, but not on high-frequencies or ultra-high-frequencies and not for volatility shocks, e. g. Pieper (2011).

2. *The proposed system does not forecast volatilities.*

   The system makes use of machine learning algorithms, but for asset price forecasts, e. g. Groth and Muntermann (2011), Božić (2013), or Barazzetti et al. (2014).

3. *The proposed system is not a monitor.*

   The system miss to make use of machine learning algorithms to identify not only the relevant news, but to train also a monitor to apply the findings on further economic applications, e. g. Boudoukh et al. (2013) and Milea (2013).

The system proposed in this thesis to monitor for high-frequency volatility shocks, is therefore a strong demarcation of existing quote and volatility forecasting applications. Thus, please note that the forecasting objects in this thesis are not directly observable like asset quotes, but statistical control instruments. Two significant points in the forecasting challenge will hence be: (1) which statistical control instruments to use and (2) how to measure and to test for changes?

1.5 Contents

The remainder of the thesis is structured as follows:

Chapter 2 starts to give the general framework to discriminate the different types of volatility, to set the assumptions on the underlying asset pricing process, to estimate the volatility, to sample data and to pre-process raw data.

Chapter 3 introduces stylized facts of volatilities, the concept of microstructure noise and the estimators for the integrated volatility respective the interday periodicity. Note, that the integrated volatility gives the actual intraday volatility while the interday volatility gives the asset specific time of the day typical volatility.

Chapter 4 is built on a descriptive analysis of asset quotes and the corresponding volatility estimates. The hereby observed characteristics are applied to a Markov-switching mixture model for autoregressive and heteroscedastic time series, originally developed by Kömm and Küsters (2015) to forecast price changes of milk products. In this thesis this new model is used in a modified variant to identify the latent data generation process.

Chapter 5 gives the link of asset quotes and ad-hoc news and the filter applied to identify relevant news. The filtered data set out of a two year survey in 2010 and 2011 is used to train, to validate and to evaluate the proposed monitor. Furthermore, this chapter describes the Wald-type test to discriminate volatility affecting incidents from non affecting incidents as well as the general framework to quantify financial text data to apply text forecasting algorithms.

Chapter 6 introduces the framework of algorithmic text forecasting. In total, three classification and three meta-learning-algorithms were selected. The algorithms are applied to the two year sample, and for comparison purposes on additional 1,000 random benchmark points.

Chapter 7 gives the benchmark. The selected algorithms are cross-validated to their out-of-sample performance and pairwise tested to determine the best fitting of the proposed algorithms. Furthermore, a confusion analysis is applied to determine the goodness of classification. The chapter concludes with a benchmark analysis of the random benchmark used to calibrate the final monitor.

Chapter 8 gives the monitor with an analysis of the proposed system, a discrimination of the data conditional shock identification and a consideration of the costs of misclassification.

Chapter 9 concludes with the primary findings, discovered weaknesses and limitations, and gives proposals to future research.

The first part of the thesis, given in the Chapters 2 to 6, introduces the applied assumptions, theories, concepts, and models, and is clarified by comprehensive, chapter connecting examples. The second part of the thesis, given in the Chapters 7 and 8, evaluates the proposed system and investigates (1) the overall quality of the monitoring system, (2) the effect of different data, different estimators, and different forecasting algorithms on the forecasting quality, and (3) the costs of misclassification. The first part establishes thus the essential tools and theories of the thesis to bring them together in the second part. For clarification, the structure of the thesis is illustrated in the architectural plan in Figure 1.2 on the next page.

Please be aware that the forecasting process is designed to run in real-time. The estimation of the integrated volatility, the determination of the best fitting zero-inflated DGP, and the classification of historical incidents are resource-intensive processes requiring supercomputing and parallelization techniques. The monitor to forecast the risk of volatility shocks, however, runs in real-time, or close to real-time, with a magnitude of seconds or milliseconds.

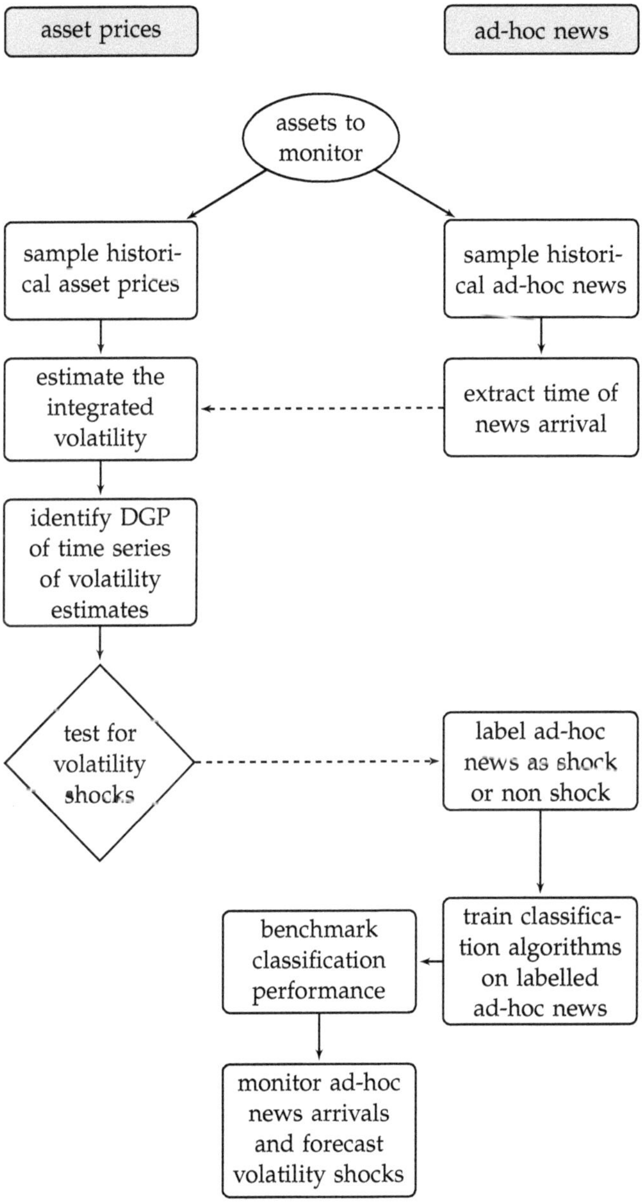

Figure 1.2: General architectural plan of the monitoring system. The left side reports the workflow based on asset quotes. The right side reports the workflow based on ad-hoc news. The combination of both is given in the centre.

2 General Framework

The purpose of this chapter is to provide the framework for the economic processes, where the processes are designed to represent the uncertainty in the market. This necessitates (1) the framework of volatility models, which, in the proposed approach are (2) built on stock prices that have (3) to be sampled and pre-processed first.

Therefore, the chapters content is threefold: Section 2.1 gives an introduction to the general classes of volatility models and the related definitions of volatility. Section 2.2 gives the methodological framework of asset pricing and the link from asset prices to latent volatility estimation. Finally, Section 2.3 presents data sampling schemes and pre-processing techniques to sample and correct for errors in raw data.

2.1 Classes of Volatility Models

The term volatility refers to the variability of an underlying stochastic process, usually the variability of a given time series. In particular, the volatility is unobservable but can be estimated. The most commonly used estimators can be classified in estimates of stochastic and non-stochastic volatility models.

2.1.1 *Time-Invariant Volatility Models*

Time-invariant volatility models assume the volatility σ to be constant within a single and specific time window. Two of them, the historical and the implicit volatility, will be explained below. The historical volatility is an explicit estimation of the volatility, while the implied volatility is the implicit result of the Black-Scholes differential equation.

Historical volatility The term historical refers to the length of the for estimation considered history n. The volatility estimate σ is simply the standard deviation s of the past n returns. The advantage of historical volatility models is in the simplicity of implementation, while the disadvantage is the arbitrary choice of the historical parameter n.

Implied volatility The implied volatility refers to a concept rather than to a model. The implied volatility proposed by Black and Scholes (1973) is the estimate of the non-observable parameter σ in the Black-Scholes differential equation such that the market value of the considered option, depending on the time and the underlying stock price value, equals the theoretical value of the option.

Please note, that the implied volatility model belongs to stock prices as well as the associated option prices. The options market, however, often shows an immense lack in liquidity what results in insufficient sporadic data sets of option prices. It seems therefore inadvisable to use implied volatility models for ultra-high-frequency volatility estimates, due to the discrepancy in the data granularities of stock and associated option prices.

2.1.2 *Stochastic Volatility Models*

A general overview of the following described class of stochastic volatility (SV) models, autoregressive conditional heteroscedasticity (ARCH) models and generalized autoregressive conditional heteroscedasticity (GARCH) models is given in Bauwens et al. (2012).

Stochastic volatility (SV) models suppose a non-constant but conditional volatility. The stochastic volatility is estimated on the observed trajectory of a hidden stochastic process.

A very early approach of stochastic volatility models is the product process of Taylor (1982, formula (3)). The product is formed by a non-negative process σ_t and a second i.i.d. process z_t having zero mean and unit variance describing the level of the process:

$$y_t - \mu = \sigma_t z_t$$
$$\log \sigma_t^2 = \omega + \beta \log \sigma_{t-1}^2 + \nu_t \qquad \nu_t \sim N(0, \sigma_u^2),$$

with μ the unconditional mean of y_t. Taylor supposes furthermore σ_s to be independent of z_t for all s and t. The random variable ν_t declaring the shocks is expected to be i.i.d. and to be uncorrelated with z_t. The factor β declares the process for volatility clusters. Today, practitioners often simply assume z_t to be standard normal distributed, i.e. $z_t \sim N(0,1)$. However, any other symmetric distribution, e.g. the t-distribution, or a symmetric mixture of distributions, would do as well, as the variability is declared by σ_t.

Conditional volatility A second class of stochastic and conditional volatility models interpret the conditional variation of the underlying process y_t as a function of the observable history. A famous representative of the time conditional stochastic volatility models is the autoregressive conditional heteroscedasticity (ARCH) model of Engle (1982, formula (18)). The model assumes the mean of the process y_t to be declared by $x_t\beta$, a linear combination of exogenous and endogenous variables embedded in the information set ψ_{t-1} available at time $t-1$:

$$
\begin{aligned}
&y_t|\psi_{t-1} \sim N(x_t\beta, h_t),\\
&\varepsilon_t = y_t - x_t\beta,\\
&h_t = \alpha_0 + \alpha_1\varepsilon_{t-1}^2 + \ldots + \alpha_q\varepsilon_{t-q}^2,
\end{aligned}
$$

with q being the order of the ARCH process, α and β vectors of unknown parameters, and $\alpha_0 > 0$ and $\alpha_1, \alpha_2, \ldots, \alpha_p \geqslant 0$ for regularity. Note, that the ARCH model is often written in the more intuitive form:

$$
\begin{aligned}
y_t - \mu_t = \varepsilon_t = \sigma_t z_t \quad z_t \sim N(0,1),\\
\sigma_t^2 = \alpha_0 + \alpha_1\varepsilon_{t-1}^2 + \ldots + \alpha_q\varepsilon_{t-q}^2.
\end{aligned}
$$

In this form, it becomes obvious that Engle's ARCH model is closely related to Taylor's SV model. The main distinction of SV to ARCH models is the knowledge of the conditional volatility σ_t within an given information set ψ_{t-1}. While $\sigma_t|\psi_{t-1}$ is known in ARCH models, this condition is unknown and an unobserved random variable in general SV models. Engle's main idea is, hence, to consider the conditional variance of random model errors as a dependency of historical realized errors.

The generalization of Engle's concept, to model the conditional variance not only as a dependency of the time series history, but also of his own history, is given in Bollerslev (1986). This model is called generalized autoregressive conditional heteroscedasticity (GARCH) model.

Stochastic volatility models are generally more flexible and allow a more natural economic interpretation than GARCH models. Empirical applications are, however, dominated by GARCH instead of SV approaches. This is due to the circumstance that in practise GARCH model estimation is often less complex than an equivalent SV model estimation.

Bauwens et al. (2012, p.33) note, that stochastic volatility models *"...are essentially parametric and usually designed to estimate the daily, weekly, or monthly volatility using data sampled at the same frequency."* Note, that Bauwens et al. are not talking about high-frequency data measured in seconds, minutes, or hours.

The authors note further, that: *"Since French et al. (1987) [..] econometricians have considered using data sampled at a very high frequency to compute ex-post measures of volatility at a lower frequency."*

The daily, weekly, or monthly volatility is not under investigation in this thesis. However, the objects under investigation are high-frequency volatility shocks, making ultra-high-frequency data the data of interest and the realized volatility described below the estimator of interest.

Realized volatility The main idea of realized volatility models is to make use of each single variation on a high-frequency or ultra-high-frequency scale. The canonical estimator of the realized volatility is the sum of the squared first differences of the logarithmic asset price process X_t:

$$RV = \sum_{i=1}^{n_t} (X_{t,i} - X_{t,i-1})^2$$

with i indicating the ith observation at period t, e. g. a day or an hour, and n_t the total number of observations in period t.

The origin of the idea, to simply sum up squared realizations to estimate the volatility, is unknown, but it dates back at least to the suggestion of Merton (1980).

2.1.3 *Integrated Volatility*

In contrast to the realized volatility, which is defined in discrete time, the deterministic integral of the quadratic stochastic process σ_s

$$IV = \int_0^t \sigma_s^2 ds \tag{2.1}$$

is defined in continuous time. This integral of the quadratic volatility process σ_s along the time interval $[0, t]$ is called the *integrated volatility (IV)*. A detailed discussion of the theoretical issues about the integrated volatility is provided below, in Section 2.2.2.

It is worth mentioning that the widely-used GARCH and SV models, belonging to the class of parametric models, infer the integrated volatility. RV models, on the other hand, belonging to the class of non-parametric models, calculate the integrated volatility. Hence, the common denominator of volatility estimation is the latent integrated volatility.

In this thesis, five different realized volatility estimators (introduced in Section 3.2) calculating the integrated volatility will extensively be discussed and evaluated for their overall performance in the final volatility shock monitoring system. The remaining volatility estimators mentioned in this chapter were given in order to understand the connections, but are no longer part of further considerations.

2.2 Framework to Model the Integrated Volatility

The given framework follows the standard financial theory on volatility modelling. It is built on the theory of stochastic processes to model asset prices, see Iacus (2008) and Iacus (2011), and the theory of integrated volatility. Further following the approach of Aït-Sahalia and Jacod (2010), it is state of the art to embed a continuous component in high-frequency stock data models. Typically, by making use of a Brownian motion.

2.2.1 *Modelling Asset Prices*

The origin of today's financial mathematics is most probably the dissertation of Bachelier (1900). The fundamental idea of Bachelier is to make use of probabilistic theory to model the motions of asset prices. In particular, to use Brownian motions to evaluate the value of asset options. Today, the *geometric Brownian motion* is the fundamental model to describe the motion of asset prices. A mathematical concept to model the motion of asset prices using stochastic processes is as follows:

Probability Space First, assume a probability space $(\Omega, \mathcal{A}, P)$. This construct describes the potential outcome of random experiments and consists of three parts:

1. A non-empty sample space Ω, which is the set of all possible outcomes of a random experiment.

2. A σ-algebra $\mathcal{A}$ on the set Ω, which is a set consisting of countable subsets of Ω.

3. An assignment of probabilities to the events of the random experiment, which is a function $P : \mathcal{A} \to [0, 1]$ from events to probabilities.

σ-Algebra Secondly, assume a σ-algebra in the probability space $(\Omega, \mathcal{A}, P)$. A σ-algebra is a system of sets $\mathcal{A}$, fulfilling the conditions:

1. $\Omega \in \mathcal{A}$.

2. $A \in \mathcal{A} \Rightarrow A^c \in \mathcal{A}$ with A^c the complementary set of A.

3. $A_1, A_2, \ldots \in \mathcal{A} \Rightarrow \bigcup_{t \in \mathbb{N}} A_t \in A$.

The intuitive function of σ-algebras in the theory of stochastic processes is to describe the potential observable information at each specific time.

Filtration Third, assume a filtration. A family of embedded σ-algebras $(\mathcal{A}_t)_{t \in \mathbb{N}}$ modelling a rising time sequence is called filtration, meaning for all $s, t \in \mathbb{N}$ with $s < t$ is $\mathcal{A}_s \subseteq \mathcal{A}_t$. Finally, adapt the stochastic process $\{S_t\}_{t \in \mathbb{N}}$ to the filtration $(\mathcal{A}_t)_{t \in \mathbb{N}}$. The intuitive function of a filtration is to guarantee that it is not possible to have more information at an earlier than actual time.

Martingale A stochastic process $\{S_t\}_{t \in \mathbb{N}}$ adapted to the filtration $(\mathcal{A}_t)_{t \in \mathbb{N}}$ is further called a martingale, if

1. $E(|S_t|) < \infty$, and
2. $E(S_{t+1} \mid \mathcal{A}_t) = E(S_{t+1} \mid S_t, \ldots, S_1) = S_t$.

The first condition ensures the existence of the expectation value, the second condition characterizes the martingale property. Simply changing the second condition to

$$E(S_{t+1} \mid \mathcal{A}_t) \geqslant S_t \text{ or}$$
$$E(S_{t+1} \mid \mathcal{A}_t) \leqslant S_t$$

is called sub-martingale ($\geqslant$), respectively super-martingale ($\leqslant$). The stochastic process $\{S_t\}_{t \in \mathbb{N}}$ is further called semi-martingale, if $\{S_t\}$ is either a sub- or an super-martingale.

Further details on probability spaces, adapted processes, filtrations, and martingales, are e. g. given in Bauer (2011).

All together, following the suggestion of Back (1991) to model the motion of asset prices, let $\{S_t\}_{t \geqslant 0}$ be the price of an asset and assume the latent DGP of $\{S_t\}$ to be a super-martingale. Corresponding to the Doob-Meyer decomposition theorem, see e. g. Protter (2005, pp.106-117), the existing condition also gives a not necessarily unique decomposition of the price process $\{S_t\}_{t \geqslant 0}$ into the sum of a stochastic process of finite variation on the one hand, and a martingale on the other hand.

Now consider a short time interval dt. The changing of the asset price process in the interval $[t, t + dt)$ is accordingly equal to $dS_t = S_{(t+dt)} - S_t$, having returns r given by the proportion of dS_t to S_t:

$$r = dS_t / S_t.$$

The Doob-Meyer decomposition property transmits directly to this return process, giving

$$r = \text{deterministic part} + \text{stochastic part}. \tag{2.2}$$

The first part, the deterministic component, is generally related to the risk free interest rate and the deterministic return in dt is μdt. The process is of finite variation for constant returns in each infinitesimal small time interval $[t, t + dt)$:

$$\text{deterministic contribution} = \mu dt. \tag{2.3}$$

The second part, the stochastic component, on the other hand, relates to the stochastic variation of the asset with non-predictable shocks. The shocks are nevertheless typically assumed to be Gaussian, i. e. symmetric with zero mean:

$$\text{stochastic contribution} = \sigma dB_t, \tag{2.4}$$

where B_t is a standard Brownian motion or standard Wiener process fulfilling $dB_t = B_{(t+dt)} - B_t$ and $dB_t \sim N(0, dt)$. A Brownian motion is furthermore a martingale and hence conform with the statement of the Doob-Meyer decomposition theorem. Fitting the equations (2.3) and (2.4) in the return process (2.2) results in:

$$dS_t/S_t = \mu dt + \sigma dB_t$$

which is equivalent to the stochastic differential form:

$$dS_t = \mu S_t dt + \sigma S_t dB_t. \tag{2.5}$$

Setting the processes $\{\mu S_t\} = \{\mu_t\}$ and $\{\sigma S_t\} = \{\sigma_t\}$, gives

$$dS_t = \mu_t dt + \sigma_t dB_t, \tag{2.6}$$

which is simply the differential form of the general Itō process

$$S_t = S_0 + \mu \int_0^t S_u du + \sigma \int_0^t S_u dB_u.$$

with S_0 as the start value of the process, see e. g. Iacus (2011, pp.8-9). Please note, that any Itō process can also be interpreted as a generalized Brownian motion with random drift and volatility.

Note further, that the *geometric Brownian motion* is the process S_t that solves formula (2.5). The differential of this process can principally be build by Riemann integration theory, but due to the non-differentiability of the Brownian motion, the differential does not exist in a single point. This warrants the use of stochastic integrals, e. g. the integration terminology of Itō. For a general introduction to stochastic integration theory, see e. g. Chung and Williams (2014).

2.2.2 *Modelling Integrated Volatility*

Taken together, each asset motion S_t, and therefore also the logarithm of the asset prices $X_t = \log S_t$, can be represented by the stochastic differential equation (2.6), which is:

$$dX_t = \mu_t dt + \sigma_t dB_t. \tag{2.7}$$

Thus, the logarithmic price changes are represented by the differential dX_t, determined by

1. a real-valued and continuous process with finite variation μ_t,
2. a strictly positive Càdlàg process σ_t (any stochastic process is called Càdlàg, if (a) each trajectory $t \to X_t$ is right-sided continuous in each point t a.s. and (b) the left-sided limits exist), and
3. a standard Brownian motion or Wiener process B_t.

The changing of the logarithmic price process X within the interval $(0, t]$ is consequently:

$$dX_t = r_t = \int_0^t \mu_s ds + \int_0^t \sigma_s dB_s. \tag{2.8}$$

Due to the short considered time intervals (e. g. one day or one hour), the deterministic component in (2.8), $\int_0^t \mu_s ds$, is supposed to be zero. The stochastic component in (2.8), $\int_0^t \sigma_s dB_s$, however, is not calculated evaluating the Itō integral, but by the quadratic variation of the Itō process, which is:

$$[X, X]_t = \int_0^t \sigma_s^2 ds. \tag{2.9}$$

Please note, that every Itō process has the quadratic variation (2.9). This fact is also known as *the representation theorem of the quadratic variation of stochastic processes* (to be discussed in Section 2.2.3). Note in particular the transition from the stochastic integral $\int(\cdot)dB_s$ to the deterministic integral $\int(\cdot)ds$ when using the quadratic variation.

What is decisive, however, is that the quadratic variation of the Itō process (2.9) corresponds to the *integrated volatility* of formula (2.1) on page 14. This integrated volatility is the object of interest, either over one or successive periods of time. The task in forecasting high-frequency volatility shocks is therefore, to estimate the latent integrated volatility (2.1) in real-time. This task demands to use intraday data.

2.2.3 *Quadratic Variation of Stochastic Integrals*

The link from stochastic integrals of the form $\int_{t-1}^{t} \sigma_s dB_s$ (Itō integrals) to deterministic integrals of the form $\int_{t-1}^{t} \sigma_s^2 ds$ (Riemann integrals) is based on the representation theorem of *continuous local martingales as stochastic integrals with respect to Brownian motions*, which is part of semi-martingale process theory. Please note the importance of this theorem in order to model stochastic volatilities.

The representation theorem states (in an abbreviated version) that each stochastic integral $\int_0^t \sigma_s dB_s$ along a standard Brownian motion B with a measurable, adapted process σ fulfilling $P(\int_0^t \sigma_s^2 ds < \infty) = 1$ for every $0 \leqslant t < \infty$ (meaning σ to be local bounded in the full domain) is a continuous local martingale with quadratic variation $\int_0^t \sigma_s^2 ds$, which is a continuous function of P a.s. The full theorem including the proof is e.g. given in Karatzas and Shreve (2007, pp.170-173).

However, the representation theorem further assumes complete markets, fulfilling the following conditions:

1. Neither regional, objective, temporal nor personal preferences.
2. Perfect market transparency.
3. Homogeneity of goods.
4. Unlimited fast reactions of all market participants to changes.

The implications in the context of this thesis are: (1) all investors will identically evaluate the impact of unexpected news, (2) all investors have full access to all news arrivals at the same moment, (3) the impact of homogeneous news is identical, and (4) there is no lagged dynamic in the return process of the assets.

Due to the restrictive assumptions, complete markets do obviously not exist. Stock markets, however, apply to be the markets which are next to the requested pure competition, see Harrison and Pliska (1981). Therefore, the sufficient attainment of complete markets to make use of the representation theorem can be regarded as fulfilled. But, inefficiencies in the considered empirical price processes are nevertheless expected.

2.3 Sampling and Pre-processing Intraday Data

The umbrella term *intraday data* envelopes all data sampled within a day, independent of the sampling frequency and independent of the sampling scheme.

The literature on intraday data is hence not clear in the definition of sampling frequencies and sampling schemes. The statistical properties of the in Section 3.2 proposed integrated volatility estimators to determine formula (2.9), however, depend on sampling frequencies and sampling schemes.

2.3.1 *Sampling Schemes*

Sampling schemes are rules of data recording. The main classification of sampling schemes is due to the concept of time, see Oomen (2005, 2006) and Griffin and Oomen (2008):

1. *Calendar Time Sampling:* Sampling in calendar time means to sample on an equidistant calendar time scale, for instance every five minutes. Public available stock price data are typically calendar time data.

2. *Business Time Sampling:* Sampling in business time means to sample in event time, but in predefined distances. The sampling frequency in business time follows an intensity process, e. g. a function describing when to sample very often or to sample moderately.

3. *Transaction Time Sampling:* Sampling in transaction time means to sample in event time, but not necessarily in predefined or equidistant distances. The sampling frequency in transaction time records every single transaction. Transaction time sampling provides the most available information.

4. *Tick Time Sampling:* Tick time sampling corresponds to the sampling scheme in transaction time, but with censoring all zero returns. Tick time samples are records of price changes, and hence based on informations, not on transactions.

One main argument to use transaction or tick time sampling is market intensity. Both sampling schemes are not necessarily equidistant, allowing a flexible sampling intensity. The principle is to sample more data in active than in calm market situations, contrary to sampling for instance once a minute.

Two corresponding analyses are provided by Oomen (2005) and Oomen (2006). Their analysis is built on the assumption, that each observable data point consists of the combination of a true but latent data point plus a random data point, called microstructure noise (defined in Section 3.1.2 on page 31). Their central finding is: The mean squared error (MSE) between observed and true data in realized volatility estimates (to be discussed in Section 3.2 on page 32) is lower on business or transaction time samples than on calendar time samples.

Patton (2011) further found that tick time samplings provide more accurate realized volatility estimates than calendar time samplings, and Griffin and Oomen (2008) found, that microstructure noise is autocorrelated in tick time, while it is close to i.i.d. in transaction time. This is due to the effect, that in transaction time the i.i.d. bias can often be explained by an first order serial correlation, such that the i.i.d. bias corrections work fine. However, in tick time second and higher order correlations can be important, making the i.i.d. bias corrections for the first order serial correlation inappropriate.

All in all is transaction time sampling the preferable sampling scheme to all realized volatility estimators that assume independent noise.

2.3.2 *Data Sampling*

Public available samples of financial data are mostly offered in calendar time. Usual patterns of public data are (1) end-of-the-day closing, or (2) open (first price of the day), high, low, close (last price of the day) prices. These four statistics of (2) are also called OHLC prices. Some free-to-use data providers even offer 15, 5 or 1 minute data. However, transaction data is generally offered exclusively by professional data providers. The most common used sampling mechanism in realized volatility literature is hence calendar time sampling using 15, 5 or 1 minute data, see Oomen (2006, p.224), but not transaction time data.

Transaction time sampled data is available commercially. But, purchasable data sets are usually pre-processed. Even if the pre-processing is documented, the original raw data is nevertheless not normally available, making any control of the pre-processing procedure impossible.

An alternative to commercial data sets are access points to professional data providers. Two famous data providers are Bloomberg and Thomson Reuters. The advantage of an access point is the full control of the data stream. The disadvantage, however, is in the immense amount of unadjusted data which show an enormous occurrence of technical errors. That is why the analysis of gathered data sets generally starts with data pre-processing.

The providers offer market data including prices and sizes for ask and bid quotes, where

1. *The bid quote* is the highest price that potential buyers are willing to pay to purchase a contract. Bid prices are therefore of primary interest for sellers.

2. *The ask quote* is the lowest price that potential sellers are willing to accept to divest a contract. Ask prices are therefore of primary interest for purchasers.

3. *The size* is the quantity of contracts offered or requested at the given price, each for ask and bid prices.

Please note, that an analysis of mid quotes, this is the mean of ask and bid quotes, would miss to differentiate the economic situation of purchases from the economic situation of sellers.

Market Data Market data can further be separated into the level of information. Level 1 information is ask and bid prices, sizes, and the last price at which the most recent trade was completed. The bid or ask price to which the security was traded is also referred as quote. These quotes correspond to transaction time sampling and hence to the stage of analysis in this thesis. Level 2 market data, this is the order book, further include the highest 5 to 10 bid and the lowest 5 to 10 ask prices and sizes, see Figure 2.1 on the next page for illustration. Whenever the best ask price hits the best bid price, a transaction is performed. The level 3 service, finally, allows to insert instantaneously new quotations into the system. This service is mainly reserved to market makers and broker-dealer firm trading rooms, see Loss et al. (2011, p.754).

Note, that using level 1 instead of level 2 data is not a lack in information when analysing realized volatilities, as the measure of interest are the executed transactions, not the potential transactions. Note further, that the trading volume is not considered to be relevant information in this thesis. Instead, it is assumed that a single trade will not have a relevant price-influencing effect when using a transaction time sampling frequency.

Implementation The raw data of asset prices used to estimate the corresponding realized volatilities are level 1 streams of transaction time quotes provided by Bloomberg, each for ask and bid quotes from January 1st, 2010 to December 31st, 2011. The used application programming interface (API) to Bloomberg comes with the R-library RBloomberg. For pre-processing purposes, the data is saved into a MySQL database, using the RMySQL package. All transactions are converted to UTC, the coordinated world time, to avoid artificial induced errors resulting from changes of summer and winter times. Support for the transformations was given by the R-libraries timeSeries and timeDate, to convert time depending data in the location and time-scale independent POSIX standard format.

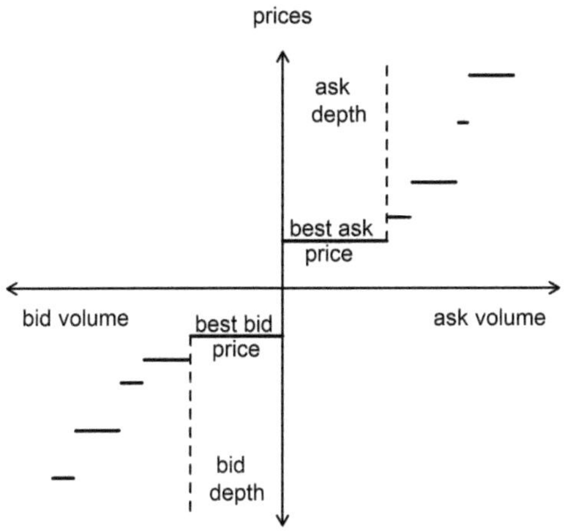

Figure 2.1: The order book. The horizontal lines above the abscissa and right of the ordinate show the different offers of the sellers (ask side). The level of the horizontal line shows the price, the length of the horizontal lines the size of the offer. The horizontal line below the abscissa and left to the ordinate show correspondingly the offer of the buyers. Whenever the best bid price hits the best ask price, the trade will be executed.

2.3.3 *Data Pre-processing*

The downloaded raw data streams of Bloomberg show an immense lack in pureness. Some errors are caused by human failure, some are caused by technical errors. Among others, potential sources of error can be:

1. *Caused by human failure:* Unintended stock price offerings, both for ask and bid prices, for instance triggered by typing errors in the asset symbol or the asset price. To give an example, this could be an ask offering to 10.50 instead of the intended 105.00.

2. *Caused by technical errors:* Transmission record breaks reporting negative or zero asset prices. Both are illogical. This technical effect seems to arise rarely (less than 1‰ of the recorded data) and bundled, e. g. in sequences of some dozen or hundred zeros.

The applied data correction mechanism consists of two steps, see Figure 2.2 on the next page: The first step is to remove outliers identified by Walsh's outlier test, see Walsh (1950, 1953). The a-priori information required for Walsh's outlier test, how many outliers have to be considered, is found using Grubbs' outlier test, see Grubbs (1950). Grubbs' test is also called the maximum normed residual test. Both tests adjust the data for errors in the tails, see Figure 2.2a, but not for errors masked through time series patterns. Hence, the second step is to widen masking outliers as atypical level records using a series of exponentially-weighted means surrounded by level conditional confidence intervals and to remove records outside the estimated confidence bounds, see Figure 2.2b.

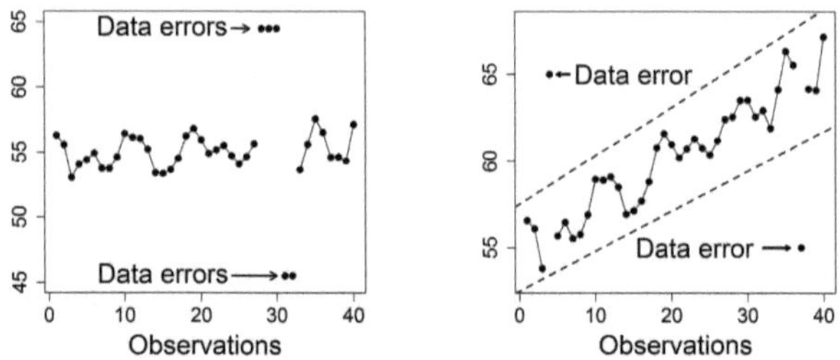

(a) The marked data errors in this figure can be identified using Walsh's outlier test.

(b) The marked data errors in this figure are due to the trend masked for Walsh's outlier test.

Figure 2.2: The pre-processing of the raw data consists of two steps. The first step, illustrated in Figure 2.2a, identifies errors in the tails of the considered data, e. g. sequences of zeros, but can not account for errors masked through a trend in the time series. The second step, illustrated in Figure 2.2b, accounts for time dependencies using a $\pm 3\sigma$ error bound (with σ the standard deviation) and identifies those observations as outliers, that are not within the error boundaries.

The Grubbs test Grubbs' test for outlier detection tests for the significance of the largest (respectively the smallest) observation in a normal distributed sample of size n. Denote the sample in order of increasing magnitude as $x_1 \leqslant x_2 \leqslant \ldots \leqslant x_n$ and assume normality for the population. The hypotheses of Grubbs' test is, that all observations in the sample come from the same normal population, see Grubbs (1969, pp.4-5). That is, that each observation x_i can be explained by a constant μ and a normal random variable $a_i \sim N(0, \sigma^2)$, giving: $x_i = \mu + a_i$ for $i = 1, \dots, n$. Writing $x_i = \mu + \Delta_i + a_i$ for $i = 1, \dots, n$ allows to write the hypothesis as:

$$H_0 : \forall_{i=1,\dots,n} \text{ is } \Delta_i = 0 \quad \text{vs.}$$
$$H_1 : \exists_{i=1,\dots,n} \text{ with } \Delta_i \neq 0.$$

For the two-sided Grubbs test, the test statistic is

$$G = \max |x_i - \overline{x}|/s$$

with $\overline{x}$ denoting the sample arithmetic mean and s denoting the sample standard deviation including the suspected outlier.

Following Stefansky (1972, p.473), the critical values C_α of the two-sided test are calculated as:

$$C_\alpha = \frac{n-1}{\sqrt{n}} \sqrt{\frac{t^2_{(\alpha/2n);n-2}}{n - 2 + t^2_{(\alpha/2n);n-2}}},$$

where $t_{(\alpha/2n);n-2}$ denotes the critical value of a t-distribution with $(n-2)$ degrees of freedom and a significance level of $(\alpha/2n)$. H_0 is discarded to α if $G \geqslant C_\alpha$.

The Grubbs' test can also be formulated as a one-sided test. To test for the highest observation x_n to be an outlier, the test statistic is:

$$T_n = (x_n - \overline{x})/s.$$

To test for the smallest observation x_1 instead of the largest observation x_n, the criterion to test for an outlier is simply

$$T_1 = (\overline{x} - x_1)/s.$$

Here, H_0 is discarded to α, if $T_n > T_\alpha$, respectively $T_1 > T_\alpha$, where T_α is the critical value substituting $t_{\frac{\alpha}{2n};n-2}$ with $t_{\frac{\alpha}{n};n-2}$ in the test statistic C_α. The publishing of the critical values is given in Grubbs and Beck (1972).

Grubbs' test and simultaneous inference Grubbs' test appears to be valuable for single outlier detection, provided the normal population assumption holds. But multiple outliers, for example sequences of technical error records (lumpy outliers) often stay undetected. This phenomenon is called masking outliers. The iterative application of Grubbs' test may hence result in the wrong classification of potential outliers as non-outliers, a type two error.

The critical values of the test reported in Grubbs and Beck (1972) are calculated for a once only application. The test should therefore only once be used. The sequential application of the test, however, increases the likelihood to monitor a rare event and therefore to reject the true null hypothesis and to reject too many outliers. This is known as swamping and a type one error.

Therefore, reduce the significance level α by the factor m, with m the number of iterations, such that for a family of hypotheses $H_1, \dots, H_m$ and corresponding p-values $p_1, \dots, p_m$ the p-value p_i is smaller than α/m:

$$p_i < \frac{\alpha}{m}.$$

Reject hypotheses H_i if $p_i \leqslant \frac{\alpha}{m}$. This well known Bonferroni correction, see e.g. Hochberg (1988), assures that rejecting all p_i will guarantee that the family-wise error rate (FWER) of the iterative application of Grubbs' test is smaller or equal to α, that is

$$\text{FWER} \leqslant \alpha.$$

The FWER is the probability of making at least one type I error among all hypotheses in the family of the considered multiple hypotheses tests. This allows to control the overall probability of type I errors at a pre-defined level.

The Bonferroni correction is a common method of simultaneous inference with the objective to control the FWER. Further methods, e.g. the Holm-Bonferroni correction which is uniformly more powerful than the Bonferroni correction, see Holm (1979), can for example be found in the review of the common methods to control the FWER in Hochberg and Tamhane (1987).

Please note, that the assumed normal population in Grubbs' outlier test can be crucial. The often observed practice to disregard the assumption without any argument on the legitimacy or to argue with the central limit theorem, but missing to justify the i.i.d. assumption of this theorem, could result in an systematic error.

Walsh test Walsh's test for outliers tests for the significance of the r largest, respectively the r smallest, observations in a sample of size n, where n is assumed to be large, independent and drawn from symmetric continuous distributions, see Walsh (1950, p.583). Walsh's test expects no specific distribution, therefore, it is a non-parametric test and free from the often found assumption of a normal population.

Initially, denote the sample in order of increasing magnitude again as $x_1 \leqslant x_2 \leqslant \ldots \leqslant x_n$. Set $c = \lfloor\sqrt{2n}\rfloor$, $k = c + r$ and

$$C = \frac{1 + K\sqrt{\frac{c-K^2}{c-1}}}{c - K^2 - 1}$$

with $K = \sqrt{1/\alpha}$, following the proposal in assumption (ii) in Walsh (1959, p.229). Please note, that for sufficient large n, which is assumed for the test, C must be positive. Hence, it is required that

$$\alpha > \frac{1}{\lfloor\sqrt{2n}\rfloor - 1}.$$

This means that at least $n > 220$ observations were required for a 5%, and $n > 5,100$ for a 1% significance level.

The test hypotheses of the r smallest observations to be outliers in Walsh's outlier test are:

H_0^{min} : The r smallest values are members of F_{n-r} vs.
H_1^{min} : The r smallest values are no members of F_{n-r},

with F_{n-r} the distribution of the remaining $n - r$ sample elements, see Walsh (1959, p.224).

The test statistic, that the r smallest observations are too small, is

$$W_{min} : x_{(r)} - (1 + C)x_{(r+1)} + Cx_{(k)}.$$

Reject H_0^{min} to a given level α, if $W_{min} < 0$. Here, a large C statistic will reject H_0, while a low C will retain the null.

The test hypotheses of the r largest observations to be outliers in Walsh's outlier test are:

H_0^{max} : The r largest values are members of F_{n-r} vs.
H_1^{max} : The r largest values are no members of F_{n-r},

and again, F_{n-r} the distribution of the remaining $n - r$ sample elements, see Walsh (1959, p.225).

The test statistic, that the r largest observations are too large, is then

$$W_{max} : x_{(n+1-r)} - (1 + C)x_{(n-r)} + Cx_{(n+1-k)}.$$

Here, reject H_0^{max} to a given level α, if $W_{max} > 0$. Here, a small C statistic will reject H_0, while a large C will retain the null.

Implementation The first step is to use Grubbs' outlier test, implemented in the R-library outliers. The significance level α is set to 0.1‰, guaranteeing the FWER to be lower or equal 1%, provided the maximum number of identified outlier candidates is lower or equal 100. This condition holds for all considered data. The detected outlier candidates are marked and the test is iterated until the test does not discard the null hypothesis for the first time. Set r with the number of marked outlier candidates, identified by Grubbs' outlier test.

To overcome the assumption of normality, set r as the a-priori identified number of potential outliers for Walsh's non-parametric outlier test for large sample sizes ($n > 220$ for significance levels of 5% and $n > 5{,}100$ for significance levels of 1%). The chosen α of the used implementation of Walsh's test is still 1%. This will confirm or reject the r largest respectively the r smallest candidates proposed by the Grubbs' test for being outliers, or not. In cases with less than the required 5,100 transactions for Walsh's outlier test, a combination of several months is used, until the requirement was fulfilled for the first time. This happened rarely, as it is illustrated in Table 4.1 on page 48. All outliers confirmed by the Walsh test were finally removed.

The second step is to consider the data for outliers masked through time series characteristics. Therefore, the exponentially-weighted mean, implemented in the package TTR was computed and all data outside the $\pm 3\sigma$ rolling corridor were marked to be outliers, see Figure 2.2b on page 24. Note, that the $\pm 3\sigma$ confidence interval corresponds to a 99.7% confidence band on normally distributed samples.

3 Integrated Volatility

Having a general framework to model asset prices, it is the purpose of this chapter to obtain the instruments to estimate the latent integrated volatility on a ultra-high-frequency scale. Using tick-by-tick data measured in milliseconds rather than in minutes, hours, or days, the most promising approach are realized volatility estimators.

Hence, the content of this chapter consists of the following three units: Section 3.1 gives a list of the primary stylized facts of volatility, the description of the concept of microstructure noise and general assumptions on the noise process. Section 3.2 describes selected realized volatility estimators to calculate the integrated volatility. Finally, Section 3.3 gives an additional estimator to determine the hour-of-the-day typical interday volatility, which is necessary to correct the volatility series for market opening, lunch time and closing effects.

3.1 Framework to Estimate Integrated Volatility

Recall, that the object of interest is the integrated volatility of formula (2.1) on page 14. The estimators of interest are the realized volatility estimators, which are conceptionally built on the sum of the historical squared returns. In addition, please recall, that the sampling scheme (see Section 2.3.1 on page 20) is crucial in terms of estimation accuracy and microstructure noise.

The effect of the sampling frequency on realized volatility estimates is illustrated with the volatility signature plot in Figure 3.1 on the next page. The realized volatility estimate is nearly identical (with a negligible variation) in increasing sampling frequencies, as long as the frequency is not greater than 30 seconds. For sampling frequencies less than 30 seconds, however, the estimates burst.

3.1.1 *Stylized Facts of Volatility*

A key aspect of financial markets volatility are stylized facts. Stylized facts are those that are not evidenced in a strong sense, meaning an analytical proof, but those facts that are often observed in empirical analysis and accepted to be a characteristic of empirical data. The vast literature on financial markets mentions a plurality of "stylized facts" on asset prices, see e. g. Cont (2001), and asset volatilities. The following stylized facts of volatility estimates, see

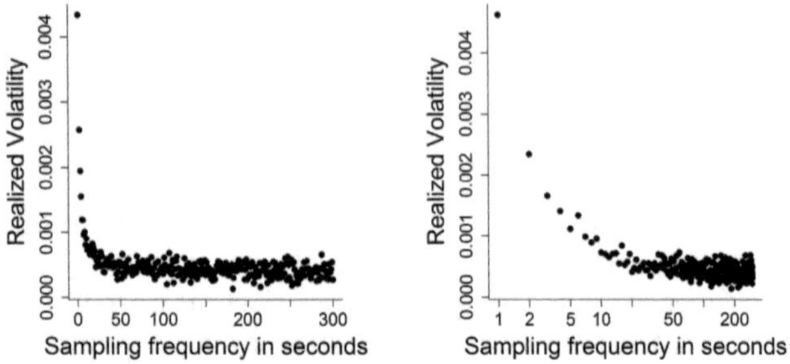

(a) Untransformed scales (b) Logarithmic abscissa

Figure 3.1: Exemplary volatility signature plots. Each dot represents a realized volatility estimate based on the data sampled in the frequency displayed on the abscissa. Figure 3.1a shows the volatility signature plot on an untransformed scale, Figure 3.1b the identical data on a logarithmic scale on the abscissa.

Engle and Patton (2001), are in-line with an ultra-high frequency analysis of the integrated volatility:

Fact 1 *Level persistence:* High levels of volatility are often followed by high levels, while small levels of volatility are often followed by small levels.

Fact 2 *Volatility as shock factor:* The changes in the volatility series often appear in increased occurrences of shocks. This allows also zeros between the shock points, as in the case of ultra-high-frequent samplings.

Fact 3 *Asymmetric impact of exogenous events:* Negative events may cause more shocks and therefore influence the volatility series stronger than positive events.

Stylized facts are often given in different contexts, which makes a clear distinction necessary. A detailed list of stylized facts on asset prices volatilities is e.g. given in Engle and Patton (2001). The authors mention two further facts, but on a *non*-ultra-high frequent scale. These are: (1) a *mean reverting feature*, which is simply a close to zero level on a transaction time scale and (2) *tail properties*, indicating non-normality. However, it is not clear whether the mean reverting feature and the tail properties also confirm to be facts on ultra-high-frequency scales or to be artefacts created through the specific volatility estimator.

Furthermore, Corsi et al. (2012) give an explicit list of stylized facts on *realized volatility series* in contrast to Engle and Patton's list of asset price volatilities.

They add (3) a *long-range dependence* to indicate that the realized volatility is also often observed to be significantly autocorrelated on long lags. However, this long-lag dependence is also found on data measured on hourly frequencies and no effort was given to analyse the effect on a minute, second or millisecond scale.

Hence, it can not be assumed that these facts mentioned in the literature beyond fact 1, fact 2, and fact 3 also hold for ultra-high-frequent sampled data. But, one further characteristic of volatility estimates on ultra-high-frequency samples, which will be discussed in Section 3.3 on page 40, namely the interday periodicity of volatility estimates, could be a candidate for another stylized fact.

3.1.2 *Microstructure Noise*

The empirical analysis of the sampling frequency effect, illustrated through the volatility signature plots in Figure 3.1 on the previous page, suggests, that financial asset returns measured in ultra-high frequencies include further latent discrepancies. The latent effects, that cause the burst in volatility on sampling frequencies less than a minute (in the given example less than 30 seconds), are discussed in the financial literature as *microstructure noise* and can primary be categorized in three groups, see Aït-Sahalia et al. (2011):

1. *Trading effects:* These can for example be bid-ask bounces, the discreteness of price changes, roundings, and tradings on different markets.

2. *Measurement effects:* For example prices entered as zeros and misplaced decimal points. This happens rarely.

3. *Informational effects:* These can be given through differences in trade sizes, content of new information (different languages), price responses to block trades (privately negotiated transactions of large blocks of shares, e. g. at least 10,000), and strategic order flow interruptions.

To account for microstructure effects, let $Y_{t,i}$ be the *observed* log-price (including microstructure noise) and $X_{t,i}$ be the *true* log-price (corrected for the microstructure noise), corresponding to the Itō process (2.7) on page 18. The index i indicates the ith observation at period t, e. g. a day or an hour, and n_t the total number of observations in period t. The observed log-price $Y_{t,i}$ is assumed to be the sum of the latent efficient (true) log-price $X_{t,i}$ plus the microstructure noise component $\varepsilon_{t,i}$. That is:

$$Y_{t,i} = X_{t,i} + \varepsilon_{t,i}.$$

It follows, with $r^*_{t,i} = X_{t,i} - X_{t,i-1}$ the latent or efficient return and $\eta_{t,i} = \varepsilon_{t,i} - \varepsilon_{t,i-1}$ the noise difference, that the return of the observed prices

$$r_{t,i} = Y_{t,i} - Y_{t,i-1}$$

is

$$\begin{aligned} r_{t,i} &= X_{t,i} + \varepsilon_{t,i} - (X_{t,i-1} + \varepsilon_{t,i-1}) \\ &= r^*_{t,i} + \eta_{t,i}. \end{aligned}$$

Please note, that the variance of the observed return $r_{t,i}$ is increased by the noise component $\eta_{t,i}$.

3.1.3 *Assumptions on the Noise Process*

Any purpose to estimate the integrated volatility should further account for the time series characteristics of noise processes. Therefore, it is recommendable to distinguish the different realized volatility estimators (considered in Section 3.2), between the following three assumptions, see McAleer and Medeiros (2008):

Assumption 1 The microstructure noise is a weak stationary (1st moment and covariance do not vary with respect to time, see e. g. Grenander and Rosenblatt (1984, p.33)) stochastic process with zero mean and restricted variance.

Assumption 2 The microstructure noise is an i.i.d. random variable with zero mean, that is independent from the price process and of restricted variance.

Assumption 3 The microstructure noise is stationary (the joint probability distribution does not vary with respect to time) strong mixing (broadly speaking, mixing can be understood as asymptotically independent, e. g. i.i.d. processes, strong mixing is an additional assumption on the mixing coefficient to tend to zero as the distance between two observations increases, see e. g. Rosenblatt and Davis (2011, pp.3-10)) stochastic process with zero mean, that is independent from the price process and of restricted variance.

3.2 Estimating Integrated Volatility

Assume the logarithmic true price process $X_t = \log S_t$ to be a continuous stochastic Itō process with Brownian motion following (2.7) on page 18 and recall, that the sum of squared first differences is a non-parametric estimator of the integrated volatility, see (2.9) on page 18. The following section will present a list of five estimators, all candidates to calculate and to analyse the latent integrated volatility.

This makes a total of five integrated volatility estimators, applied separately on ask and bid quotes of assets measured in transaction time. In sum, roughly 2,000 time series of quotes covering four hours each will be uniformly divided in 960 intervals of each 15 seconds. The realized volatility will be calculated on each of these 960 intervals, such that 960 estimates constitute one new time series of integrated volatilities. In total, roughly 2,000 time series of integrated volatility estimates based on ask quotes and the same number of time series based on bid quotes are calculated.

The 15 seconds windows on which the realized volatility estimators are applied habitat between zero and some hundred observations. Estimates on windows without any observation return zero as volatility estimate. Many small changes in the price process lead to an increased volatility estimate, whereas one single high change may be estimated by a low level of volatility, see Figure 1.1 on page 3. This effect, however, depends on the volatility estimator. For example, the canonical realized volatility estimator, see Section 3.2.1, measures the realized sample-path variation of the squared return process and would therefore not correct for fluctuations caused by single high level changes.

Therefore, the fundamental phenomenons are (1) the measuring characteristics mapped by the volatility estimator, and (2) the resulting zero-inflation (to be discussed in Section 4.2).

3.2.1 *Canonical Estimator*

The first estimator discussed is the canonical estimator of semi-martingale processes built on the quadratic variation $[X, X]$. The quadratic variation of any Itō process (2.7) of the time window $[0, t]$, with observations $X_{t,i} = \log S_{t,i}$, is:

$$\begin{aligned}
[X, X]_t &= \sum_{i=1}^{n_t} \left(X_{t,i} - X_{t,i-1}\right)^2 \\
&= \sum_{i=1}^{n_t} (r^*_{t,i})^2,
\end{aligned}$$

see e. g. Protter (2005, p.70). This canonical estimator $[X, X]_t$ is called *realized volatility* or *realized variance* estimator. The usual acronym of this estimator is $\text{RV}^{(\text{all},X)}$ with "all" describing all sampled data which is sampled in this thesis in transaction time, and "X" indicating the true process X_t. In other words,

$$\widehat{\text{RV}}^{(\text{all},X)} = [X, X]_t.$$

This estimator is in cases of *no* microstructure noise consistent, given that $\sup_{i \geqslant 0}(X_{t,i} - X_{t,i-1}) \to 0$ and $\sup_{i \geqslant 0}(X_{t,i-1}) \to 0$ with probability one, see Andersen et al. (2003), that means:

$$\widehat{RV}^{(all,X)} \xrightarrow{P} IV. \tag{3.1}$$

But, this results holds if, and only if, the true process X_t coincides with the observed process Y_t. The implication for the volatility signature plot in Figure 3.1 on page 30 would be, that the volatility estimates on high frequencies greater than 30 seconds and on windows without any or only moderate observations will not burst to infinity, but hold the overall level.

In the presence of microstructure noise, however, $\widehat{RV}^{(all,Y)}$ is biased. The extended return process set-up

$$r_{t,i} = r^*_{t,i} + \eta_{t,i}$$

gives in the case of microstructure noise

$$\begin{aligned}
\widehat{RV}^{(all,Y)} &= \sum_{i=1}^{n_t} (Y_{t,i} - Y_{t,i-1})^2 \\
&= \sum_{i=1}^{n_t} (r_{t,i})^2 \\
&= \sum_{i=1}^{n_t} \left[(r^*_{t,i})^2 + 2r^*_{t,i}\eta_{t,i} + \eta^2_{t,i} \right].
\end{aligned} \tag{3.2}$$

Bandi and Russell (2008) showed, that given assumption 1 in Section 3.1.3 on page 32 holds,

$$\widehat{RV}^{(all,Y)} \xrightarrow{a.s.} \infty \quad \text{as} \quad n_t \to \infty.$$

Note, that this assumes the noise process η_t to be equipped with a positive probability measure, that is $P(\eta_t) > 0$. Otherwise, the process Y_t would be free of microstructure noise. Requesting further $\eta_t \to \infty$ will guarantee relatively small distances between the individual observations and result in a volatility signature plot as it is illustrated in Figure 3.1.

Increasing the sampling speed to ultra-high-frequencies with transactions in seconds and milliseconds rather than in minutes, hours, or even days, and taking into account the empirical observed microstructure noise, will thus distort the canonical estimator.

However, $\widehat{RV}^{(all,Y)}$ does not estimate the true volatility, but, as Zhang et al. (2005) proved, consistently the variance of the latent noise, $V(\varepsilon) = E(\varepsilon^2)$, with:

$$\widehat{E\varepsilon^2} = \frac{1}{2n_t}\widehat{RV}^{(all,Y)}. \tag{3.3}$$

Note, that the pre-factor 2 results from the induced doubling of the variance when considering differences, that is, see formula (3.2):

$$E\left(\sum_{i=1}^{n_t} \eta_{t,i}^2\right) = E\left(\sum_{i=1}^{n_t} (\varepsilon_{t,i} - \varepsilon_{t,i-1})^2\right) = 2n_t E(\varepsilon^2).$$

Remark on the canonical estimator All in all that means, that simply summarizing the squared first difference of contaminated processes leads to an accumulation of noise in ultra-high-frequent samples. In this case, the canonical estimator provides a consistent estimate of the variance of the noise, instead of an unbiased estimate of the integrated volatility.

It is recommendable to assume empirical data sets to be noise contaminated. An indication for the contamination is the volatility signature plot in Figure 3.1 on page 30. It is therefore not advisable for practical purposes to make use of the canonical realized volatility estimator in combination with ultra-high-frequency samples.

Note, that the popular variant to sample not in transaction but in calendar time and to estimate $RV^{(5,Y)}$, which "5" indicating to sample once every five minutes, will reduce the microstructure noise caused bias but at the cost of missing to use most of the data. This procedure is also known as *sparse sampling*. But, sampling once each five minutes instead of once a second will reduce the sample size by factor 300. Sampling every transaction possibly even more. Please note the discussion on sampling schemes and the benefits of transaction time sampling given in Section 2.3.1 on page 20. It is hence recommendable to use all available data and to model the noise, even if the noise distribution is misspecified, see Aït-Sahalia et al. (2005).

3.2.2 *Averaging Estimator*

The second estimator makes use of the idea to estimate the integrated volatility not by a single, but by multiple grids. The idea is to use not a consecutive sequence but an interrupted sequence of observations. For example, start with observation 1 in grid 1 and use every 5th following observation, having the observations 1, 6, 11 etc. in grid 1, and the observations 2, 7, 12 etc. in grid 2 with a total of 5 grids. Using multiple grids, instead of a single grid, allows to stay with the transaction time approach and simultaneously to avoid the accumulation of noise.

Following the notation in Zhang et al. (2005), suppose the index set of the full grid to be $\mathcal{G} = \{t_0, \ldots, t_n\}$ and $\mathcal{G}^{(k)}$ for $k = 1, \ldots, K$ to be a partitioning of $\mathcal{G}$ in K non-overlapping sub-grids. Getting

$$\mathcal{G} = \bigcup_{k=1}^{K} \mathcal{G}^{(k)}, \quad \text{where } \mathcal{G}^{(k)} \cap \mathcal{G}^{(l)} = \emptyset \text{ for all } k \neq l.$$

To select sub-grid $\mathcal{G}^{(k)}$, start with an index t_{k-1} and pick thereafter every Kth transaction, until T. That is

$$\mathcal{G}^{(k)} = \{t_{k-1}, t_{k-1+K}, t_{k-1+2K}, \ldots, t_{k-1+n_k K}\},$$

where n_k is the integer making $t_{k-1+n_k K}$ the last element in $\mathcal{G}^{(k)}$.

Accordingly is the realized volatility estimator applied on the observations Y_t in sub-grid k, that is $t \in \mathcal{G}^{(k)}$:

$$\widehat{RV}^{(k,Y)} = \sum_{t_j, t_{j,+} \in \mathcal{G}^{(k)}} \left(Y_{t_{j,+}} - Y_{t_j} \right)^2, \tag{3.4}$$

where if $t_i \in \mathcal{G}^{(k)}$, then $t_{i,+}$ denotes the following element in sub-grid $\mathcal{G}^{(k)}$. The arithmetic mean of the K sub-grid statistics (3.4), finally, gives the average realized volatility estimator:

$$\widehat{RV}_K^{(avg,Y)} = \frac{1}{K} \sum_{k=1}^{K} \widehat{RV}^{(k,Y)}. \tag{3.5}$$

Define $\bar{n}_K$ to be the average number of elements over all sub-grids, in other words:

$$\bar{n}_K = \frac{1}{K} \sum_{k=1}^{K} n_k,$$

with n_k being the number of observations in sub-grid $\mathcal{G}^{(k)}$. Using formula (3.3) in the single grid case, $E\varepsilon^2$ can further be consistently approximated by

$$\widehat{E\varepsilon^2} = \frac{1}{2n_t} \widehat{RV}^{(all,Y)}.$$

Hence, in the multi grid case, and now assuming assumption 2 holds, which means the noise process to be independent of the price process such that the bias is explained by $\eta_{t,i}^2$ (see formula (3.2)), the bias of the average estimator can be consistently estimated by

$$2\bar{n}_K \widehat{E\varepsilon^2}. \tag{3.6}$$

For the proof see also Zhang et al. (2005).

Remark on the averaging estimator The multi grid averaging estimator (3.5) assumes a noise process following assumption 2, and remains a biased estimator of the integrated volatility. But, the averaging estimator is preferable to the canonical estimator because of $\bar{n}_K \leqslant n$. Hence, the bias increase is slower in the average than in the canonical estimator.

Please note, that the assumed assumption 2 is more restrictive to the distribution of the observations due to the grid structure, with the effect, that it is additionally assumed that the noise process is independent of the price process. This comes with the no longer existent (except of insignificant) short-lag autocorrelation due to the artificial interruption in the sequence of observations using multiple grids.

Note further, that any search for an optimal $\bar{n}$ in order to reduce the MSE of the estimator would only balance the coexistence of bias and variance, but not correct the estimator for the bias. This procedure, however, is common in practical applications.

3.2.3 *Two-Time-Scales Estimator*

The third estimator, the two-time-scales realized volatility (TSRV) estimator of Zhang et al. (2005), is the natural advancement of the results presented so far.

Assume again, a noise process following assumption 2. The bias-corrected estimator of the integrated volatility comes with the combination of (3.3) with (3.6) to:

$$\widehat{\mathrm{TSRV}}^{(\mathrm{classic},Y)} = \widehat{\mathrm{RV}}_K^{(\mathrm{avg},Y)} - \frac{\bar{n}_K}{n_t}\widehat{\mathrm{RV}}^{(\mathrm{all},Y)}, \tag{3.7}$$

combining the two time scales of the average and the canonical estimator.

Aït-Sahalia et al. (2011) proposed to generalize this estimator with the definition of an *average lag J realized volatility estimator*, similar to the sub-grid estimator of equation (3.5), which is:

$$\widehat{\mathrm{RV}}_J^{(\mathrm{avg},Y)} = \frac{1}{J}\sum_{j=1}^{J} \widehat{\mathrm{RV}}^{(j,Y)},$$

but with $1 \leqslant J < K \leqslant n_t$. The authors propose to choose J in order to minimize the asymptotic variance (numerous other variants possible) as:

$$\lim_{n_t \to \infty} \sup \frac{J}{K} = 0.$$

Another approach is to declare the grade of dependency m first, and to set $J = m + 1$. The generalization of the TSRV estimator is hence simply

$$\widehat{\text{TSRV}}^{(\text{avg},Y)} = \widehat{\text{RV}}_K^{(\text{avg},Y)} - \frac{\bar{n}_K}{\bar{n}_J} \widehat{\text{RV}}_J^{(\text{avg},Y)}, \tag{3.8}$$

thereby combining the two time scales J (fast time scale) and K (slow time scale). Note, that the generalized TSRV estimator (3.8) is identical to the first classic TSRV estimator (3.7) in the special case where $J = 1$ and $K \to \infty$ for $n_t \to \infty$. Both variants are popular in the literature as TSRV estimators. All further work is done with the generalization (3.8).

This estimator corresponds further to the *conditional quadratic variation*, see e.g. Protter (2005, pp.124-125), or integrated volatility, of X_t, written in the symbol $\langle X, X \rangle$. In other words,

$$\widehat{\text{TSRV}}^{(\text{avg},Y)} = \langle X, X \rangle_t^{\text{TSRV, avg}}.$$

Remark on the two-time-scales estimator The TSRV estimator is unbiased and hence, in the context of the theory discussed so far, an acceptable candidate of a consistent estimator to determine the latent integrated volatility in the empirical relevant case with microstructure noise. Please note, however, that the classic as well as the adjusted TSRV estimator (introduced in Section 3.2.4) still assume the noise process to be i.i.d. according to assumption 2. But, Aït-Sahalia and Mancini (2008) could show in direct comparison of the canonical and the classic, respectively the average TSRV estimator, that the two-time-scale estimators outperforms the canonical realized volatility estimator in estimation and forecasting of the integrated volatility. They also confirmed their results in cases where the noise is autocorrelated and strong mixing (corresponding to assumption 3 in Section 3.1.3 on page 32) with the true return process.

3.2.4 *Adjusted Two-Time-Scales Estimator*

The fourth estimator comes with the proposed adjustment of Zhang et al. (2005)

$$\left(1 - \frac{\bar{n}_K}{n_t}\right)^{-1}$$

to adjust the TSRV estimator $\widehat{\text{TSRV}}^{(\text{avg},Y)}$ to correct for grid effects by choosing K and J. With the generalization of Aït-Sahalia et al. (2011), this gives the adjusted TSRV estimator

$$\widehat{\text{TSRV}}^{(\text{adj},Y)} = \left(1 - \frac{\bar{n}_K}{\bar{n}_J}\right)^{-1} \widehat{\text{TSRV}}^{(\text{avg},Y)}. \tag{3.9}$$

Remark on the adjusted two-time-scales estimator The average (3.8) and the adjusted (3.9) TSRV estimator behave asymptotically identical. The difference comes with the number of grids K on finite samples. Reducing the number of grids increases the sub-grid mean $\bar{n}$ and hence the adjustment factor. The estimated volatility in this case will be scaled up. The adjustment factor is especially important in situations where the grid number is defined to be conditional on time or on the observed transactions.

3.2.5 *Area Adjusted Two-Time-Scales Estimator*

The average and the adjusted TSRV estimator both assume assumption 2. This especially includes i.i.d. noise. This assumption is at least disputable.

The fifth estimator, proposed by Zhang (2006) and Aït-Sahalia et al. (2011), generalizes the TSRV context to the area adjusted TSRV estimator following assumption 3. This estimator no longer expects i.i.d., but stationary and strong mixing noise. The estimator is given as:

$$\widehat{\text{TSRV}}^{(aa,Y)} = \frac{n}{(K-J)\bar{n}_K}\widehat{\text{TSRV}}^{(avg,Y)}.$$

Remark on the area adjusted two-time-scales estimator The area adjusted estimator inherits the properties to be unbiased and consistence from the classic TSRV estimator. The noise, however, is now allowed to be autocorrelated in the form that is characterized in assumption 3 in Section 3.1.3 on page 32.

Concluding remarks Due to the immense literature on volatility estimation, the presented estimators reflect those, that expand a conjoint basic model with additional characteristics in order to discriminate the differences, but that follow also a common data generation process. One further estimator that assumes a different data generation process will be introduced in Section 3.3.

Implementation Note, that the economic challenge of this thesis is to forecast ultra-high-frequent volatility shocks triggered through unexpected but publicly observable events. But, any estimation of model parameters requires also a suitable quantity of observations. To accomplish these requirement, is each estimator of the integrated volatility determined in non-overlapping fifteen second intervals, 480 times in total, each ex-ante and ex-post of any logged ad-hoc news reported incident. Some support to calculate the proposed estimators was further received by the R-library realized developed by S. Payseur. Moreover, xts, a R-library for time series representations, is used for data conversions.

3.3 Estimating Interday Periodicity

A referee pointed out, that a main characteristic of volatility estimates on asset quotes could be a type of *interday periodicity*. This is a time-of-the-day specific characteristic of the volatility estimates, which is different for each asset and periodically observable. It is therefore recommendable to assign the existence of interday periodicities to the stylized facts of volatility.

To give an example: Common patterns of interday periodicity are high levels of volatility with market opening (which is, at the FSE, actually at 9.00 am) and shortly before closing (which is, at the FSE, actually at 5.30 pm). Some, but not all, assets also show an increased volatility around midday.

Therefore, it could be recommendable to discriminate an asset typical volatility level at market opening or closing from unexpected volatility levels that could be explained by exogenous factors. Hence, it seems to be advisable to estimate the asset individual interday periodicity first, and to scale thereafter the volatility estimates of Section 3.2 by the asset and time-of-the-day specific "natural" volatility level. Remaining shocks, finally, are assumed to be unexplained volatility shocks.

3.3.1 *Modelling Interday Periodicity*

To specify the interday periodicity it is assumed that the logarithm of the asset price $\log S_t = X_t$ follows a diffusion with deterministic mean $\mu_t dt$ and stochastic variance $\sigma_t dB_t$, with B_t the standard Brownian motion, following formula (2.7) on page 18, but with an additional additive associated jump process $\kappa_t dJ_t$.

Note, that it is not the intention of the interday periodicity estimation to explain shocks, but to explain systematic characteristics. The task of the additional jump component is to explain extraordinary peaks by the jump component, and not by the diffusion. Furthermore, the jump process is supposed to be finite and independent of the diffusion. The jump size is determined by κ_t, the jump intensity is governed by a finite counting Poisson process J_t with time varying intensity $\lambda(t)$, that is $P(dJ_t = 1) = \lambda(t)dt$. This model is also used in Andersen et al. (2007).

All in all, the log price diffusion admits the representation:

$$dX_t = \mu_t dt + \sigma_t dB_t + \kappa_t dJ_t. \tag{3.10}$$

These mixtures of *jump-diffusion-models* using both, (1) continuous variance and (2) discrete jump processes to explain the underlying return series, were first proposed by Merton (1976), which is still a recommendable reference for first inspections. The intuitive inclusion is, that in formula (3.10) the jump component is modelled by a distribution describing a pulse.

Recall, that the deterministic component is related to the risk free interest rate. The following operations on ultra-high-frequent scales is therefore sufficient to set the deterministic component to $\mu_t = 0$, assuming a non-significant mean process.

Let further the discrete, and with period Δ, sampled returns be denoted by $r_{t,\Delta} = X_{t,\Delta} - X_{(t-1),\Delta}$. To ease the notation, normalize the time interval of one day to unity. All further notations within this section running from t to $t+1$ will therefore describe a full day. For example, using a five minute sampling, makes

$$\Lambda = \frac{1}{8.5 \times 60/5} = \frac{1}{102}$$

the sampling frequency (a trading day on the FSE has 8.5 hours) and $1/\Delta = 102$ the number of observations within a day. $1/\Delta$ is assumed to be integer, if not, use $\lfloor 1/\Delta \rfloor$ instead.

Under the assumption that the log price process follows (3.10), showed Andersen et al. (2007), that for $\Delta \to 0$:

$$\mathrm{RV}^{(\mathrm{all},Y)}{}_{t+1} \xrightarrow{P} \int_t^{t+1} \sigma_s^2 ds + \sum_{t<s\leqslant t<t+1} \kappa_s^2. \tag{3.11}$$

Please note, in contradiction to formula (3.1) on page 34, the additional jump size parameter κ.

Note, that the authors used five minute returns to reduce the influence of microstructure noise. This was discussed before as sparse sampling, see Section 3.2.1 on page 33. The implementation used in this thesis to determine the interday periodicity follows this strategy.

However, Barndorff-Nielsen and Shephard (2004, 2006) propose for jump diffusion models according to (3.10), to use their *Bipower Variation (BPV)* estimator of the integrated volatility that allows especially to separate between the components of formula (3.10). The standardized realized bipower variation is, for $\Delta \to 0$, given by:

$$\widehat{\mathrm{BPV}}_{t+1} = \frac{\pi}{2} \sum_{t=2}^{n} |r_{t,\Delta}||r_{(t-1),\Delta}|$$

with

$$\widehat{\mathrm{BPV}}_{t+1} \xrightarrow{P} \int_t^{t+1} \sigma_s^2 ds \tag{3.12}$$

see Andersen et al. (2007). Hence, combining formula (3.11) and formula (3.12), the discrete jumps can be consistently estimated for $\Delta \to 0$ by

$$\widehat{RV}^{(all,Y)}_{t+1} - \widehat{BPV}_{t+1} \xrightarrow{P} \sum_{t<s\leqslant t<t+1} \kappa_s^2,$$

see Barndorff-Nielsen and Shephard (2004) and Andersen et al. (2007).

It is now the objective to determine the from jump effects separated interday periodicity. Andersen and Bollerslev (1997) suggest for this purpose to impose additional structure on the spot volatility, assuming that the local volatility can be explained by an interday periodicity factor $f_{i,\Delta}$ (non-constant but identical for every day) and a daily volatility factor (identical within a day but usually non-identical on different days). Here, the index i denotes the window under analysis, e. g. a 5 minute window, within the one day interval [0,1], see Boudt et al. (2012):

$$\int_{(i-1),\Delta}^{i,\Delta} \sigma_s^2 ds = f_{i,\Delta}^2 \int_0^1 \sigma_s^2 ds.$$

Under the DGP of formula (3.10), with $\Delta \to 0$ and within an interval without jumps, are the returns r_i conditional normal distributed with variance

$$\sigma_i^2 = \int_{(i-1),\Delta}^{i,\Delta} \sigma_s^2 ds,$$

see Boudt et al. (2011). Setting $s_i = \sigma_i / f_i$ makes s_i the periodically adjusted volatility estimate of the returns r_i. Common estimators of s_i on data generation processes following (2.7) are the realized volatility estimators discussed in Section 3.2.

Here, however, Boudt et al. (2011) suggest the following normalized version of the BPV estimator over the local window i, with $r_{j+1}, \ldots, r_{j+\lfloor 1/\Delta \rfloor}$ the $\lfloor 1/\Delta \rfloor$ returns within the given window. Assuming the window under analysis to be of one day, this is:

$$\hat{s}_i = \sqrt{\frac{\pi}{2} \frac{1}{\lfloor 1/\Delta \rfloor - 1} \sum_{l=j+2}^{j+\lfloor 1/\Delta \rfloor} |r_l||r_{l-1}|}. \tag{3.13}$$

To estimate in the next step the interday periodicity f_i, first standardize the observed high-frequency returns r_i to

$$\bar{r}_i = r_i / \hat{s}_i$$

using $\hat{s}_i$ from formula (3.13). In the following, two suggestions developed by Taylor and Xu (1997) (non-parametric) and Andersen and Bollerslev (1997) (parametric) to estimate the interday periodicity f_i are concerned.

3.3.2 *Non-Parametric Periodicity Estimation*

The first proposal is non-parametric. This estimator scales those standardized returns that are observed at identical times, but on different days, with the average standardized return of the proposed periodicity window averaged over all considered days.

Following the notation of Boudt et al. (2011), let $\bar{r}_{1,i}, \ldots, \bar{r}_{n_i,i}$ denote the standardized returns observed at identical times of the day and day of the week at which r_i is observed. Further, let N_i denote the index set of those indices, that belong to the identical time as index i, having $\lfloor 1/\Delta \rfloor$ observations. The non-parametric interday periodicity estimator of one day, proposed from Taylor and Xu (1997), is then given by:

$$\hat{f}_i = \frac{\sqrt{\frac{1}{n_i}\sum_{j=1}^{n_i} \bar{r}_{j,i}^2}}{\sqrt{\frac{1}{\lfloor 1/\Delta \rfloor}\sum_{j \in N_i}\left(\frac{1}{n_i}\sum_{j=1}^{n_i} \bar{r}_{j,i}^2\right)}}. \tag{3.14}$$

The nominator gives the square root of the average quadratic standardized return observed at identical times, but on different days. The denominator gives the square root of the average standardized returns in the corresponding periodicity window, averaged over all considered days. The denominator accounts further for the standardization:

$$\lfloor 1/\Delta \rfloor \sum_{j \in N_i} f_j^2 = 1. \tag{3.15}$$

The intuitive meaning of the standardization (3.15) is, that the final interday periodicity estimate will be a vector of estimates surrounding the value 1.

Note however, that this non-parametric estimator only makes use of a subset of the given data. Namely only of those with identical periodicity windows. This reduction of data results in inefficient estimates.

But, Andersen and Bollerslev (1997) were able to show, that more efficient estimates can be obtained when using the proposed parametric periodicity estimator of Section 3.3.3, and with this the full domain of the considered time series, see Boudt et al. (2011).

3.3.3 *Parametric Periodicity Estimation*

The second proposal of Andersen and Bollerslev (1997) to estimate the interday periodicity is parametric and makes use of the full domain of the considered time series. They propose to model the logarithm of the periodicity factor $\log f_i$

using a linear function of a vector of variables x_i, (e. g. a polynomial or trigonometrical transformation of the time of the day), that is $\log f_i = x_i^{'}\theta$, where θ is the true parameter vector. Therefore, the authors consider the regression

$$\log |\bar{r}_i| - c = x_i^{'}\theta + \varepsilon_i$$

with i.i.d. error terms ε_i having zero mean and a density function of an absolute log-normal distribution and the parameter c the mean of the absolute log-normal distribution, which is approximately $c \approx$ -0.63518, see Boudt et al. (2011).

Boudt et al. (2011) suggest to use the Truncated Maximum Likelihood (TML) estimator introduced by Marazzi and Yohai (2004) instead of an OLS or ML estimator to determine θ. Their arguments are, that (1) an OLS estimation would not be efficient, due to the non-normality of the error vector ε_i, and that (2) the efficient ML estimator was shown to be biased in the presence of jumps in the simulation study of the authors, while the proposed TML estimator makes use of the shortest half scale estimator proposed by Rousseeuw and Leroy (1988). This estimator is shown to be robust in the sense, that jumps cause the minimum of the possible bias, see Martin and Zamar (1993). The correction is finally done by weightings, giving identified jumps the weight zero, see Boudt et al. (2011) for further details.

The TML estimator proposed by Boudt et al. (2011) is then given by:

$$\hat{\theta}^{\text{TML}} = \arg\min_{\theta} \frac{1}{\sum_{i=1}^{n} \delta_i} \sum_{i=1}^{n} \delta_i \rho^{\text{ML}}(\varepsilon_{i,\theta}),$$

with

$$\delta_i = \begin{cases} 1 & \text{if } \rho^{\text{ML}}(\varepsilon_i^{wn}) \leqslant \rho^{\text{ML}}(q) \text{ and} \\ 0 & \text{else,} \end{cases}$$

$$\rho^{\text{ML}}(z) = -0.5 \log(2/\pi) - z - c + 0.5 \exp(2(z + c)),$$

$$\varepsilon_i^{wn} = \log |\bar{r}_i| - c - \log f_i^{wn},$$

with f_i^{wn} the weighed and hence outlier corrected variant of the non-parametric estimator (3.14), n denoting the number of equally-spaced return observations r_i over all days, and q denoting an extreme upper quantile of the distribution of ε_i. Note, that ε_i is distributed to an absolute log-normal. Hence, considering the upper quantiles also includes the lower quantiles. For example, setting q to the 99.5% quantile will give all observations with $\rho^{\text{ML}}(\varepsilon_i^{wn}) > 3.36$ a weight of zero, see Boudt et al. (2011).

The proposed parametric TML estimator for the interday periodicity is finally

$$\hat{\hat{f}}_i = \frac{\exp(x_i^{'}\hat{\theta}^{\text{TML}})}{\sqrt{\frac{1}{\lfloor \lambda/\Delta \rfloor} \sum_{j \in N_i} \exp(x_i^{'}\hat{\theta}^{\text{TML}})}}. \tag{3.16}$$

Concluding remarks Please note, that the periodicity factor f_i is above one in periods with periodically high volatility and below one in periods with periodically low volatility, see formula (3.15) and compare the exemplarily estimation of the interday periodicity in Figure 3.2. Recall, that it was a referee who

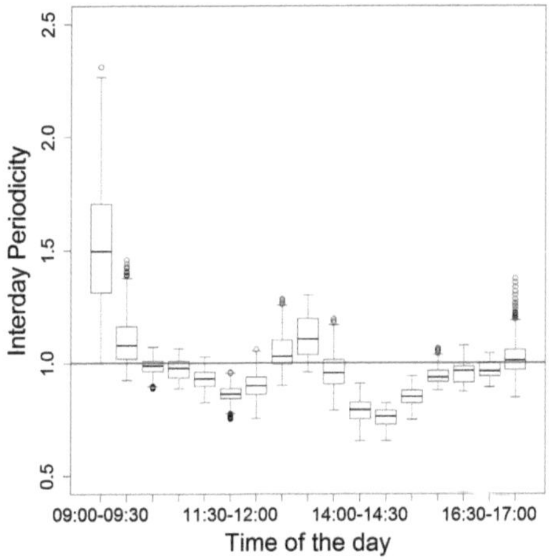

Figure 3.2: Rolling interday periodicity estimates of the SDAX asset Amadeus Fire using the non-parametric periodicity estimator (3.16). The estimates are associated on a half year rolling window of transaction prices in 2010 and 2011 (1st rolling window is from January 2010 to June 2010, the last rolling window from July 2011 to December 2011). Each periodicity estimation is based on six months of five minute records over 8.5 trading hours each day. The boxplots represents hence each 510 interday periodicity estimates.

pointed out, that a main characteristic of volatility estimates on asset quotes could be a type of *interday periodicity*. But, it is still unclear whether the correction of an interday periodicity effect is recommendable for the task under analysis in this thesis to forecast high-frequency volatility shocks. Inspecting the values domain of the estimates in Figure 3.2, it is obvious that (1) the time of the day has considerable effects on the "natural level" of the asset typical volatility, but also that (2) the level is (using the median statistic as a-priori information to correct for the interday effect), in relation to the shocks under analysis, relatively small. It seems nevertheless advisable to account for the time of the day effect when inspecting the reaction of the latent integrated volatility to the arrival of unexpected events at different times. Therefore, all integrated volatility estimates (Section 3.2) are corrected by the time of the day specific interday periodicity factor.

Implementation Support for the parametric and the non-parametric interday periodicity estimation is given by the R-library RTAQ, developed by K. Boudt and J. Cornelissen. The interday periodicity factor is determined by the TML estimator of formula (3.16), whereas the daily volatility factor is calculated twice, once by the BPV-type estimator of formula (3.13) and once by the RV estimator of formula (3.2).

4 Zero-inflated Data Generation Processes

The estimation of the integrated volatility implies two phenomenons, (1) the estimation characteristics coming with the selected volatility estimator, and (2) the zero-inflation coming with the ultra-high-frequency measurement, meaning the agglomerated appearance of zeros. Zero-inflation occurs especially in situations where the frequency of transaction records is substantially larger than the frequency of price changes, and can be observed in the transaction records as well as in the resulting volatility estimates.

Hence, the purpose of this chapter is to affiliate the new model of Kömm and Küsters (2015) to take two aspects into account: (1) the zero-inflation of the volatility estimates based on ultra-high-frequency data measured in transaction time and (2) the time series characteristics of volatility estimates especially autocorrelation.

The content of the chapter is threefold: Section 4.1 gives a descriptive analysis of the considered assets separated for the indices, both for transaction quotes respectively returns as well as corresponding volatility estimates. Section 4.2 introduces the methodological framework of zero-inflated models in discrete, semi-continuous, and continuous time. Section 4.3 presents the new Markov switching mixture model for zero-inflated and autoregressive time series, and emphasizes the difference to the common zero-inflation models introduced in Section 4.2.

4.1 Descriptive Analysis

The purpose of a descriptive analysis is to present the object of interest in few meaningful statistics, together with a fundamental analysis of the considered object. Therefore, the descriptive analysis is positioned between the data sampling and the application of models.

4.1.1 *Data Description*

The sampling scheme used for all further analysis is transaction time sampling, providing the largest possible data set. The assets under analysis are all companies listed in one of the Frankfurt stock exchange (FSE) indices DAX, MDAX, SDAX or TecDAX. All companies listed in one of these indices belong to the prime standard, which is a market segment of the FSE having high levels of transparency standards. These affect e. g. the duty of quarterly instead of yearly reporting and ad-hoc disclosures in both, German and English, instead of disclosures in German only, as it is sufficient for the general standard.

The analysis of the transaction frequencies (this is the number of transactions, not the trading volume) of the assets listed in the indices DAX, MDAX, SDAX and TecDAX starts with a summary statistic of the monthly records of the assets sampled in transaction time in 2010 and 2011, and is reported in Table 4.1:

	DAX	MDAX	SDAX	TecDAX
ASK				
Minimum :	130,132	11,125	1,156	1,902
1st Quartile :	561,046	234,742	58,902	146,272
Median :	795,788	318,789	113,489	217,140
Mean :	1,052,407	371,176	133,003	235,735
3rd Quartile :	1,292,727	443,164	184,553	298,368
Maximum :	4,445,282	2,732,277	772,127	1,009,841
BID				
Minimum :	130,066	8,875	964	901
1st Quartile :	558,706	232,567	58,247	147,793
Median :	791,304	318,752	112,456	214,037
Mean :	1,046,156	367,825	129,479	232,272
3rd Quartile :	1,274,221	440,079	181,258	289,082
Maximum :	4,408,586	2,685,271	604,018	935,527

Table 4.1: Monthly transaction frequencies of the assets listed in the indices DAX, MDAX, SDAX and TecDAX, sampled in transaction time in 2010 and 2011 and separately for ask and bid quotes.

More than 50% of the reported transactions accumulate in the large-cap stock index DAX. This index unites the 30 most frequently traded assets on the FSE. The non-technology indices MDAX, standing for mid-cap DAX, and SDAX, standing for small-cap DAX each further unite 50 companies. The technology index TecDAX is, according to the quantity of transaction records, to be settled between MDAX and SDAX. The TecDAX is made up by 30 companies from the technology sector.

In total, these are 160 companies recorded in 2010 and 2011, each for bid and ask quotes, which makes a two year dataset of about one hundred million records per month.

4.1.2 *Data Presentation*

Note, that the relevant information is: What is the proportion of zeros in the return series and what is the resulting proportion of zeros in the volatility estimates, based on the asset quote records measured in transaction time?

The records considered in Table 4.1 include sequences of successive trades at identical prices. The returns of these trades, this is the first difference of the logarithm of the recorded prices, should therefore show a substantial proportion of zeros. Figure 4.1 on this page shows, for comparison purposes, the monthly frequency of trades, and Figure 4.2 on the next page the corresponding proportion of zero changes in the corresponding return series. Both figures are given for the DAX ask quotes. An inspection of bid quotes yields in very similar results.

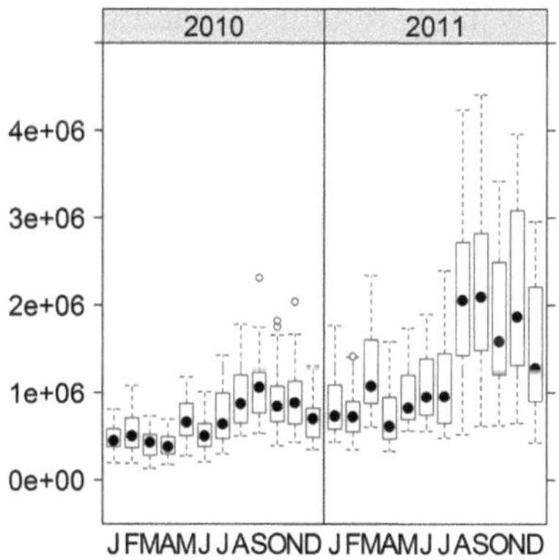

Figure 4.1: Transaction frequencies of the ask quotes for the DAX assets from January 2010 to December 2011. Note, the significant increase of zeros from July to August 2011, which can be explained by a new automated trading service introduced by the Deutsche Börse Group.

Please note the shock in the total number of transactions illustrated in Figure 4.1. An explanation of this effect might be the new service for ultra-fast

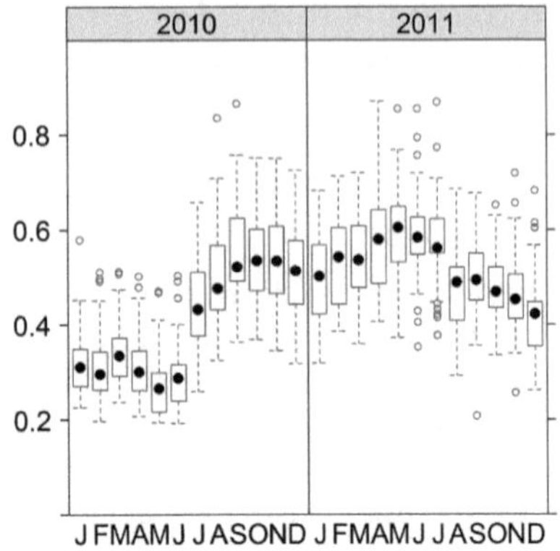

Figure 4.2: Proportion of zeros in the ask quote return series of DAX assets from January 2010 to December 2011.

processing of new information started by the Deutsche Börse Group in August 2011, see Petring and Bayer (September 9th, 2011). The corresponding effect on the proportion of zeros in the return series is given in Figure 4.2. The effect of the proportion of zeros in the resulting volatility estimates relevant for this thesis is given in Figure 4.3 on page 52.

A potential cause of the observed effect could be, that the increased trading speed, due to the new service for ultra-fast processing of new information, called Alpha Flash, also increased the number of executed trades. Best bid and best ask prices in the order book, see Figure 2.1 on page 23, are more likely to hit. The increased trading speed will hence also increase the spread of bid to ask quotes. This increased spread straddles the fluctuation in the returns series and leads to a significant increase of the assets volatility, which means a decrease of zero volatility estimates. An inspection of the indices MDAX, SDAX, and TecDAX confirms the general findings on zero proportions, but the effect of the new service is only found for the DAX.

4.1.3 *Characterising Zero-inflated Data*

Zero-inflation indicates a disproportionately high number of zeros in the data. Here, the add on *inflation* refers to a comparison of the empirical with a theoretical distribution. The number of zero counts in the empirical observations is in a zero-inflated data set far beyond the expected value in a theoretical distribution.

Meaning that the observed frequency of zeros clearly exceeds the theoretically expected value.

The canonical assumption on the distribution of financial returns is the normal distribution. Even though the non-normality of financial returns was subject to a variety of research papers, see e. g. Esch (2010) for a discussion of models that account explicitly for the non-normality of returns. But, the probability of an observation to be exactly zero is, due to the continuity of normal distributed random variables X, equal to zero, in other words, $P(X = 0) = 0$. This is true for each single-point measurement on continuous distributions. It is hence questionable, whether a pure (not mixture) continuous distribution is able to account for zero-inflation.

The DAX returns in Figure 4.2, however, show a significant proportion of zero returns. Please note, that the reported zero returns are exactly zero, and not a small aberration close to zero. Therefore, it is convincing to assume that financial returns of asset prices measured in transaction time follow a zero-inflated DGP, and that the normal distribution alone will not be able to account for this characteristic.

Note, however, that the object of interest is not the return series but the series of estimated integrated volatilities. But, the proportion of zeros in the returns recorded in Figure 4.2 should transfer to the proportion of zeros in the estimates of the integrated volatility in Figure 4.3 on the next page. Note, that the volatility estimation in this figure is based on an area-adjusted TSRV estimate, see Section 3.2.5 on page 39. Inspecting the results of the remaining volatility estimators described in Section 3.2 yields very similar results, for both, ask and bid quotes.

The significant increase in the number of transaction records, see Figure 4.1, from July to August 2011 has had a much more resounding effect on the zero to non-zero proportion in the volatility estimate in Figure 4.3a, than in the return series in Figure 4.2. The proportion of zeros in the MDAX, Figure 4.3b, seems to be affected too, but weak. The effects in the indices SDAX and TecDAX are similar to the effect in the MDAX.

That means, that the assets within the four indices DAX, MDAX, SDAX and TecDAX show a substantial proportion of zeros in the transactions, the returns and the corresponding volatility estimates. Any model designed to monitor the integrated volatility on a ultra-high frequency scale should therefore especially account for zero-inflation.

Concluding remarks It is noteworthy, that the jump from July to August 2011 in the total number of observations in Figure 4.1 only shows a small effect in the proportion of zeros in the corresponding returns in Figure 4.2, but a significant decrease in the corresponding volatility estimate in Figure 4.3a. A

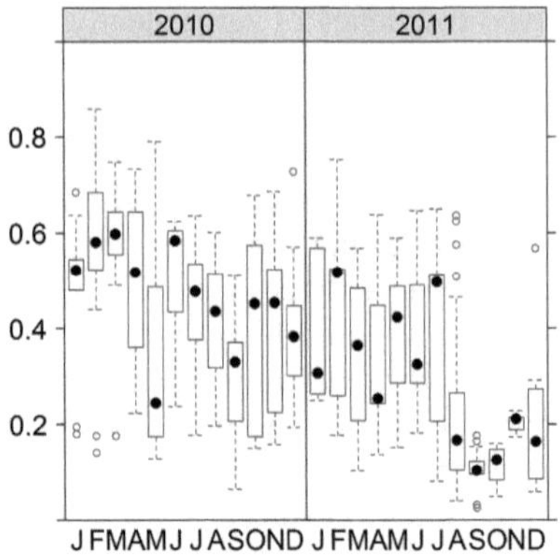

(a) DAX zero volatility.

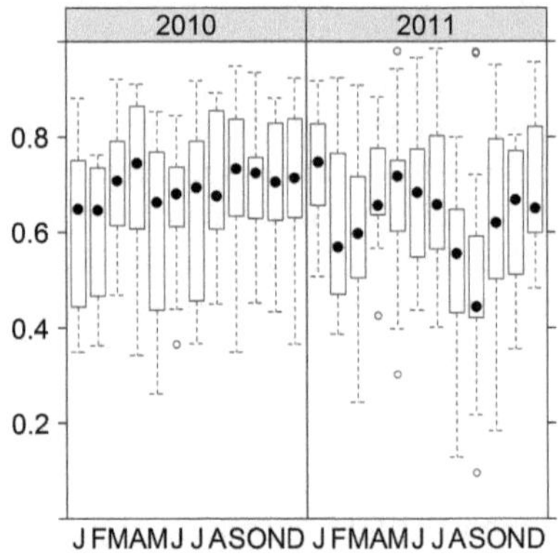

(b) MDAX zero volatility.

Figure 4.3: Proportion of zeros in the volatility estimates of the assets in the indices DAX and MDAX. Estimated with the area adjusted TSRV estimator, Section 3.2.5 on page 39, on ask quotes, both for 2010 and 2011.

possible explanation could be, that the starting of the new service for ultra-fast processing of new information increased the number of transactions, but only with low effect on the proportion of zeros in the return series. However, the for microstructure noise corrected TSRV estimate accounts for this high-frequency effect, resulting in a significant decrease in zeros.

Therefore, it can be assumed that the starting of the new service also increased the market volatility, because of the reduced proportion of zeros. This consequence is in line with the position of high-frequency trading proponents arguing, that algo-trading-systems improve the market efficiencies and increase therefore the number of contract conclusions (increased number of transaction, Figure 4.1). It also supports, however, the position of high-frequency opponents, arguing that algorithmic controlled trading strategies also increase the market volatility, especially in uncertain times (decreased proportion of zeros in volatility estimates, Figure 4.3a).

4.2 Zero-inflated Models

Zero-inflation accounting models are common in micro-econometrics and intermittent demand literature. An important distinction of the models refers to the value-domain, which is either (1) continuous, (2) semi-continuous, or (3) discrete. All models in common is a positive and not negligible probability mass at zero.

In the following, an exemplary outline is given for models common to use for the value-domains: (1) non-negative and semi-continuous, (2) non-negative and discrete, see Min and Agresti (2002), as well as (3) continuous on the entire real axis, see McLachlan and Peel (2000).

However, for continuous time series data, that are also autoregressive or heteroscedastic, it is proposed to use the new approach of Kömm and Küsters (2015), which accounts especially for these characteristics.

The purpose of this section is to introduce a selection of common models accounting for zero-inflation, and to tell the difference of each of these approaches in comparison with the new model of Kömm and Küsters.

4.2.1 *Semi-continuous Data*

The first considered value-domain is semi-continuity. This is a weaker property than continuity and can roughly be explained with the following example: Assume f to be a continuous and real-valued function, but with a single jump in x_0. The function f is, because of the jump in x_0, either left or right continuous at x_0. But the function is semi-continuous in x_0 (for an upper (lower) jump, f is called to be upper (lower) semi-continuous). Discrete distribution functions, for example, are upper semi-continuous.

Tobit models Tobin (1958) was the first who proposed a hybrid of (1) *probit analysis* and (2) *multiple regression* models to model semi-continuous data. Probit models belong to regression models, but with binary restricted responses, e. g. a simple yes or no decision (response values are also known as dependent variables in regression models). Hence, Probit models alone do not regard for the entire non-negative real axis under analysis. The proposal of Tobin is, to assume the existence of a latent variable that is linear dependent of one or more independent variables with corresponding parameter vectors. This concept is well known from linear regression models. But, contrary to linear regression models is the observed variable defined to be identical to the latent variable in all cases where the latent variable is positive, and to be zero, if the latent variable is zero or negative. This proposal is known as *Tobit*-model, in imitation on *Tobin* and the affinity to the binary decision of *Probit* models. Here, the interesting idea is the introduction of a latent variable with the real-axis as value-domain, but to censor the latent variable in two states, positive and non-positive, in this way modelling zero-inflation.

Further developments of non-negative and semi-continuous models accounting for zero-inflation are for example (1) two-part models, see Duan et al. (1983), (2) compound Poisson exponential dispersion models, see Jørgensen (1987), or (3) ordinal threshold models, see McCullagh (1980).

This type of modelling restricts the value-domain to be the non-negative real axis. The object under analysis, however, is the changing (measured by the first difference) of the integrated volatility estimate. Hence, the value-domain of the object under analysis needs to account for positive as well as negative values.

4.2.2 *Discrete Data*

The second considered value-domain are discrete values. Zero-inflated count data models, for example, belong to this domain. An introduction to the general analysis of count data is e. g. given in Winkelmann (2008).

Hurdle-at-Zero Models Mullahy (1986) introduced Hurdle count data models in general, and Hurdle-at-zero models in particular. Hurdle-at-zero models are two-part models with a truncated count component for positive responses and a Hurdle component for zero responses. The first part of the model classifies the response to be zero or positive, usually using a probit or logit regression. The second part of the model determines the level of positive responses, using a truncated-at-zero model with strictly positive responses. Often using a truncated Poisson or a truncated negative binomial regression.

Further developments of non-negative and discrete models accounting for zero-inflation are for example (1) zero-inflated Poisson models, see Lambert (1992) and (2) zero-inflated binomial models, see Hall (2000).

This type of modelling restricts the value-domain to be the non-negative discrete axis. But, the volatility estimates under analysis are high-frequency time series and hence assumed to be quasi-continuous. Discrete data models therefore also seem to be unsuitable to account for the requirements of this thesis.

4.2.3 *Continuous Data*

The third considered value-domain is for continuous data, not constrained to value-domain subsets and not restricted to be discrete.

Finite Mixture Models The common approach to model zero-inflated models in continuous time are finite mixture models. These models suppose an existing representation of the response density function through the convex combination of two or more individual density functions. The applied weights are called mixing proportions, are positive and sum to one while the individual densities are called component densities. Details are e. g. provided in Everitt and Hand (1981) and McLachlan and Peel (2000). Zero-inflated models for count data are finite mixture models on discrete distributions, using two discrete densities with one of them degenerated at zero. When using continuous instead of discrete distributions, or a mixture of both, these are finite mixture models in continuous time.

Note, that this type of modelling does not restrict the value-domain, neither to be non-negative nor to be discrete. Finite mixture models are therefore principally suitable to model the relevant changes of the integrated volatility estimates. But, the time series of volatility estimates also show time series typical characteristics, especially autocorrelation. Therefore, an extension of the mixture models to a new model that accounts for (1) zero-inflation, (2) a quasi-continuous value-domain, and (3) autocorrelation is required.

4.3 Modelling Zero-inflated Volatility Estimates

Kömm and Küsters (2015) proposed a *Markov switching mixture model*, that not only accounts for a two-state discrimination of zeros and non-zeros, but also for autoregression and heteroscedasticity, both common characteristics in time series analysis.

The new proposal combines elements of zero-inflated models with traditional ARIMA-GARCH models and accounts in the full parametrization for (1) zero-inflation, (2) autoregression, and (3) heteroscedasticity in continuous time on the entire real axis. Fur this purpose, the model in the given form makes use of a truncated normal distribution and a censoring component. The censoring component reports small fluctuations in the prices as zero, that can not be explained by a revaluation of the market, but by natural price fluctuations due to the high-frequency measurement. This censoring component strengthens therefore the zero-inflation.

This section summarizes the model of Kömm and Küsters.

4.3.1 *Markov Transition Probabilities*

Let $z_t = \nabla\widehat{IV}_t = \widehat{IV}_t - \widehat{IV}_{t-1}$ denote the first difference of the time series of integrated volatility estimates. Note, that the estimate can be done by any of the discussed integrated volatility estimators in Section 3.2. The first difference will moreover measure the change, not the absolute level, of the estimated volatilities between two sequenced time points $t-1$ and t. That means, that the estimate of the integrated volatility $\widehat{IV}_t$ is based on the transaction records observed between $t-1$ and t. Note, that the estimate of the integrated volatility is zero if there are no observations in $(t-1, t]$.

Markov chain states The Markov chain, inserted to the model to account for the zero-inflation, has two states: (1) the zero change state, $z_t = 0$, and (2) the non-zero change state, $z_t \neq 0$.

Markov Transition matrix The time dependencies of the Markov chain are modelled by the conditional transition probabilities ω_{i1} for $i \in \{0, 1\}$ where $\omega_{01} = P(z_t \neq 0 \mid z_{t-1} = 0)$ and $\omega_{11} = P(z_t \neq 0 \mid z_{t-1} \neq 0)$, and combined to the transition matrix as given in Table 4.2:

ω_{i1}	$z_t = 0$	$z_t \neq 0$
$z_{t-1} = 0$	$1 - \omega_{01}$	ω_{01}
$z_{t-1} \neq 0$	$1 - \omega_{11}$	ω_{11}

Table 4.2: Markov transition matrix.

Example To demonstrate, how the Markov switching component will account for zero-inflation, exemplary consider the time series of Biotest on March 22nd, 2011 from 11:02:00 a.m. to 3:02:00 p.m. GMT. Note, that the time window covers exactly four hours, namely two hours before and two hours after the arrival of an unexpected news at 1:02:00 p.m. Note further, that two of the measures of interest will be the changings of the transition probabilities estimates ω_{01} and ω_{11} from the earlier to the later window. The time series as well as the corresponding area-adjusted TSRV estimates of this series are given in Figure 1.1 on page 3.

Table 4.3 exemplarily reports the corresponding 2×2-contingency tables of zero and non-zero frequencies h_{ij}, as well as the conditional frequencies ω_{01} and ω_{11} of the estimated integrated volatilities. The estimates are separated in pre-incident (left hand side) and post-incident (right hand side) estimates.

h_{ij}	$z_t = 0$	$z_t \neq 0$
$z_{t-1} = 0$	441	12
$z_{t-1} \neq 0$	12	14

(a) Absolute frequencies

h_{ij}	$z_t = 0$	$z_t \neq 0$
$z_{t-1} = 0$	358	28
$z_{t-1} \neq 0$	27	66

(b) Absolute frequencies

$\hat{\omega}_{i1}$	$z_t = 0$	$z_t \neq 0$
$z_{t-1} = 0$	.97	.03
$z_{t-1} \neq 0$	.46	.54

(c) Conditional frequencies

$\hat{\omega}_{i1}$	$z_t = 0$	$z_t \neq 0$
$z_{t-1} = 0$	.93	.07
$z_{t-1} \neq 0$	.29	.71

(d) Conditional frequencies

Table 4.3: Transition matrices of the area-adjusted TSRV estimates of Biotest AG bid quotes measured in transaction time on March 22nd, 2011. The tables on the left hand side report the values from 11:02:00 a.m. to 1:02:00 p.m. GMT. The tables on the right hand side report the values from 1:02:01 p.m. to 3:02:00 p.m. GMT. Please note the increased transition probabilities ω_{01} and ω_{11} from .03 to .07 respectively from .54 to .71, indicating an increased volatility in the later time window.

It can be concluded, that the arrival of the unexpected news at 1:02:00 p.m. has had an increasing effect on the latent volatility, which is measured by the microstructure noise corrected area-adjusted TSRV estimator. However, it can hitherto not been concluded, whether the observed increase is significant, or explained by random variation. Therefore, further analysis on the latent DGP and the significance of changes in the context of the DGP is required.

Please note, that a natural fluctuation in price time series measured in transaction time, e. g. a sequence of price fluctuations by one cent, will also be part of the estimated volatility. The fluctuations, however, may be caused by technical reasons, e. g. two competing algorithmic trading systems, and are therefore not necessarily caused by company revaluations. Small price changes in high-frequent time series should therefore not be attributed to changed market conditions, but to a natural discrepancy in the subjective fair evaluation of an asset. It is therefore proposed, that the DGP describing model holds a parameter τ to filter small volatility estimates caused by small fluctuations in the price process.

Information Augmentation To advance the idea, it is recommendable to further discriminate between periods of information augmentations and constant states. Constant states do not change the volatility, which is equivalent to $z_t = 0$. States of information augmentations can, but must not change the volatility. Therefore, it should be differentiated between observable values z_t and latent values z_t^*, linked by the regulation:

1. z_t^* observations outside the interval $[-\tau, \tau]$ are reported as observable, i. e. $z_t^* = z_t$.

2. z_t^* observations inside the interval $[-\tau, \tau]$ are reported as $z_t = 0$.

No change states $z_t = 0$ can hence result out of two sources: (1) Either by constant states without new information or (2) by states of information augmentations, but with changes too small to be considered, e. g. on the above described natural fluctuation on small levels often found in high-frequency time series. This characteristic is in contrary to the given example of Biotest, but typical for MDAX and in particular for DAX assets. Note, that the critical barrier of natural fluctuation $\pm\tau$ is no a-priori information, but estimated as asset specific characteristic together with the remaining model parameters.

Modelling the latent variable z_t^* further assumes to postulate an assumed DGP. It is therefore assumed, that the first difference of the DGP is symmetric and mesokurtic, as long as there are no other rationale to account to asymmetric, leptokurtic or platykurtic pattern. The canonical choice of a symmetric and mesokurtic distribution is the normal. The DGP of the latent variable z_t^* is therefore assumed to be $N(\mu, \sigma^2)$. Fat-tail distributions, however, can be used as well.

Model parameters The proposed specification makes the latent variable z_t^* outside the interval $[-\tau, \tau]$ a random variable. Kömm and Küsters (2015) suggest to describe the process with a canonical normal distribution $\phi(z_t^* \mid c + \rho z_{t-1}, \sigma^2)$, with $c + \rho z_{t-1}$ denoting the expectation value of the latent variable z_t^* at time t given by the prior observation z_{t-1} at time $t - 1$,

- c denoting the intercept,
- ρ denoting the autoregressive coefficient to incorporate an AR(1),
- σ^2 denoting the natural variation (fluctuation), and
- ϕ denoting the density of a normal distribution.

Figure 4.4 illustrates the two-state Markov switching mixture model proposed by Kömm and Küsters (2015), where the additional parameter I_{t-1} denotes the information set available at time $t - 1$.

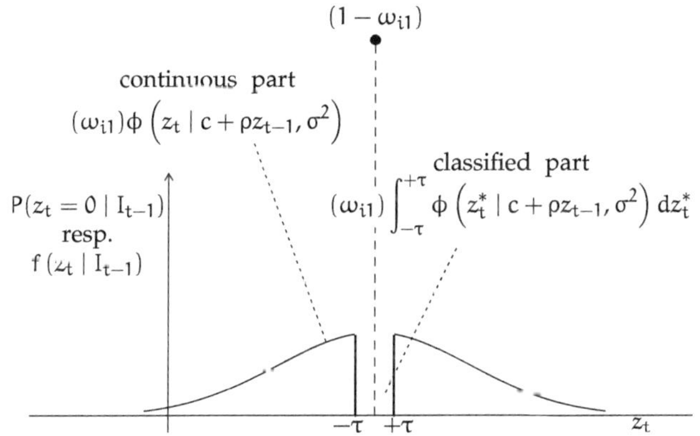

Figure 4.4: The Markov switching mixture model proposed by Kömm and Küsters (2015), mixing a discrete and degenerated at zero with a truncated normal distribution. Here, I_{t-1} denotes the information set available at time $t - 1$.

Please note, that the parametrization of the transition probabilities used in this thesis differs from the parametrization used by the authors in Kömm and Küsters (2015), e. g. using 1-ω_{01} instead of ω_{00}. The main argument for the reparametrisation is, that the parameter of interest in this thesis is the probability of a non-zero state, which maybe represents a shock, not the zero state, which is of primary interest in Kömm and Küsters (2015).

The corresponding log-likelihood function, representing the model in Figure 4.4, is hence given by

$$\ell(\omega_{01}, \omega_{11}, c, \rho, \sigma^2, \tau) = \ell_{00} + \ell_{01} + \ell_{10} + \ell_{11}$$

where

$$\ell_{00} = \sum_{t \in \Omega_{00}} \ln \left((1 - \omega_{01}) + \omega_{01} \int_{-\tau}^{+\tau} \phi \left(z_t^* \mid c, \sigma^2 \right) dz_t^* \right)$$

$$\ell_{01} = \sum_{t \in \Omega_{01}} \ln \left((\omega_{01}) \, \phi \left(z_t \mid c, \sigma^2 \right) \right)$$

$$\ell_{10} = \sum_{t \in \Omega_{10}} \ln \left((1 - \omega_{11}) + \omega_{11} \int_{-\tau}^{+\tau} \phi \left(z_t^* \mid c + \rho z_{t-1}, \sigma^2 \right) dz_t^* \right)$$

$$\ell_{11} = \sum_{t \in \Omega_{11}} \ln \left((\omega_{11}) \, \phi \left(z_t \mid c + \rho z_{t-1}, \sigma^2 \right) \right)$$

with $\Omega_{ij} = \{t \in \{2, \ldots, T\} : z_{t-1} = i \wedge z_t = j\}$ for $i, j \in \{0, 1\}$ denoting the index sets corresponding to the four states of the transition matrix in Table 4.2 on page 56.

Note, that the model is designed to account for an autoregressive component of order one, but not of higher orders. This is due to the two transition probabilities ω_{01} and ω_{11}, resulting in a 2×2-transition matrix. Any higher order of autocorrelation would require to use additional transition probabilities and accordingly to extend the transition matrix as well as the log-likelihood function.

But, volatility estimates, as well as the underlying returns, show a non-negligible level of first order autocorrelation. Merging elements of Markov switching models with finite mixture models to a single holistic model including an autoregressive parameter, simultaneously allows to account for zero-inflation and autocorrelation in the latent DGP.

The time series characteristics, however, are further subject to permanent changes triggered through natural variations in time and structure-changing events. This requires the computation of partially nested sub-models, each representing individual characteristics, in order to search for the most suitable model to represent best the true, but latent DGP.

Nested sequence of sub-models The proposed Markov switching mixture model is hence not only a single model, but a nested sequence of sub-models, a dozen in total. The smallest possible model "M" explains the latent DGP exclusively by a natural variation σ. This base model is extended by further characteristics typical for zero-inflated and autocorrelated time series. The additional parameters are:

1. "C" to add a non-zero constant $c \in \mathbb{R}$. The absence of "C" includes the restriction $c = 0$.
2. "R" to add autocorrelation $\rho \in (0, 1)$. The absence of "R" includes the restriction $\rho = 0$.
3. "W2" to add a two-state Markovian model with non-equal parameters $\omega_{01}, \omega_{11} \in (0, 1)$.
4. "W" to add a two-state Markovian model without memory with $\omega_{01} = \omega_{11}$, and $\omega_{01}, \omega_{11} \in (0, 1)$.

The absence of either "W" or "W2" include the restriction to a model without Markovian characteristics. The structure of the nested sequence of sub-models is illustrated in Figure 4.5.

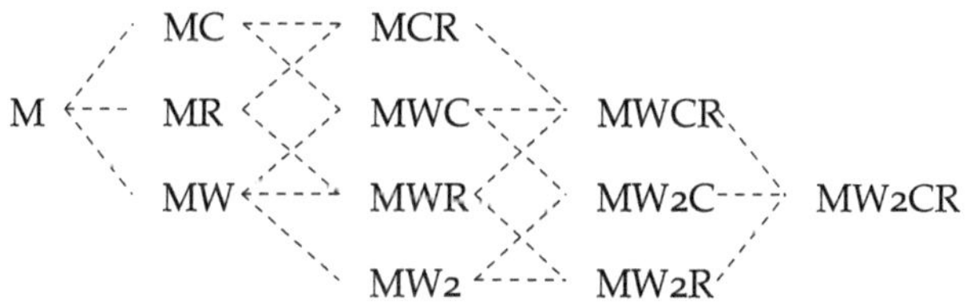

Figure 4.5: Partially nested sequence of sub-models. A dozen in total. Starting with model "M", modelling the latent DGP with a single variation parameter σ, and expanding to the full model "MW2CR", modelling the latent DGP with parameters for variation "M", constant level shifting "C", autocorrelation "R", and a two-state Markovian model without memory "W" respectively with memory "W2". Each dashed line represents the model on the left hand to be a nested sub-model of the model on the right hand. Based on Kömm and Küsters (2015).

4.3.3 *Model Estimation and Computation*

The model parameters are obviously constraint to individual restrictions. Hence, some effort must be given to the numerical parameter optimization.

Parameter Restrictions The optimization is due to the model design subject to the following restrictions:

- $\omega_{01}, \omega_{11} \in (0,1)$
- $c \in \mathbb{R}$
- $\rho \in (-1,+1)$
- $\sigma, \tau \in \mathbb{R}_+$

The first restriction, $\omega_{01}, \omega_{11} \in (0,1)$, ensures the Markov transition probabilities to be in a canonical probability space. The constant c is unrestricted and no additional effort must be given here. The autocorrelation coefficient $\rho \in (-1,+1)$ ensures the process to be stationary. The last restriction, $\sigma \in \mathbb{R}_+$ is canonical for standard deviations. $\tau \in \mathbb{R}_+$ restricts the truncation area $[-\tau,+\tau]$ to be symmetric. An asymmetric truncation would also be possible.

Hence, two types of parameter restrictions have to be considered: The first will ensure that the estimates are within a pre-defined interval, the second will ensure the estimates to be non-negative.

Transformations and Restrictions The first restrictions of the form $\vartheta_i^* \in (a_i, b_i)$ can be considered using the logit transformation:

$$\vartheta_i^* = \frac{a_i + b_i \exp(\vartheta_i)}{1 + \exp(\vartheta_i)}, \quad i = 1, 2, \ldots, K_1 \tag{4.1}$$

with unrestricted $\vartheta_i \in \mathbb{R}$ and K_1 the number of considered parameters. This allows to hold for the restriction on the transition probabilities $\omega_{01} \in (0,1)$ and $\omega_{11} \in (0,1)$ and the stationarity condition on the autocorrelation coefficient $\rho \in (-1,1)$.

The second restriction, the non-negativity of the standard deviation and the truncation parameter τ holds, when using the modified inequality transformation:

$$\vartheta_i^* = \vartheta_i^2 > 0, \quad i = 1, 2, \ldots, K_2 \tag{4.2}$$

with unrestricted $\vartheta_i \in \mathbb{R}$ and K_2 the number of considered parameters. An overview of these and further transformation techniques accounting for different restrictions is given in Küsters (1987).

Significance and Multivariate δ-Method However, restricting the parameter estimates will also cause a challenge to derive the standard deviations of the estimates. The technique to derive the required standard deviations of the restricted parameters is the multivariate δ-method, see e. g. Serfling (1980, pp.122-124).

Maximum likelihood estimators are, if existent, asymptotically efficient, i.e. the estimators converge in distribution to a normal distributed random variable and the variance of the estimators is given by the inverse of the Fisher-information-matrix $\mathcal{I}(\vartheta)$. Therefore, for the maximum likelihood estimation of a consistent estimator vector ϑ^* holds:

$$\sqrt{n}(\vartheta^* - \vartheta) \xrightarrow{D} N(0,\ \mathcal{I}(\vartheta)^{-1})$$

with n the number of observations, $\mathcal{I}(\vartheta)^{-1}$ the inverse of the Fisher-information-matrix and D convergence in distribution. Further may $h(\cdot)$ be an absolutely continuously differentiable function, e.g. a transformation function, and ∇ be the gradient. Then the multivariate δ-method implies, that:

$$\sqrt{n}(h(\vartheta^*) - h(\vartheta)) \xrightarrow{D} N(0,\ \nabla h(\vartheta)^T\ \mathcal{I}(\vartheta)^{-1}\ \nabla h(\vartheta)).$$

Roughly Interpretation Start with an unrestricted maximum likelihood estimate $\hat{\vartheta}_i$, for $i = 1, 2, \ldots, K$, where K is the total number of parameters, i.e. $K = K_1 + K_2$, and $\hat{\sigma}_{\vartheta_i}$ the corresponding estimates of the standard deviations. First, retransform the unrestricted estimates $\hat{\vartheta}_i \in \mathbb{R}$ using the appropriate transformations according to (4.1) and (4.2) for all parameters requested to be restricted, this is for $i = 1, 2, \ldots, K$. Secondly, calculate the corresponding standard deviations $\hat{\sigma}_{\vartheta_i^*}$ of the restricted estimates $\hat{\vartheta}_i^*$ by applying the multivariate δ-method. This will correct the inverse of the Fisher-information-matrix for the applied restrictions. The square root of the diagonal of the corrected inverse of the Fisher-information-matrix, finally, gives the corresponding standard estimates.

Further details to the DGP, the maximum likelihood estimation, the inference as well as forecasting and evaluation techniques are given in Kömm and Küsters (2015).

Computing Task The time series under analysis are the time series of volatility estimates, and the object under analysis is the arrival of shocks, identified by the model parameters of the Markov switching mixture model proposed by Kömm and Küsters (2015). Therefore, estimate (1) for each of the five time series of volatility estimates, (2) for both, ask and bid quotes, (3) for each of the twelve proposed sub-models (4) the model parameters twice, but simultaneously, once before the arrival of an unexpected news and once after the arrival of the news for (5) each of the considered news arrivals.

Implementation Kömm and Küsters (2015) propose to obtain the maximum likelihood estimates of the parameters via the BFGS algorithm, see e.g. Dennis and Schnabel (1996) followed by one Newton-Raphson step, see e.g.

Kennedy and Gentle (1980). This highly computing intensive estimation process demands for parallelization techniques and supercomputing. The necessary support for the supercomputing task was offered from the Leibniz Supercomputing Centre (LRZ) Munich, operating

1. the Linux cluster system and
2. the national supercomputing system SuperMUC, see Bode et al. (2012).

These supercomputing systems allow the parallelized processing of the computing task in a manageable time, which is less than 24 hours for a full sequence of models as illustrated in Figure 4.5 on page 61. Support for the maximum likelihood estimation was provided by the maxLik library and for the parallelization by the snowfall library.

5 Volatility Shock Causing Incidents

The identification of the latent data generation process (DGP) of each series of volatility estimates, also determines the forecasting object, which in this thesis is the changing of the parameters of the Markov switching mixture model discussed in Section 4.3.2. Note, that the task is not to forecast the statistical control parameters, but to identify the latent process explaining the estimated volatility and to test for structural breaks in the identified process that can be explained with the appearance of unexpected news.

The forecasting task is therefore twofold: (1) Identify historical news that caused a break in the DGP of historical volatility estimates and (2) predict the effect of new and unexpected news arrivals, assuming that the historically observed changing in the DGP of the volatility series is a proxy for the expected changing affected by the new and unexpected news.

Here, the central idea and assumption is, that market participants react similarly in their uncertainty to surprising news that are similar in their statement, and this independent of the underlying asset. Please be aware, that the expected reaction is not based on the asset prices, but solely on the uncertainty of how to evaluate the fair value of new information.

But, not every new arrival of news affects the markets and not every change in the volatility series can be traced back to a specific news. The objective is hence to split relevant from irrelevant events and to forecast the risk of a significant change, before the market has had time to react. This demands to consider classification techniques in order to separate irrelevant from relevant news.

Therefore, the content of this chapter is as follows: Section 5.1 gives the definition of the statistical test used to classify historical incidents in those, that triggered in the past a volatility shock and those, that did not. Section 5.2 engages the task to quantify text data and to define the type of text news used in this thesis. Section 5.3 constitutes the distinction of unsupervised and supervised pattern recognition techniques in order to use texts for prediction.

5.1 Filtering Ad-hoc News

A main issue of supervised pattern recognition, which will be part of Section 5.3, is to possess an adequate data set with sufficient separation properties to account for training purposes. Therefore, first fit the Markov switching mixture model of Section 4.3.2 to the time series of volatility estimates in order to approximate the true but latent DGP. But, fit the model twice and simultaneously, once on the two hours before and once on the two hours after the arrival of the news under analysis. Afterwards, test the pre-incident DGP against the post-incident DGP for structural breaks explaining an increased level in the underlying volatility series. The classification of the historical news in shock and non-shock triggering events determines the training set.

5.1.1 *Selected Sample*

A 2 year exhaustive survey of potential candidates in 2010 and 2011 was conducted. Because each of the events should be capable to account for significant structural changes in the underlying DGP, the events were initially checked to comply with the following conditions:

1. The announcement concerns at the time of release to one of the assets listed in the prime standard indices DAX, MDAX, SDAX, or TecDAX.
2. The announcement is published by dpa-AFX, a news agency for German and English real-time financial and economic news.
3. The announcement includes a unique asset assigning international securities identification number (ISIN).
4. The announcement is marked to be an ad-hoc news (discussed in Section 5.2.1).
5. The announcement includes a unique time stamp of first publishing.
6. The announcement is between 11:00 a.m. and 3:30 p.m. local Frankfurt time, to ensure at least two pre-incident and two post-incident trading hours at the FSE and hence 480 volatility estimates in 15 second windows.

Figure 5.1 gives, for completeness, the histogram of all by dpa-AFX in 2010 and 2011 published ad-hoc news, concerning at least one of the assets listed in the prime standard indices DAX, MDAX, SDAX, or TecDAX.

Population This final sample comprised a population of 2,036 news.

Applying the Markov Switching Mixture Model The computations of the Markov switching mixture model proposed in Section 4.3 on each of this 2,036 news were further checked for the return codes of the optimization algorithms. The purpose of this check is to ensure that the computations were stopped because of a converged optimization algorithm, and not because of the maximum permissible computing time, or because of the non-convergence of the algorithm.

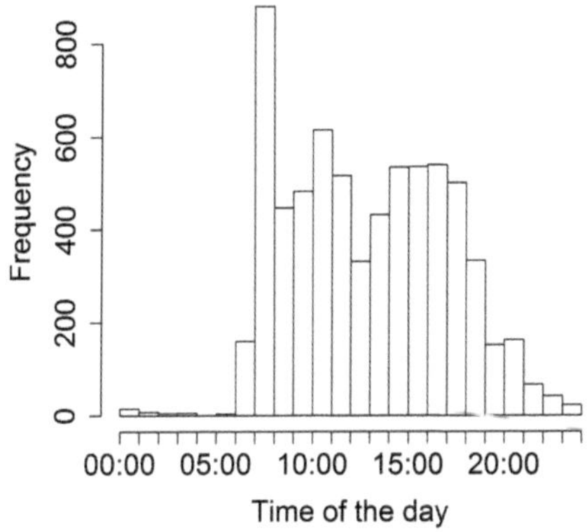

Figure 5.1: Histogram of all by dpa-AFX in 2010 and 2011 published ad-hoc news, concerning at least one of the assets listed in the prime standard indices DAX, MDAX, SDAX, or TecDAX. Note, that not all of these ad-hoc news include a unique ISIN.

This check returned 1,938 of the 2,036 news. And this is the final set of news that will be used in all further considerations.

5.1.2 *Identifying the Data Generation Process*

Time series characteristics are subject to permanent changes. Therefore, the task is to identify the model, that fits the latent DGP best. The proposed Markov switching mixture model of Section 4.3.2 consists of 12 sub-models, each accounting for specific characteristics.

The common technique to determine the best fitting of these 12 models is the likelihood ratio test, see Greene (2003, pp.484-486). The idea is, to compare a restricted sub-model with an unrestricted full model and to test for the statistical significance of the restrictions.

Likelihood-Ratio-Test Let P_ϑ be a population of probability distributions, depending on the unknown parameter vector ϑ, and ϑ be estimated by maximum likelihood. Set further $R(\vartheta)$ to be the restriction of ϑ, where r is the number of constraints. This gives the test hypotheses:

$$H_0 : R(\vartheta) = 0 \quad \text{vs.}$$
$$H_1 : R(\vartheta) \neq 0.$$

A valid restriction $R(\vartheta) = 0$ should therefore not lead to a large reduction of the log-likelihood function. The test statistic is consequently based on the difference of the log-likelihood values of the restricted model and the unrestricted model $\ln L_R - \ln L_U$, where L_U is the likelihood value of the unrestricted and L_R the likelihood value of the restricted model. The test statistic λ is then given by:

$$\lambda = \frac{L_R}{L_U},$$

with the test decision rule to reject the null, if

$$-2 \ln \lambda \geqslant \chi^2_r.$$

Where r gives the degrees of freedom equal to the number of restrictions imposed, and χ^2 the chi-squared distribution.

The log-likelihood value of the restricted model $\ln L_R$ is theoretically lower than the log-likelihood value of the unrestricted model $\ln L_U$. Hence, the difference $\ln L_R - \ln L_U$ should also always be positive. But, it can be observed in empirical applications that the difference can also become negative. In this case, this is a strong indication of a flat on the summit likelihood-function, causing numerical difficulties to the optimization algorithms in finding the global maximum. The value of the difference, however, should be close to zero.

The full testing sequence of the proposed sub-models is given in Figure 4.5 on page 61. Each dashed line in the figure corresponds to one likelihood ratio test. Making a total of 20 tests for each news arrival under analysis.

Information Criteria It is common in applied statistics and econometrics to use, in addition to likelihood ratio tests, one or more information criteria. Information criteria calculate a trade-off between (1) the goodness of fit and (2) the complexity of the model to judge the fit. It is, in this regard, common to use the likelihood function L to determine the adjustment accuracy of the model to the underlying data, and to determine the complexity of the model by the number of model parameters k. A famous representative of the class of information criteria is the Akaike Information Criteria (AIC), see Akaike (1981):

$$\text{AIC} = 2k - 2\ln(L).$$

A preferable model is, in this context, one with a good trade-off between (1) maximal adjustment accuracy expressed through the value of the likelihood function L and (2) minimal complexity expressed through the number of parameters k. The preferred model is hence the one with the minimum AIC. With the AIC compete, among others:

1. The corrected Akaike information criteria (AICc), which is a AIC correction for finite sample sizes using a greater penalization of additional parameters, see Hurvich and Tsai (1989).

2. The Bayesian information criteria (BIC), which accounts, contrary to the AIC, for an overestimate of the model order using a sample size depending penalization for additional parameters, see Schwarz (1978).

3. The Hannan-Quinn information criteria (HQC), which is a variant of the BIC using a smaller penalty factor than the BIC, but a higher penalty factor than the AIC, see Hannan and Quinn (1979).

The value-domain of the penalty factor is in the interval (0,1], and depends on the sample size. For low sample sizes (smaller 10), the AIC penalty dominates the AICc, the BIC, and the HQC criteria. This is why the AIC is often mentioned to overestimate the model order. In the asymptotic, however, all information criteria mentioned here behave identically.

Further insights to information theory and information criteria, including a detailed comparison of AIC and BIC, are given in Burnham and Anderson (2010).

Model Rankings However, information criteria are no statistical tests. But they help to select the model whenever pure testing procedures are difficult to apply. The task to identify the model that describes the latent DGP of the time series of volatility estimates best, is hence the task to identify the model with the minimal AIC. Boxplots of the minimal AIC model of the 2 year sample, separated for each of the used volatility estimators of Section 3.2, are presented in Figure 5.2 on page 70 and page 71.

The left side of the Boxplot diagrams show models with a restriction to autocorrelation, while the right side shows models including autocorrelation, for example model "M" on the left side and model "MR" on the right side, with "R" indication the autocorrelation parameter, see Section 4.3.2 on page 58. The ranking of the models on the right side is obviously improved in comparison to the left side. The additional autocorrelation component improves therefore the estimated likelihood strong enough, to improve the AIC ranking for all model comparisons of models with and sub-models without autocorrelation component.

When considering the models from top to bottom compare the models with and without restrictions on the constant "C", for example model "M" with model "MC" or model "MW" with model "MWC" and so forth. This holds for the left as well as the right side. The additional constant parameter drops the AIC ranking in any case.

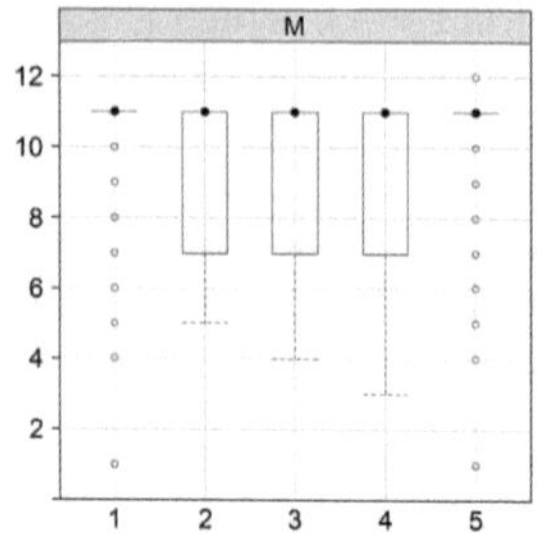

(a) Model "M".

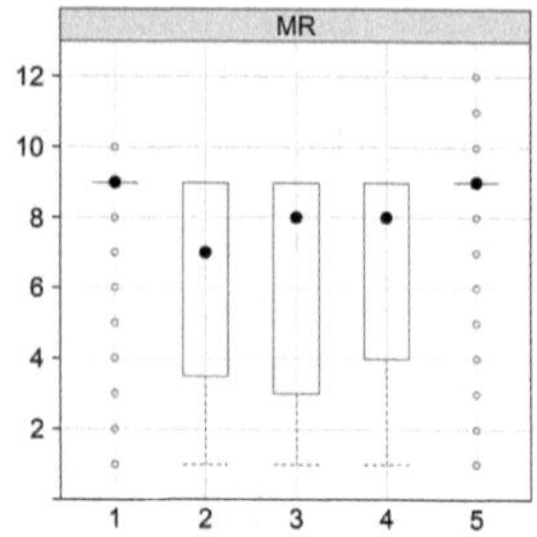

(b) Model "MR".

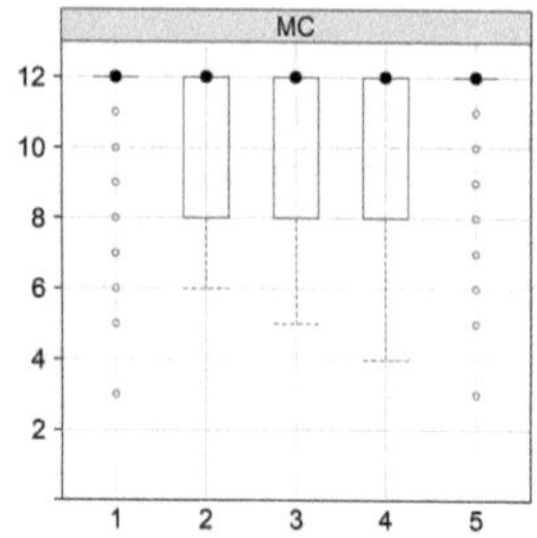

(c) Model "MC".

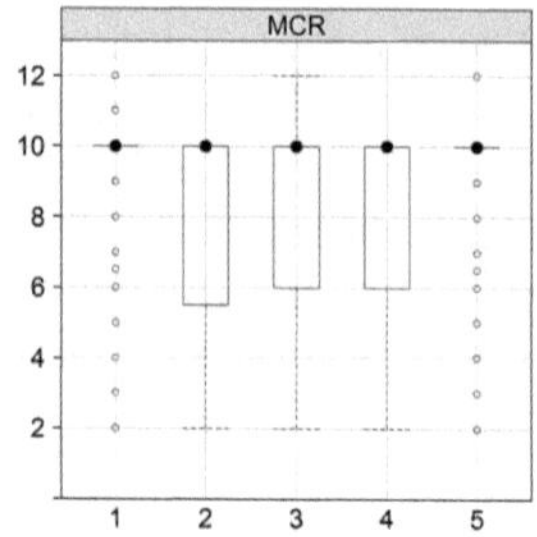

(d) Model "MCR".

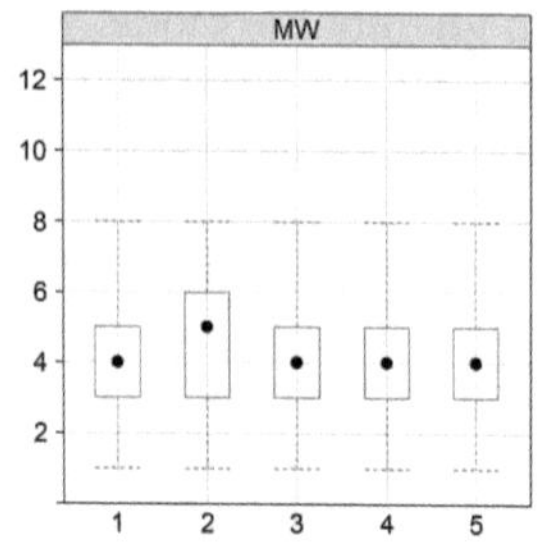

(e) Model "MW".

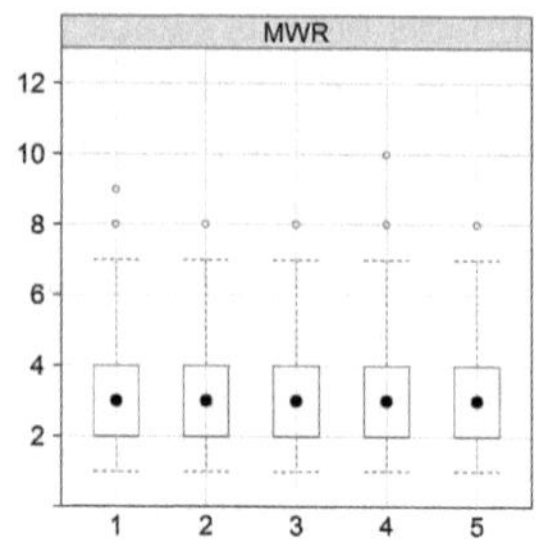

(f) Model "MWR".

Figure 5.2: AIC ranking of the Markov switching mixture model of 12 different sub-models. The abscissa carries the different volatility estimators, the ordinate the AIC ranking of the sub-model. The coding on the abscissa is corresponding to Section 3.2: 1 canonical estimator, 2 averaging estimator, 3 two-time-scales estimator, 4 adjusted two-time-scales estimator, and 5 area adjusted two-time-scales estimator. The preferred model is the one with minimum AIC, receiving rank 1 while the maximum AIC model receives rank 12.

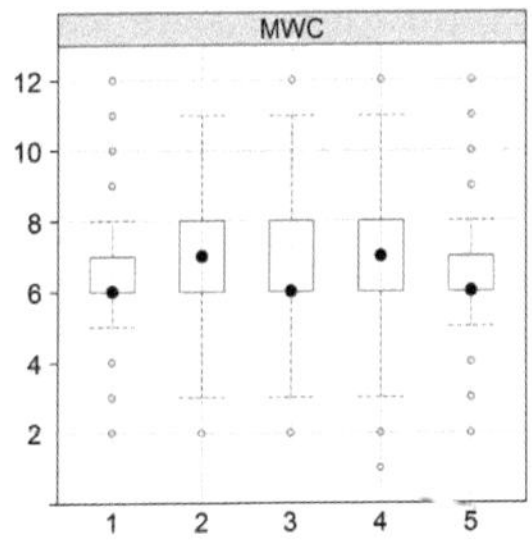

(g) Model "MWC".

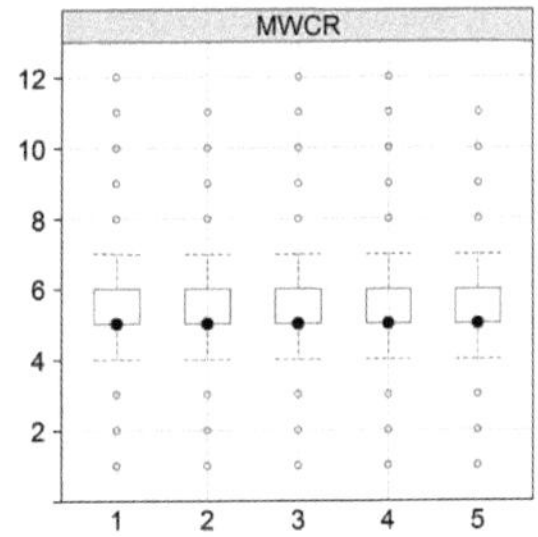

(h) Model "MWCR".

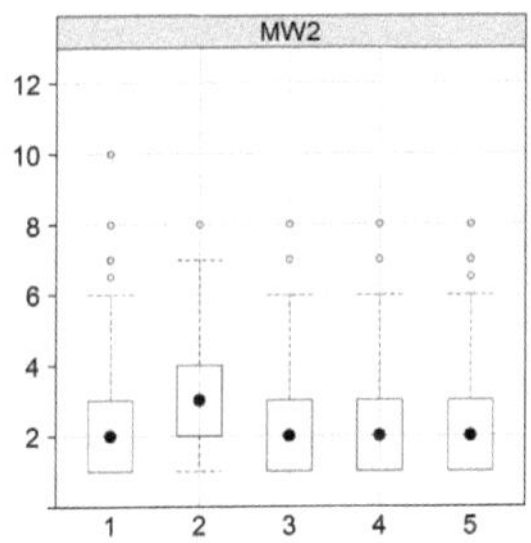

(i) Model "MW2".

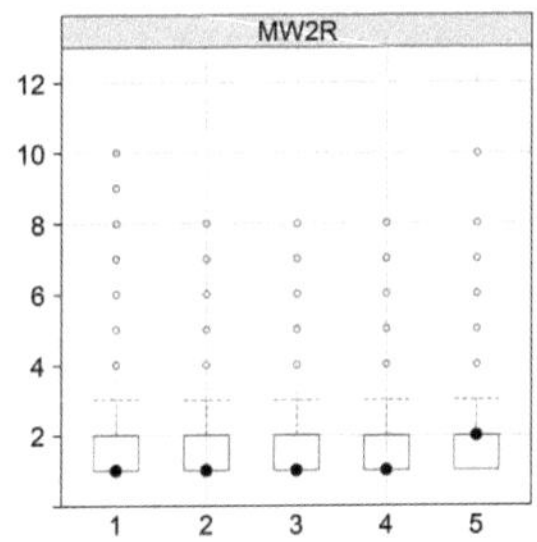

(j) Model "MW2R".

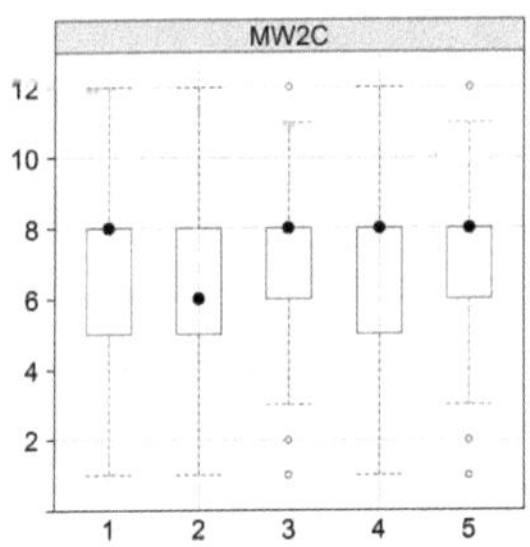

(k) Model "MW2C".

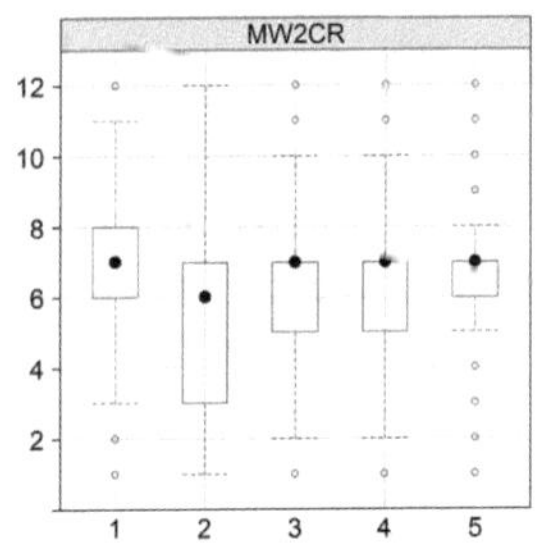

(l) Model "MW2CR".

Dominating Model The dominating model is "MW2R", accounting for zero-inflation with memory and autocorrelation.

Using a traditional finite mixture model alternatively to account for zero-inflation, see Section 4.2.3 on page 55, instead of the proposed Markov switching mixture model, would therefore miss to account for the significantly relevant autocorrelation.

Note, that the proposed model can further account for heteroscedasticity by modelling the fluctuation σ not as a parameter, but as a function of historical 1-step error forecasts, provided by the GARCH framework. For further details to this extension, see Kömm and Küsters (2015). However, applying this extended model to the time series of volatility estimates could weaken the transition effects of the Markov switching mixture model, measured by the transition probabilities ω_{01} and ω_{11}, which are used to identify shocks. It is therefore recommendable, for the classification task in this thesis, to account for autocorrelation, but not explicit for heteroscedasticity.

5.1.3 *Testing for Volatility Shocks*

To apply the proposed model to classification approaches, it is advisable to estimate simultaneously the pre-incident parameters ϑ and post-incident parameters ϑ^* of the model, using one likelihood for both parameter vectors. The parameters in the proposed model accounting for structural changes in the DGP of the volatility series are

1. the transition probabilities ω_{01} and ω_{11}, accounting for changes in the frequencies of zero and non-zero states, and

2. the natural variation parameter σ, accounting for changes in the amplitude of non-zero states.

The constant c and the autocorrelation parameter ρ may differ between the pre-incident and post-incident periods. Nevertheless, any differences between the periods of these parameters can not be used to explain volatility shock causing incidents. These parameters remain therefore unconsidered for the classification task.

Test Approach The approach of the test is to inspect the time series of volatility estimates for measurable shocks, occurring in the two hours after the arrival of an unexpected news. Here, measurable is to be understood in the sense of changes in the parameter estimates and shocks in the sense of statistically significance.

In order to test for changes of the pre-incident estimates $\hat{\vartheta}$ to the post-incident estimates $\hat{\vartheta}^*$, the parameters need to be restricted first. The restrictions on the pre-incident parameters

$$\vartheta = (\omega_{01},\ \omega_{11},\ c,\ \rho,\ \sigma,\ \tau)'$$

remain unchanged to Section 4.3.2. Post-incident parameters relevant for the classification purposes, however, are represented as the additive link of the pre-incident parameter estimates $\hat{\vartheta}$ and the non-negative changing-parameters ω_{01}^*, ω_{11}^* and σ^*. These post-incident parameters, relevant for the identification of volatility shocks, are restricted to be non-negative, to account only for the shock relevant volatility increases, but not for decreases. The post-incident constant c^* and the post-incident autocorrelation ρ^* are independent of the pre-incident estimates and subject to identical restrictions as c and ρ. The pre-incident and post-incident truncation parameter, however, are fixed to be identical, i. e. $\tau = \tau^*$, ensuring identical truncation areas.

The post-incident parameter vector ϑ^* consequently has the form:

$$\vartheta^* = (\omega_{01} + \omega_{01}^*,\ \omega_{11} + \omega_{11}^*,\ c^*,\ \rho^*,\ \sigma + \sigma^*,\ \tau = \tau^*)'.$$

The parameters, the transformations and the corresponding domains are summarized for an overview in Table 5.1 on the next page.

The task to test for volatility increasing incidents is thus a task to test for parameter changes. A suitable test for this purpose is the parametric Wald test.

Please note, that any maximum likelihood estimation under the assumption of the application of suitable regularity conditions, see Greene (2003, p.474), is asymptotically efficient and normal distributed. This feature is implicit used in the following test.

Wald Test The Wald test formulated as a test for multiple parameters is based on the distance between the pre-incident parameter estimates $\hat{\vartheta}$ and the post-incident parameter estimates ϑ_0. The canonical formulation of a Wald test hypotheses would hence be

$$H_0 : \vartheta = \vartheta_0 \quad \text{vs.} \quad H_1 : \vartheta \neq \vartheta_0.$$

The Wald test statistic is, where $\Sigma_{\hat{\vartheta}}$ is the asymptotic non-singular variance-covariance matrix of the maximum likelihood estimate, given by:

$$W_0 = (\hat{\vartheta} - \vartheta_0)' \Sigma_{\hat{\vartheta}}^{-1} (\hat{\vartheta} - \vartheta_0). \tag{5.1}$$

Under the null hypotheses the Wald statistic (5.1) further follows a limiting chi-squared distribution, where the degree of freedom is equal to the number of restrictions imposed.

Applied Wald Test With the conditioning on the for classification purposes relevant parameters ω_{01}, ω_{11} and σ, and the restrictions imposed on δ =

PRE-INCIDENT		
Parameter	Transformation	Domain
ω_{01}	$\omega_{01} \curvearrowright (4.1)$	$(0,1)$
ω_{11}	$\omega_{11} \curvearrowright (4.1)$	$(0,1)$
c		$\mathbb{R}$
ρ	$\rho \curvearrowright (4.1)$	$(-1,1)$
σ	$\sigma \curvearrowright (4.2)$	$\mathbb{R}_+$
τ	$\tau \curvearrowright (4.2)$	$\mathbb{R}_+$
POST-INCIDENT		
Parameter	Transformation	Domain
$\omega_{01} + \omega_{01}^*$	$\omega_{01}^* \curvearrowright (4.2) \wedge \omega_{01} + \omega_{01}^* \curvearrowright (4.1)$	$(0,1)$
$\omega_{11} + \omega_{11}^*$	$\omega_{11}^* \curvearrowright (4.2) \wedge \omega_{11} + \omega_{11}^* \curvearrowright (4.1)$	$(0,1)$
c^*		$\mathbb{R}$
ρ^*	$\rho^* \curvearrowright (4.1)$	$(-1,1)$
$\sigma + \sigma^*$	$\sigma^* \curvearrowright (4.2) \wedge \sigma + \sigma^* \curvearrowright (4.2)$	$\mathbb{R}_+$
$\tau^* = \tau$	$\tau^* \curvearrowright (4.2)$	$\mathbb{R}_+$

Table 5.1: Pre-incident and post-incident parameter restrictions. The logit transformation (4.1) on page 62 ensures the parameter estimates to be within the given domain (interval). The inequality transformation (4.2) on page 62 ensures the parameter estimate to be positive. The symbol "$\curvearrowright$" denotes the transformation according to the corresponding transformation rule.

$(\omega_{01}^*, \omega_{11}^*, \sigma^*)'$ to be non-negative, the Wald type hypotheses are to be tested to apply the test for classification purposes, modified to:

$$H_0 : \delta = 0 \quad \text{vs.} \quad H_1 : \delta > 0. \tag{5.2}$$

Please note, that the modification of $H_1 : \delta > 0$ is due to the test approach identical to $H_1 : \delta \neq 0$, when taking into account that the parameters in δ are non-negative. The corresponding statistic of the applied Wald test is furthermore given by:

$$W_1 = \delta' \Sigma_{\hat{\delta}}^{-1} \delta. \tag{5.3}$$

The Wald statistic (5.3) is under the null chi-squared distributed with three degrees of freedom, i. e. $W_1 \sim \chi_3^2$. Therefore, decline H_0 if $W_1 > \chi_3^2$.

Implementation The proposed Wald-type test, applied to the specificities of the Markov switching mixture model, allows to take into account a total of three states. Each volatility shock would be expressed in the post-incident parameters of the model either in one, a combination of two, or all three volatility accounting parameters ω_{01}, ω_{11} and σ. The parameter combination that needs to be tested is given by the best AIC fitting model selection. The estimates of the parameters and the variance-covariance matrix come with the maximum likelihood estimation routine in the maxLik library. Note, however, that the maximum likelihood parameter estimates and the variance-covariance matrix of the estimates are returned as unrestricted estimates. The re-transformation of the unrestricted estimates and the corresponding unrestricted variance-covariance matrix follows the paragraphs about transformations and restrictions and the multivariate δ-method in Section 4.3.3 on page 61.

Finally, please note that a two hour time window before and after the arrival of news is chosen to receive in total 480 observations when using 15 second volatility estimates. A shorter window is possible, but would also reduce the number of observations used to estimate the parameters in the Markov switching mixture model.

Alternatively, it is thinkable to use the day before and next day asset prices to receive at every time point a full ± 2 hour window of transaction time records, e. g. for news arrivals at 9:00 a.m. This, however, would also mean to mix the effects of overnight price changes with the effects measured in the ongoing trading and to accept large over-night price changes as relevant and explainable shocks.

5.2 Quantifying Financial Text Data

Financial news, or news in general, is mostly distributed in form of text. The task to transform the essential statement of text in machine interpretable quantities is a well known challenge in natural language processing, see e. g. Manning and Schütze (2003).

5.2.1 *Sampling*

Filtering for market affecting news starts with filtering for news,

1. that will reach all market participants simultaneously and
2. that was previously unknown to all market participants.

A missing in (1) would lead to asymmetric trading transactions and price adjustments. Informed traders would benefit from time advantages. A missing in (2) would suppose the existence of information insiders.

Ad-hoc News The ad-hoc-publicity, regulated in §15 WpHG of the German securities trading act, regulates the duty of public disclosures for all emitters, see e. g. Beck (2014).

The concept of ad-hoc news pledges emitters to the immediate release of facts, that could affect the price of any accredited asset of the corresponding company. This accounts for (2).

The dissemination of ad-hoc news is handled by ad-hoc service providers, as soon as the federal financial supervisory authority (BaFin) and the local stock exchange management grant the release. A typical service provider is the "German society for ad-hoc-publicity" (DGAP). This accounts for (1).

Ad-hoc news is factual, short and concise explanations news about changes that will or could change the price of the underlying assets. Ad-hoc news is in their proper use free of irony, sarcasm and humour.

Implementation Ad-hoc news is publicly available. The relevant news applying at least one of the assets listed in the prime standard indices DAX, MDAX, SDAX, or TecDAX is scraped from DGAP and parsed with the XML-parser of the R-library XML.

XML-parser analyse the structure of a XML-document and provide the included information for further processing. Parsing techniques are standard in computer science and rampant in statistical software, see e. g. Ekstrøm (2012) for a detailed application of the XML-parser in R. The R-object generated by the XML-parser represents the structure of the underling XML-tree, which is the hierarchical structure of an XML-document, and provides access to the branches including the atomized information.

The XML-structure of the ad-hoc news under analysis shows, for example, nodes for (1) the title of the news, (2) the number of words used for the news, (3) the date and the time of first news publishing, (4) the language of the news, (5) the service provider disseminating the news, (6) the ISIN, if existend, of the underlying asset the news is about, and (7) the news itself as pure text information.

Note, that not every published news is equipped with an unique ISIN identifier. But, in this thesis, only those news are taken into account, that can be clearly assigned to a single asset. To handle the unstructured text of the ad-hoc publication, the text is further broken in streams of characters, words, or tokens. For an introduction to the analysis of unstructured text data, see e. g. Weiss et al. (2010).

5.2.2 *Pre-processing*

An initial process when working with tokens is pre-processing. This is the process of cleaning and simplifying to increase the goodness of the subsequent processing. Text pre-processing techniques are common in text analytics and text data mining, see e. g. Feldman and Sanger (2008). Three popular techniques to pre-process text data are the allocation of meta information, the removal of stopwords, and stemming:

1. *Allocation of Meta Data* The allocation of meta data to each single news simplifies the subsequent real-time analysis, especially through the allocation of unique identifiers. There are two types of meta data: (1) Structural meta data and (2) descriptive meta data. Generally speaking, meta data is data, that includes information about other data. Structural meta data or data about the containers of data is about the arrangement of data, e. g. information about the document type or the font set of the text. Descriptive meta data, on the other hand, is about the content of the data, e. g. information about the number of words in the document or the language of the text.

2. *Removal of Stopwords* Stopwords are single words having no impact on the orientation of the text. Stopwords provide no contribution, but can lead to distortions in subsequent processing, e. g. classifications. Typical stopword representatives are articles like "the", "a", "my", and word fillers like "as", "after", "or", etc. Some literature distinguish the removing of stopwords from the removing of numbers, punctuations and extra white-space. The principle, however, is identical. Remove all elements in the text that do not contribute to improve the subsequent processing.

Note however, that it can be risky to remove words that could have a significant role in the interpretation of the orientation of the text, for example words like "or". It is therefore not recommendable to remove all potentially stopwords per se. Stoplist generators ease the process to identify the content specific stopwords by automatically build-up stopword lists, see e. g. Berry and Kogan (2010, pp.11-15).

3. *Stemming* Stemming is the process to normalize the non-consistent representation of words identical in statement but different in spelling. Stemming is thus the process to reduce the morphological variants of words to a single and unique word stem. A famous candidate is Porters stemming algorithm, Porter (1980). This in concept very simple algorithm determines weather a suffix of a word should be removed, e. g. suffixes of the form *"ies"* $\rightarrow$ *"i"* or *"s"* $\rightarrow$ *"" ""*, reducing plural to singular forms and generating a unique word

stem. A second rule of Porter's stemming algorithm would be to substitute "y" with "i" to guarantee, that, for example, "dummies" → "dummi" and "dummy" → "dummi" will be stemmed to identical word stems.

Porter developed alongside the stemmer for English documents a whole series of stemmers for further European languages, see Willett (2006) and combined them in the high-level computer programming language Snowball.

Implementation The most support for the pre-processing was given by the tm library developed by I. Feinerer and K. Hornick, which allows the allocation of meta information to tm documents, considering them as a corpus of documents. Primary meta tags are the date time stamp and the unique ISIN to assign each ad-hoc news clearly and unmistakeably to the corresponding asset and the definite time of news announcement.

Please note, however, that some news, e. g. the publishing of analyst reports, often include more than one ISIN. These reports can hence not be unambiguously assigned to a single asset and remain therefore unconsidered.

Note further, that the date time stamp of ad-hoc news published by DGAP is always reported in GMT, requiring transformations to account for local trading times, especially to account for summer and winter time.

Porter's stemmer as well as the stopword list come with the R-library SnowballC developed by M. Bouchet-Valat. The stopword list was further extended with words accounting for particularities of DGAP ad-hoc news, for example the words WpHG, ad-hoc and DGAP.

5.2.3 *Quantification*

A main challenge of computational text analytics is the sufficient quantification (in form of numbers) of qualitative data (in form of texts). A common process to break the qualitative text document in interpretable unities is tokenization. A token is a characterband attributed by a pre-specified grammar. A token can for example be a word, a string of characters, phrases, a symbol, or numbers. For word-type tokens, it is common to represent an ensemble of documents in a term-document-matrix.

Term-Document-Matrix The term-document-matrix is a matrix having a list of tokens in form of terms in the rows, and a list of considered documents in the columns. The terms are usually words, but can also be phrases or symbols. The selection depends on the application. Phrases can be for example of interest, if the text mining task is not on puristic ad-hoc-news, but on text documents full of sarcasm and irony.

The (i, j)-th element of the term-document-matrix represents the frequency word i occurring in document j. If, for example, word number one occurs twice in document number three, then is the value of element (1,3) of the term-document-matrix 2. Words that did not occur in a document keep the starting value 0.

Removal of Sparse Terms Term-document-matrices are often sparse, meaning they are often primarily populated with zeros. Sparse terms are therefore terms that have occurred in only a few documents. But, contrary to stop-words which are defined in a dictionary, sparse terms are those words that have occurred at a lower than a predefined frequency, e. g. 90%. For example, removing sparse terms at a 90% level removes all rows (Terms) in the term-document-matrix that have, at least in 90% of all documents, a zero entry. This means, the higher the sparsity level the less terms will be removed.

Weighting Schemes The value of absolute word frequencies, however, is questionable. An established approach is hence to interpret not only the absolute term frequencies, but to evaluate (1) the document exhaustivity and (2) the term specificity, following the approach of Jones (1972). These are:

1. *Document exhaustivity* is the coverage of its content through the allocation of terms.

   For example, the exhaustivity increases, if a document gets longer but only because of words, that have already been used. Hence, more words are assigned to a document but the number of different terms stays constant. The idea is, that the permanent repetition of a statement increases the importance of the statement.

2. *Term specificity* is a semantic property. The specificity of a term is the level of detail to express a statement.

   The term "announcement", can for example be adhered by the terms "profit announcement" or "loss announcement". The more general term "announcement" will hence appear to be used more often in content descriptions than "profit" or "loss". Term specificity is hence the concept that the merit of less frequent, but more specific terms is greater than the merit of frequent, but unspecific terms.

A typical application of weighting schemes on a term-document-matrix is therefore, to first determine the term-document-matrix using all documents under analysis with the absolute term frequencies, and to apply thereafter a weighting to account for the document exhaustivity and another weighting to account for the term specificity, see e. g. Dumais (1991).

Local Weighting The weighting corresponding to the document exhaustivity is called *local weighting*. The local weighting is applied to each cell of the term-document-matrix. Common local weightings are (1) *Term frequency* (Tf), a proportional scaling measure, (2) *Binary* (Binary), an existence measure, and (3) *Logarithm* (Log), which can be interpreted as a compromise of (1) and (2). The function $tf(i,j)$ shows the term frequency of term i in document j. The function $l_k(i,j)$ for $k = 1,2,3$ gives the corresponding local weighting, see Table 5.2:

Function	Formula	Mapping
Tf	$l_1(i,j) = tf(i,j)$	$\mathbb{N}_0 \to \mathbb{N}_0$
Binary	$l_2(i,j) = \begin{cases} 1, & \text{if } tf(i,j) \geqslant 1 \\ 0, & \text{otherwise} \end{cases}$	$\mathbb{N}_0 \to \{0,1\}$
Log	$l_3(i,j) = \log(tf(i,j)+1)$	$\mathbb{N}_0 \to \log(\mathbb{N})$

Table 5.2: Local weightings of the term-document-matrix. The function $tf(i,j)$ gives the term frequency of term i in document j. The function $l_k(i,j)$ for $k = 1,2,3$ gives the corresponding local weighting.

Global Weighting The weighting corresponding to the term specificity is called *global weighting*. The global weighting is applied to the whole row (terms) of the term-document-matrix having n documents. Common global weighting functions are (1) *Normal* (Normal), (2) *Global frequency, Inverse document frequency* (GfIdf), (3) *Inverse document frequency* (Idf), and (4) 1 - *Entropy or noise* (Entropy). The function $tf(i,j)$ shows the term frequency of term i in document j. The total number of documents is n. The function $gf(i)$ gives the global number of times that term i occurs over all documents. The function $df(i)$ describes the number of documents in which term i occurs. The function $p(i,j) = tf(i,j)/gf(i)$ maps the ratio of term i occurring in document j to the overall frequency of term i. The function $g_l(i,j)$ for $l = 1,\ldots,4$ gives the corresponding global weighting, see Table 5.3 on the next page:

Function	Formula	Mapping
Normal	$g_1(i) = \frac{1}{\sqrt{\sum_{j=1}^{n} tf(i,j)^2}}$	$\mathbb{N}_0 \to (0,1]$
GfIdf	$g_2(i) = \frac{gf(i)}{df(i)}$	$\mathbb{N} \to [1, gf(i)]$
Idf	$g_3(i) = 1 + \log\left(\frac{n}{df(i)}\right)$	$\mathbb{N} \to [1, 1 + \log(n)]$
Entropy	$g_4(i) = 1 + \sum_{j=1}^{n} \frac{p(i,j)\log(p(i,j))}{\log(n)}$	$\mathbb{N}_0 \to [0,1]$

Table 5.3: Global weightings of the term-document-matrix. The function $tf(i,j)$ shows the term frequency of term i in document j. The total number of documents is n. The function $gf(i)$ gives the global number of times that term i occurs over all documents. The function $df(i)$ describes the number of documents in which term i occurs. The function $p(i,j) = tf(i,j)/gf(i)$ maps the ratio of term i occurring in document j to the overall frequency of term i. The function $g_l(i,j)$ for $l = 1, \ldots, 4$ gives the corresponding global weighting.

Weighted Term-Document-Matrix The role of the local and the global weighting is to standardize the term frequencies. Therefore, both weightings are multiplicatively combined and applied on each cell a_{ij} of the term-document-matrix A, returning a new weighted cell w_{ij} of the weighted term-document-matrix W. That is:

$$w_{ij} = l_k(i,j) \cdot g_l(i),$$

for $k \in \{1,2,3\}$ and $l \in \{1,\ldots,4\}$, with $l_k(i,j)$ being one of the local weightings of Table 5.2 and $g_l(i)$ being one of the global weightings of Table 5.3. Note, that a zero entry in the term-document-matrix A will also return a zero entry in the weighted term-document-matrix W. That means, the weighting scheme shows no effect on the sparsity level of the term-document-matrix.

Implementation The functionalities to convert tokenized ad-hoc news in term-document-matrices, the weighting functions to account for the exhaustivity of document descriptions and term specificities, and the function to remove sparse terms from given term-document-matrices come with the R-library tm. Note, that it is one of the main challenges to find a trade-off between the sparsity level and the available memory capacity.

Two common combinations of local and global weightings, are (1) the Tf-Idf and (2) and Log-Idf weighting scheme. The Tf-Idf combination is:

$$\begin{aligned} w_{ij} &= l_1(i,j) \cdot g_3(i) \\ &= tf(i,j) \cdot \left[1 + \log\left(\frac{n}{df(i)}\right)\right], \end{aligned} \tag{5.4}$$

where the Log-Idf combination is:

$$\begin{aligned} w_{ij} &= l_3(i,j) \cdot g_3(j) \\ &= \log(\mathrm{tf}(i,j)+1) \cdot \left[1 + \log\left(\frac{n}{\mathrm{df}(i)}\right)\right], \end{aligned} \tag{5.5}$$

see Nakov et al. (2004).

But, it is still unknown which of these weighting schemes and which level of sparse term removal works best for the classification task of this thesis. Therefore, further best fitting analysis in the given classification context is required.

5.3 Predictive Text Mining

Due to the financial market regulations, in particular due to §15 WpHG, in the case of assets listed in Germany, all stock exchange listed companies are obliged to publicly announce any change in business processes, even if the change exclusively relates to the expectations. This leads to a multitude of non-stop announcements with inconsistent topics. Many, if not even most of them, play at best a minor role.

Few news, however, may have the potential to affect the concerned assets and hence, also the volatility estimate under analysis. The task is to identify those ad-hoc news that affect the concerned assets and to split them from those, that do not. The statistical technique to account for this task is pattern recognition for classification. The classification outcome, however, is determined by (1) the used volatility estimator, (2) the significance level of the applied Wald test separating shocks from non-shocks, and (3) the text mining control instruments stopwords, stemming, sparse terms, and weightings. The focus in the following Section 5.3.1 will hence be, which effect these control instruments have on the outcome of the text prediction.

Pattern recognition further discriminates unsupervised and supervised learning. The used technique in this thesis is supervised learning, which is discussed in Section 5.3.3 and which will be applied in Chapter 6. For completeness, however, the technique of unsupervised learning is also introduced in Section 5.3.2.

5.3.1 *The Pattern Recognition Task*

In pattern recognition for classification, all is about design. A poor, or even wrong design leads at least to questionable results. But, without the experience of a trained expert, it is often difficult to track down the cause of fail classification. Typical mistakes in pattern recognition designs can be:

1. Missing to split the data set in training and independent test data. The role of the training set is to optimize a predefined goodness of fit criterion for model selection and parameter estimation, the role of the test set is to determine the power of the fit, see e. g. Webb and Copsey (2011, p.582). These, and a third type of data, the validation set, are further described below.

2. Splitting the data $x_1, \ldots, x_n$ in a training set $x_1, \ldots, x_k$ and a test set $x_{k+1}, \ldots, x_n$, with $1 \leqslant k \leqslant n$, but missing to cross-validate the separating point x_k. That means, missing to evaluate the effect of the index k on the outcome on the training and test data.

3. Applying several algorithms for classification on training- and test-data and evaluating the power of the algorithms, but missing to account for the variance of the classification errors.

4. Missing to take into account an intuitive baseline outcome of a random classification.

5. Evaluating the performance of the algorithms by a single measure, but neglecting to account for the specific features of type I and type II errors.

This section will emblaze the fragmentation in training, validation and test data sets and account therefore to (1). The other potential mistakes will be addressed in Chapter 7.

Training Set Training data is used to determine estimates of model parameters. For this purpose, training data is "seen" and the model is trained on the data to fit best. Training data should hence not be used to evaluate the performance of algorithms or the performance of classification.

Validation Set The requirement of extra validation data depends on the application and the algorithm in use. Some applications and algorithms require to already test in the trainings phase to determine the algorithms parameters. To avoid that the validation is done on the test data, some seen, i. e. already known, training data is separated to test the process in the trainings phase.

Test Set Test data is "unseen" and unknown. The trained model is applied on the test data to evaluate the classification algorithm. The outcome of the algorithm on the test data determines the power of fit, not the outcome on the training data.

5.3.2 *Unsupervised Learning*

Despite the fact that the following class of unsupervised learners is not applied to the classification task under analysis in this thesis, the class is nevertheless illustrated to show the differences to the in the following used class of supervised learning.

Unsupervised learning is learning *without* instructor making unsupervised classification the classification without prior information on classes. Typical applications for unsupervised learning are input pattern clustering, to form instinctive groups with similar characteristics, and control clustering, to confirm the adequacy of a-priori given groups. The central critic on the clustering algorithms is, that different clustering algorithms generally split up in different clusters, see Duda et al. (2006, p.17).

Clustering Cluster analysis is the task to group elements that are more similar to each other than to others in one group, or cluster. Central questions on clustering are:

1. *How to determine the similarity?*

   It is common to determine the similarity with metric measures, e. g. the euclidean distance. Hierarchical clustering methods group those elements to a cluster, that are closest to the cluster.

2. *How to determine the cluster centre?*

   Centroid-based methods separate the clusters by vectors, which need not to be part of the clusters. A famous representative of centroid-based methods is the k-means clustering.

   Density-based methods on the other hand separate the clusters by elements belonging to a pre-defined theoretical density.

3. *How to choose the 'right' number of clusters* k*, the 'right' density or the 'right' distribution?*

   Unfortunately, there is no "best way" to determine these questions. The common technique to determine the control parameters is hence to evaluate the competing clustering algorithms that distinguish internal and external evaluation.

Clustering Evaluation *How to evaluate competing clustering algorithms?*

1. Internal evaluation indexes for clustering algorithms are the Davies-Bouldin index, see Davies and Bouldin (1979), and the Dunn index, see Dunn (1973). Both indexes use an inter-cluster distance metric as quantitative interpretation of the cluster similarity of all in cluster elements to evaluate the performance of the competing algorithms.

2. External evaluation indexes are used in both, in unsupervised and supervised learning algorithms. A detailed description of the external evaluation measures will hence be given in Chapter 7, but in a more general context than solely for clustering. For further readings on clustering analysis, see e. g. Everitt (2011).

5.3.3 *Supervised Learning*

Another general class of pattern recognition algorithms belongs to the class of supervised learning methods, which is used in this thesis to discriminate volatility shock causing from non-shock causing events.

Supervised learning is, contrary to unsupervised learning, the learning *with* instructor, i. e. the additional use of an endogenous variable declaring the explanatory outcome of the classification. Each pattern in the training set is hence a-priori not a single point of data but a pair of data, consisting of the input object and the desired output value. This allows to train the algorithms on the training set in order to optimize the algorithms selectivity. Major issues of supervised learning are (1) the trade-off of bias and variance, (2) the dimensionality, (3) the complexity and the design of the classifiers, and (4) over fitting.

Bias-variance trade-off A learning algorithm will have a low bias, if it is flexible enough to respond to all particularities of the data. The flexibility, however, requires a strong differentiation capacity, which can result in a high variance. Learning algorithms are therefore characterized by the ability to adjust a trade-off between bias and variance, e. g. by learning the number of parameters to use.

A learning algorithm with too few parameters could be inaccurate because of a large bias. A learning algorithm with too many parameters, however, could be inaccurate because of a large variance. The required adjustment of bias and variance is well known as the bias-variance trade-off, see Dougherty (2013, pp.159-160).

Dimensionality The task to train the learning algorithm is aggravated further by the dimensionality of the input feature vectors. Although it is sometimes obvious to assume that further features will improve the classification performance, it is observed in practice that the inclusion of features worsen rather than improve the overall performance, see Duda et al. (2006, pp.107-111).

A common strategy to increase the classification performance of a given set of features is hence to downward select the dimensionality by reducing the given set of features piece by piece. The attempt is to map the data in a lower dimensional space prior to the task of supervised learning. For the concerns of this thesis, and in cases of term-document-matrices in general, this downward selection strategy accounts for the removal of sparse terms prior to the application of the supervised learning algorithms.

Complexity of the Classifier Design The more complex the classification task, the more training data is required for sufficient trainings. While on the one hand non-complex algorithms often lead to low bias and high variance, complex algorithms on the other hand often lead to an increased bias, but low variance. The trade-off is hence again to adjust the variance/bias offset of function complexity and training data availability. The common proportion of observations to parameters is 30:1. Meaning to use at least 30 observations per model parameter.

Over-fitting Measuring for over-fitting means in general to evaluate the output values. The idea is, that incorrect output values could be caused, because of the learning algorithm trying to find a function that considers perfectly to all observations. The attempt to fit a function describing each observation perfectly, however, leads to an over-adjustment of the algorithm, which starts to describe random errors and noise, but not the searched causal relationship.

6 Algorithmic Text Forecasting

The test for a structural break in the DGP describing the time series of volatility estimates explained by the arrival of an unexpected news, unites the quantitative information of asset quotes with the qualitative information of text news through the two joint information units, ISIN and time.

The test outcome, determined by a statistical control parameter, namely the significance level of the applied Wald test in formula (5.3) on page 74, determines the label of the text news which can either be (1) shock causing or (2) non-shock causing. The clear allocation of a unique label to each text news determines thus the training set used to train the supervised learning algorithms.

The following chapter introduces the supervised learning algorithms used in this thesis. The composition is as follows: Section 6.1 introduces non-ensemble algorithms. The corresponding ensemble learning algorithms are introduced in Section 6.2. The idea to use ensemble learning algorithms is simply to use a combination of non-ensemble algorithms to achieve more accurate prediction outcomes than a single non-ensemble algorithm can reach. Section 6.3, finally, concludes the chapter with the training of the selected algorithms on the pre-classified training data and the application of the trained algorithms on the test data.

The determination of the most suitable algorithm and the evaluation of the classification accuracy are dedicated to Chapter 7.

6.1 Classification Algorithms

The task in supervised learning is to train the algorithm on the training set to explain the associated labels as accurately as possible, while simultaneously adjusting the bias-variance trade-off.

In this thesis, the training set consists of tuples of (1) text news represented in a weighted term-document-matrix, with (2) each news associated by one of the two states: "No shock", if the applied Wald test holds the null hypothesis that the arrival of the unexpected ad-hoc news did not cause a break in the underlying DGP of the volatility estimates, and "Shock", if the null hypothesis is refused.

The supervised learning algorithm will therefore try to explain the vector of associated binary labels "No shock", coded with 0, or "Shock", coded with 1, of each text document under analysis by the term-document-matrix representing the terms used in the news. The central idea is, that words used in news that caused a shock differ clearly from words used in news that caused no shock.

6.1.1 *Multinomial Regression*

The first algorithm used for classification is the multinomial regression (MNR), which is a generalization of the logistic regression to categorical rather than binary responses, or labels, (that means, there are K, not 2 possible outcomes of the regression) and measures the relationship between the dependent categorical variable and one or more independent variables. The model is used to determine the probabilities of the a-priori appointed classes of categorical distributed dependent variables, ensuring at the same time that the probabilities are elements of the interval [0,1] and on the other hand that the probabilities sum up to one. The independent variables are not restricted to be categorical. This makes the logistic regression and the multinomial regression suitable to classify nominal dependent variables, see e. g. Hastie et al. (2011, pp.119-122). The multinomial regression fulfils in this thesis the role of a standard model.

Implementation The multinomial regression for classification, which is also called maximum entropy, is implemented in the R-library maxent of T. P. Jurka and Y. Tsuruoka. The library is, strictly speaking, a wrapper to the memory efficient C++ library for maximum entropy classification maxent. For an overview of the R-library, see Jurka (2012). Please note, that the variant of a binary classification used in this thesis is a specialisation of the multinomial regression to a logistic regression.

6.1.2 *Single-Hidden-Layer Neural Networks*

The second algorithm selected for classification are neural networks (NN). Roughly speaking: Neural networks consist of at least two regression models connected in series. The first regression extracts linear combinations of input parameters as essential characteristics to model in a second regression a non-linear function determining the output, see Hastie et al. (2011, p.389). A main characteristic of neural networks is hence the "ability to learn the form of a non-linear function".

But, it is also the characteristic of neural networks to approximate any given smooth function by a high number of parameters. If the network has too many parameters, however, it will over-fit the data. A common technique to avoid the over-fitting is early stopping, meaning to stop the training before the "optimal" parametrization on the training data is found. Neural networks make for this purpose use of validation sets to determine when to stop. The training often stops when the validation error fails to decrease but starts to increase, see Hastie et al. (2011, p.398).

The "vanilla", or canonical neural network is a single-hidden-layer feed-forward back-propagation network. The vanilla network has (1) an input layer with p units $X_1, \ldots, X_p$, (2) an output layer with k units $Y_1, \ldots, Y_k$, which are in a binary classification $k = 2$ units, and (3) a single hidden layer with m units $Z_1, \ldots, Z_m$. The units of the hidden layer $Z_1, \ldots, Z_m$ are derived by linear combinations of the input units $X_1, \ldots, X_p$, and then used to model the non-linear function returning the output layer $Y_1, \ldots, Y_k$. For classification purposes, each unit in the output layer $Y_1, \ldots, Y_k$ is further allocated with the probability to be in the corresponding class $k \in K$, see Hastie et al. (2011, pp.392-393).

Feed-forward is a characteristic of the network design and refers to the transfer of information in the network, which is in a feed-forward network always one directional. A feed-forward network has no autoregressive loops (in contrast to iterative loops), in demarcation to recurrent neural networks, which may also provide autoregressive loops.

Back-propagation is a network training technique, standing for "backward propagation of errors". The training is based on a minimization of squared model errors and the calculation of the corresponding error minimum, see Hastie et al. (2011, pp.395-397).

Implementation An R-implementation of a single-hidden-layer feed-forward back-propagation neural network is given in the nnet library of B. Ripley, which is e. g. introduced in Venables and Ripley (2004).

6.1.3 *Stabilized Linear Discriminant Analysis*

The third algorithm selected for classification is the stabilized linear discriminant analysis (SLDA).

The linear discriminant analysis (LDA) was first proposed by Fisher (1936) and considers the ratio of two primary quantities: (1) the inter-group variance and (2) the intra-group variance. The inter-group variance is the variance between the groups. Intra-group variance, in contrast, is the variance within each group. The inter-group variance should be high while the intra-group variance should be low to maximise the discriminatory power between the groups, see Venables and Ripley (2004, p.332). Note, that the decision boundary in a binary classification is a simple linear function and the class density in a linear discriminant analysis is commonly assumed to be Gaussian, see Hastie et al. (2011, p.108).

Läuter et al. (1998) additionally proposed to evaluate not the observations (which can be high-dimensional), but to evaluate linear score coefficients representing the observation. This proposal allows to evaluate compressed low-dimensional score-coefficients instead of the high-dimensional observations in order to increase the stability of the solutions and to reduce the computing requirements. This stabilizing approach to reduce the dimensionality for the discriminant analysis as well as the corresponding score function was first proposed in Läuter (1992).

Implementation The linear discriminant analysis of Fisher is implemented in the MASS library of B. Ripley, B. Venables, D. M. Bates, K. Hornik, A. Gebhardt, and D. Firth. The stabilizing technique of Läuter et al. (1998) is implemented in the ipred library of A. Peters, T. Hothorn, B. D. Ripley, and T. Therneau.

6.2 Ensemble Learning Algorithms

In addition to the hitherto suggested ordinary learning algorithms, the following section proposes three further ensemble learning algorithms for classification. Ensemble learning algorithms not only train a single, but multiple learners on a single classification request, and combine the resulting set of hypothesis to a single classification outcome. An overview of ensemble methods is e. g. given in Zhou (2012).

6.2.1 *Boosting*

The first of the selected ensemble or meta learning algorithms is boosting (BOO). The central idea of boosting is to combine a set of m base classifiers B_m with $m = 1, \ldots, k$, or weak classifiers, of binary prediction. Base classifiers often take only a single measure into account, e. g. the number of words in a document to be higher or lower than a pre-defined value, or for a non-expert-knowledge implementation one of the ordinary learning algorithms introduced in Section 6.1. Base classifiers are very fast to compute, but for the price of return error rates often only slightly better than random guessing. The outcome of these k weak classifiers is combined to a new ensemble classifier B using weighting functions, that ignores bad, but pays particular attention to good results. Most boosting algorithms determine the weights simply according to the training data accuracy.

This concept of ensemble classification was introduced for the first time by Schapire (1990). The phenomenon, however, has long before been known in additive modelling, see for example Hastie et al. (2011, pp.295-336). The primary concept of boosting can be summarized as a method to fit an additive expansion of a set of individual classifiers, or basis functions. The concept of boosting is hence very similar to the concept of single hidden layer neural networks, see Hastie et al. (2011, p.341).

Implementation The R-library caTools by J. Tuszynski provides an adoption of the LogitBoost algorithm of Friedman et al. (2000) and follows the application of the algorithm as given in Dettling and Bühlmann (2003). The weak classifier of the LogitBoost implementation is a decision stump, that is a one node decision tree, see Breiman et al. (1993).

Massive criticism on boosting algorithms was given in Long and Servedio (2010). This critic, primary addressed to convex weighting functions, also concerns the LogitBoost algorithm. According to this critic, any convex potential booster with a random classification rate of pure noise data unequal to zero can not be trained to learn accuracies better than a coin-flip. Branching boosters, see e. g. Mansour (2002) and Kalai and Servedio (2005), are not affected by this criticism.

The implication of this critic for the engineering approach in this thesis is, that it can already be assumed that the control parameters will have a significant influence on the classification outcome. The analysis of these effects, is part of Chapter 7 and Chapter 8.

6.2.2 *Bagging*

The second selected ensemble learning algorithm is bootstrap aggregation, or bagging (BGG). The main idea of bagging is to take B samples of size n and to generate B predictions m_i for $i = 1, \ldots, B$ of each sample. The arithmetic mean of the B predictions gives the outcome of the ensemble classification. The classification of the single replication is often done on decision tree methods, but can generally also be done with any other classification method. The first proposal to use bootstrap aggregation was given in Breiman (1996).

Bootstrap aggregation can generally help reduce the variance of the classification. Therefore, consider the following distinction of unstable and stable classifiers: (1) Unstable classifiers show a low bias but a high variance. A typical example for unstable classifiers are decision trees. (2) Stable classifiers have a low variance, but often at the price of a high bias. A typical example for stable classifiers is the linear discriminant analysis. The ordinary decision tree algorithm relevant for the bootstrap aggregation, hence belongs to the class of unstable classifiers, having typically a high variance, but low bias, see Breiman (1998). Imposing the bagging meta algorithm on decision tree classifiers, reduces the variance of the unstable decision trees, but also preserves the low bias.

Implementation An implementation of the recursive partitioning of decision trees is given within the R-library rpart by T. Therneau, B. Atkinson, and B. Ripley, where the implementation closely follows the proposed tree construction rule by Breiman et al. (1993). The ipred library heritages the tree construction and provides the final bagging algorithm for classification.

6.2.3 *Random Forests*

The third ensemble learning algorithm is random forests (RF). Random forests are very similar to bagging, but allow a more flexible computing of the underlying decision trees. Random forests were first proposed by Breiman (2001). The major difference between random forests and bagging is generally to select the best split of a node within the algorithm.

Random forests start similar to bagging with bootstrap sampling and the construction of regression trees on each sample. The B sample trees grow to a forest of trees. Each tree in the forest returns a single classification outcome m_i for $i = 1, \dots, B$ and the modus (in contrast to the often used arithmetic mean in bagging algorithms) of the set of predictions $\{m_i\}_{i=1}^{B}$ gives the final classification.

Implementation The random forecast algorithm is implemented in the R-library randomForest by A. Liaw and M. Wiener, which is based on the Fortran code of L. Breiman and A. Cutler.

Further Classification Algorithms The algorithms considered here represent just a small subset of the classification procedures. Further common algorithms are, for example, in the field of

1. *Unsupervised learning:*
   a) K-means clustering, for example presented in Wu (2012) and the
   b) Principal component analysis (PCA), which is for example discussed in Jackson (2005).
2. *Supervised learning:*
   a) Decision trees (DT), which can be found in Breiman et al. (1993),
   b) Support vector machines (SVM), see e. g. Abe (2010), and
   c) K-nearest neighbours (k-NN), which can be found in Duda et al. (2006).

The selection of the presented algorithms in Section 6.1 and Section 6.2 was primarily because of a self-imposed boundary to use not more than 6 classification algorithms to keep the diversity not wider than necessary. For a general survey of text classification algorithms, see e. g. Aggarwal and Zhai (2012).

6.3 Real-Time Classification

The task of real-time classification is to classify any new incident (in this thesis, this is to classify ad-hoc news, but it could also be any other incident equipped with a time stamp and a corresponding textual event) in seconds or milliseconds.

The training of the algorithms puts (using the supercomputing systems of the LRZ) no serious restrictions on the computational times, which is less than 24 hours for each incident.

The task of the classification of new and unseen data, however, is to minimize the required computational times of the classification algorithms, to forecast any high-frequency volatility shock, even before the market has had time to react to the changed market situation.

6.3.1 *Labelling the Sample*

The task of supervised classification requires a pre-labelled training set. Testing the sample of Section 5.1 on page 65 for volatility process affecting incidents and incidents of random noise, while simultaneously taking into account the process' specific characteristics of autoregressive and zero-inflated time series, supplies the thereto required labels

- 0, if the arrival of the news seemed not to trigger a volatility shock, and
- 1, if the test decision suggests the conclusion that the arrival of the unexpected news caused a shock.

Note however, that the labels depend massively on the significance level of the Wald test of formula (5.2) on page 74. Any analysis of the algorithms quality should therefore especially account for the dependence of the classification outcome from the significance level of the applied Wald test.

6.3.2 *Training the Algorithms*

A random subset of 1,500 of the 1,938 incidents under analysis, see Section 5.1.1 on page 66, labelled as random noise (label 0) and volatility shock triggering (label 1) incidents, form the set to train the presented algorithms of supervised classification.

The purpose of the training is to find the algorithms parameters that minimize the error of classification, determined on the training set by the now known "true" labels. The predicted values, not labels, of the classifiers, is between 0 and 1, reflecting the conviction of the algorithms to predict the true label. A probability value in the interval [0, 0.5] will be labelled as non-shock causing (label 0), a value in the interval (0.5, 1] will be labelled as shock causing (label 1). The level that splits the labels, here it is 0.5, is also called the cutoff level. The default cutoff level in a binary classification is 0.5. This is also the cutoff level that is used in the following analysis. The analysis of the effect of different cutoff levels is part of Chapter 7.

That means, that volatility elevating incidents will be interpreted as volatility shock causing events, while volatility neutral incidents will be interpreted as those, if the post-incident re-evaluation of the market differs not at all, or only marginal but insignificant, from the initial pre-incident evaluation.

The training is carried out on each of the 6 classification algorithms (1) multinomial regression, (2) single-hidden-layer neural networks, (3) stabilized linear discriminant analysis, (4) boosting, (5) bagging, and (6) random forests. All these algorithms are introduced in Section 6.1 and Section 6.2.

6.3.3 *Classifying Unexpected Incidents*

The performance of the competing algorithms on the training set, however, is no appropriate measure to evaluate their prediction performance. The trained supervised learning algorithms are therefore applied on the remaining 438 incidents of the 2 years sample described in Section 5.1.1. Note, that 1,500 of 1,938 incidents were randomly drawn to form a training set. Therefore, another 438 incidents appearing in 2010 and 2011 can be used, to form the test set.

The probability computed by the algorithms, to classify the training set in volatility elevating incidents, or "Shocks", and volatility neutral incidents, or "No shocks", is given for the sparsity values 0.6, 0.7, 0.8, 0.9, 0.925 and 0.95 according to Section 5.2.3 on page 78. These sparsity levels correspond to the number of non-sparse and sparse entries as well as the resulting number of terms in the term-documents-matrix, and are reported in Table 6.1 on the next page. The reported number of terms is exclusively the previously removed stopwords.

Note further, that the probabilities of the used binary classification are all within the interval [0.5, 1], as only the probability of the predicted label is

Level of sparsity	Non-sparse entries	Sparse entries	Number of terms
.6	20,930	31,396	27
.7	34,303	80,039	59
.8	52,714	210,854	136
.9	81,784	736,052	422
.925	90,844	1,120,406	625
.95	107,171	2,036,257	1,106

Table 6.1: Number of non-sparse and sparse entries and the corresponding number of terms in the term-document-matrix in dependence of the sparsity level. The underlying number of documents is 1,938.

reported. For example, let the probability of label 0 be 0.3 and the probability of label 1 be 0.7. The predicted label is 1, the corresponding probability 0.7. Assume now the probability of 0 to be 0.8 and the probability of 1 to be 0.2. The predicted label is 0, while the corresponding probability is 0.8. The reported probability is therefore a label conditional probability, and the reported label depends on the used cutoff level.

The probabilities computed by the algorithms are illustrated for the different sparsity levels in Figure 6.1 on the next page. All calculations are from the test data consisting of 438 incidents. The number of cases in the no volatility box and the corresponding volatility box sum for each sparsity level and each algorithm exactly to 438. Meaning, the corresponding two boxes represent exactly the 438 incidents of the test set.

The computing is determined on transaction time sampled (see Section 2.3.1) ask quotes (see Section 2.3.2) with an area-adjusted TSRV estimates (see Section 3.2.4) of the latent integrated volatility, and an unstemmed, Log-Idf weighted term-document-matrix (see Section 5.2.3). The significance level of the shock and no shock discriminating Wald test of equation (5.2) is fixed with $\alpha=0.01$.

Similar results also emerged for stemmed terms and different weightings, e. g. Tf-Idf. A decreasing of the significance levels, e. g. $\alpha=0.001$ (note, the reduction from 0.01 to 0.001), shifted the computed probabilities of "No shocks" and "Shocks" upwards, and vice versa for an increased significance level. The findings further hold for any other integrated volatility estimator of Section 3.2.

Interpretation The estimated probabilities of predicting "No volatility shock" or "Volatility shock" sum to one. An algorithm returning the probability of 0.7 to be an element of the class "No volatility shock" returns, thus the probability of 0.3 to be an element of the competing class "Volatility shock". Therefore,

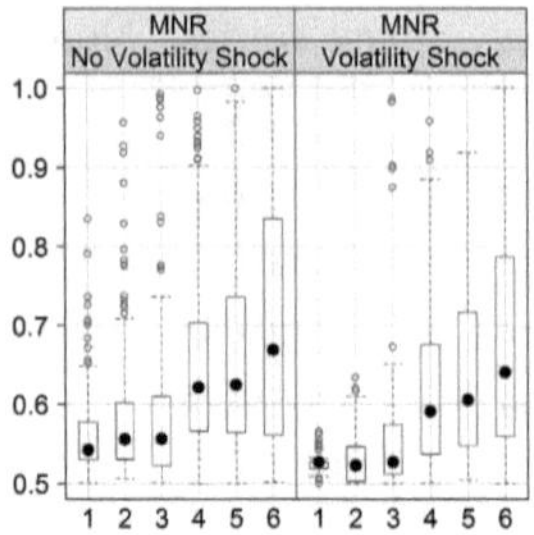

(a) "Multinomial (Logistic) Regression (MNR)".

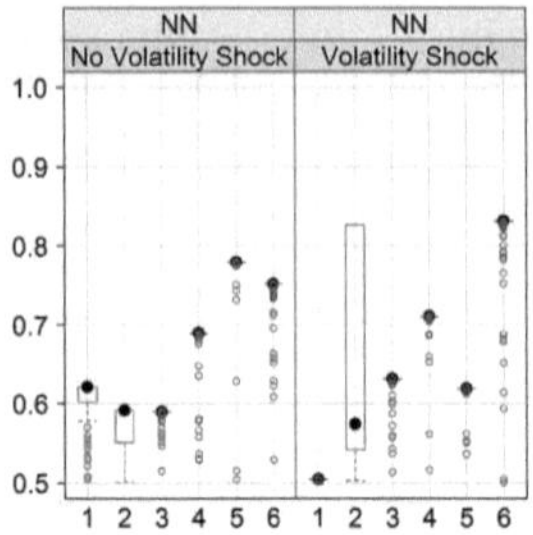

(b) "Single-Hidden-Layer Neural Networks (NN)".

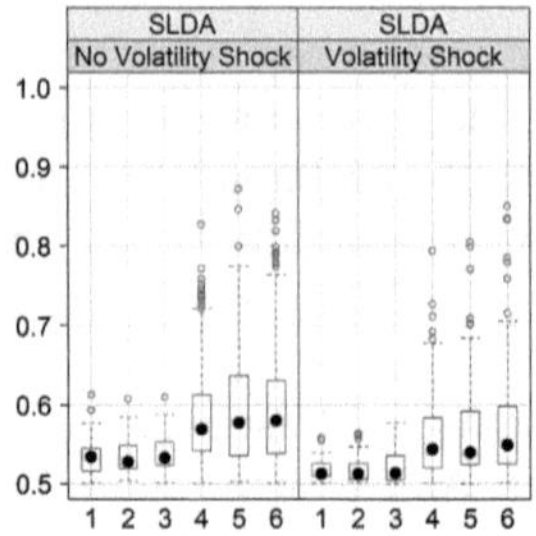

(c) "Stabilized Linear Discriminant Analysis (SLDA)".

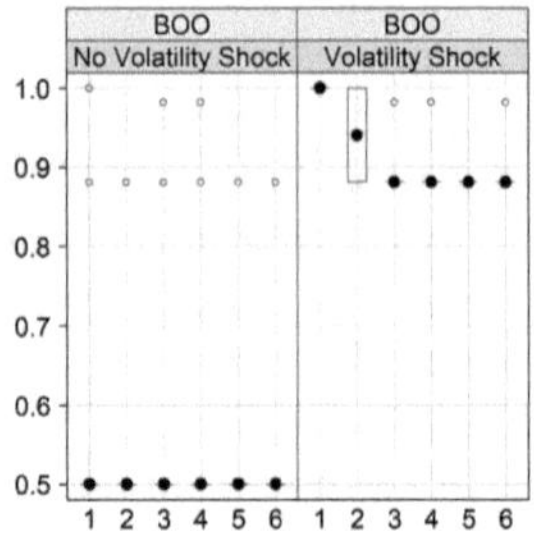

(d) "Boosting (BOO)".

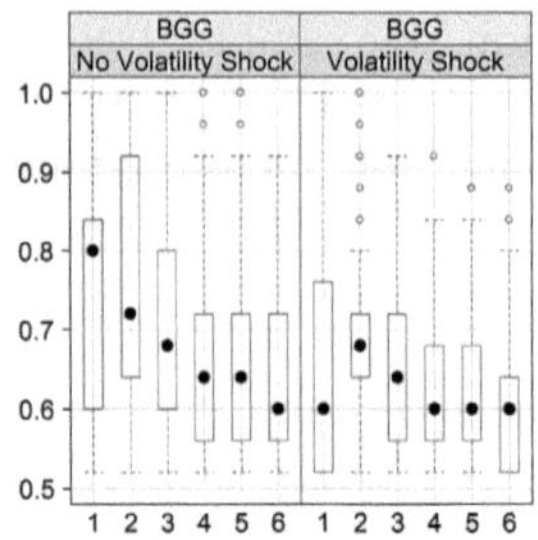

(e) "Bagging (BGG)".

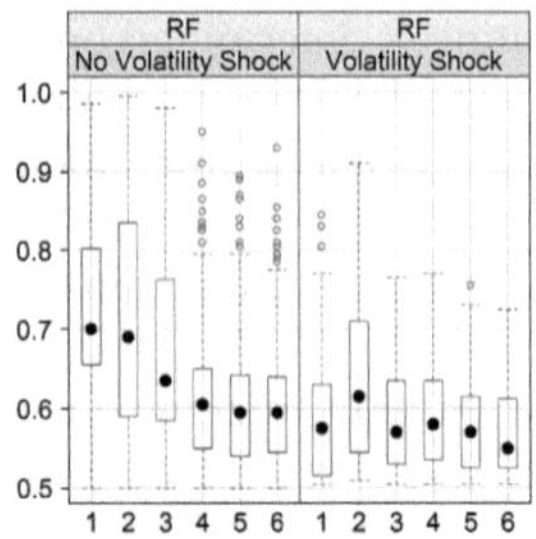

(f) "Random Forests (RF)".

Figure 6.1: Computed probabilities of binary classification of the supervised learning algorithms introduced in Section 6.1 and Section 6.2. The abscissa carries the different sparsity levels, the ordinate the probability of label 0 (left side of each graphic, corresponding to no volatility shock) or label 1 (right side of each graphic, corresponding to volatility shock). The coding on the abscissa corresponds to the sparsity levels: 1=0.6, 2=0.7, 3=0.8, 4=0.9, 5=0.925, 6=0.95.

the value gives the discriminating power of each algorithm. Values close to one indicate a high discriminating power, while values close to 0.5 indicate a low discriminating power. Solely the value of the predicted label is illustrated. Probabilities of exactly 0.5 are reported as "No volatility shock", which means they are labelled with 0. Three main findings emerge from the visualisation:

1. The calculated probabilities are highly dependent on the sparsity level and the considered supervised learning algorithm.

2. The ensemble learning algorithms bagging and random forests benefit from low sparsity levels, whereas the ordinary learning algorithms benefit from high sparsity levels. In a weakened variant, this also holds for the boosting algorithm.

3. The boosting algorithm determines very clearly between the two considered cases. But, the fact that the cutoff level is set to 0.5 and that all predictions with a probability of 0.5 are labelled as 0, raise doubts against the discriminating power of the boosting algorithm.

Implementation Some support for the implementation of the presented algorithms was given by the R-library RTextTools of T. P. Jurka, L. Collingwood, A. E. Boydstun, E. Grossman, and W. van Atteveldt, which mainly serves as a wrapper to unit the implementations of the algorithms into a single library.

The detailed evaluation of the algorithms performance is part of Chapter 7, where the fitting of the algorithms on the independent test set is compared with further minimum benchmark statistics.

7 Benchmarking

The system intrinsic true label of the effect of an unexpected news on the time series of volatility estimates determines the class of news, which can either be a "No volatility shock" or "Volatility shock" causing event. The class of news, in turn, is used to train the supervised learning algorithms on historical incidents, which will then be used to predict the class of a new and unexpected news.

In order to evaluate the performance of the competing supervised learning algorithms, however, it is essential to consider not only the computed probability of classification, but also the performance of the algorithms measured in terms of prediction error rates.

Therefore, this chapter considers the following units: Section 7.1 introduces the instrument to compute test set depending prediction error rates, with particular attention to the computed errors variance. Section 7.2 evaluates the classification accuracy of the algorithm with the minimal prediction error according to Section 7.1, and compares the accuracy of the selected algorithm with the accuracy of a random baseline model. Section 7.3, finally, compares volatility shock inducing incidents with random incidents.

This analysis accounts for the typical mistakes (2) - (5) in pattern recognition for classification exposed in Section 5.3.1 on page 82. For introductory literature about methods of error estimation, see e. g. Japkowicz and Shah (2011).

7.1 Cross-Validation

Cross-validation techniques are model-validation techniques. The main idea of cross-validation is to evaluate how the results, these are the predicted classes in a classification context, would generalize on an independent data set. For this undertaking, the cross-validation technique tries to evaluate the degree of dependence of the statistical method under analysis, here it is the supervised learning algorithms, from the training set. The cross-validation technique is very common in two different applications:

1. To skip the necessity to build an extra validation set. This is very common in practical applications, where the pure number of labelled data is often too small to split a sub-set of extra validation data, see Mohri et al. (2012, p.5).

2. To evaluate competing supervised learning algorithms, using suitable statistical tests built on the cross-validation statistics, see Lavesson (2006, pp.38-39).

In this thesis, the data set is sufficiently large for all considered applications. Hence, there is no need to use cross-validation to split an extra validation set. For the evaluation of competing supervised learning algorithms, however, two different tests applied on the computed cross-validation-errors will be discussed in Section 7.1.3.

7.1.1 *K-Fold Cross-Validation*

The k-fold cross-validation principle, where a fold is a subset of the data, is according to the following scheme to:

1. Split the full data set in k folds of approximately the same size.
2. Train the algorithms on k-1 folds and test the algorithms on the remaining fold.
3. Iterate the process k times, such that every fold is used for testing exactly once.
4. Estimate the expectation value of the k folds.

A $k = 5$ or $k = 10$ fold cross-validation is common, see McLachlan et al. (2004, p.214) and Mohri et al. (2012, p.6), but not compulsory. Please note, that cross-validated models simultaneously account for over-fitting if the folds are randomly selected.

Leave-one-out cross-validation Setting the number of folds to $k = m$ in a k-fold cross-validation, where m is the number of data minus one, is called leave-one-out cross-validation. Each observation will hence represent the whole test set exactly once. The average leave-one-out error then gives an approximately unbiased estimator of the average algorithm error. The computational requirements, however, can be very cost intensive, see Mohri et al. (2012, p.6).

The leave-one-out cross-validation technique can furthermore return wrong predictions in a binary classification context, if the training set is uniformly distributed. Let, for example, M be the number of elements in the whole sample. The training sample has therefore M-1 elements. Suppose further, that M/2 elements of the training sample belong to class 0, while the remaining M/2-1 elements of the training sample belong to class 1. The classification algorithm will return the class 0, because of the additional element in this class. The correct class, however, would be class 1, which is the class of the leave-one-out element.

Due to the binary classification of this thesis, the used technique in the following is a k-fold cross-validation with k=10 folds.

7.1.2 *Cross-Validating the Algorithms*

The cross-validation of the competing algorithms is based on an evaluation of miss-classified and correctly-classified instances. The function to measure the loss of predicted to true labels is the loss function, see Mohri et al. (2012, p.4).

Loss function Let S be the set of all labels and S' be the set of potential predictions. Any loss function L is a mapping $L : S \times S' \to \mathbb{R}_+$. The loss function used in this thesis is the indicator loss function $L(s, s') = 1_{s \neq s'}$, with $s \in S$ and $s' \in S'$. For the binary prediction of this thesis, this means: If the prediction is correct, then the return value of the loss function is 0, if the prediction is wrong, the loss function returns the value 1.

Computing the Cross-Validation Errors The error of the cross-validation is computed on the basis of the loss function $L(s, s') = 1_{s \neq s'}$. Let s_{ij} be the true label of the incident j which is element of fold i for $i = 1, \ldots, k$. The total number of observations within fold i is denoted by n_i. Computing the k-fold cross-validation on all but the ith fold returns the error of hypotheses h_i applied on incident r_{ij}, where $h_i(r_{ij})$ represents the predicted label of the algorithm on the corresponding incident. Then, the estimated error of fold i is:

$$\widehat{\text{error}}_i = \frac{1}{n_i} \sum_{j=1}^{n_i} L(s_{ij}, h_i(r_{ij})),$$

and the average error of all hypotheses h_i for $i = 1, \ldots, k$ gives the k-fold cross-validation error $\hat{R}_{CV}$, see Mohri et al. (2012, p.5):

$$\hat{R}_{CV} = \frac{1}{k} \sum_{i=1}^{k} \widehat{\text{error}}_i. \tag{7.1}$$

The computed 10-fold cross-validation errors of the presented algorithms are reported in Table 7.1 on the next page. The listed results are calculated for the time series of area-adjusted TSRV estimates based on ask quotes measured in transaction time. The significance level of the applied Wald test in formula (5.2) on page 74 is set to $\alpha = 0.01$. Stopwords were initially removed on all calculations.

	MNR	NN	SLDA	BOO	BGG	RF
.6	.379/.037	.374/.042	.373/.049	.379/.041	.459/.030	.430/.041
.7	**.373**/.055	.375/.045	.374/.036	.384/.047	.434/.028	.407/.020
.8	**.367**/.031	.386/.033	.371/.038	.381/.045	.401/.035	.403/.038
.9	**.355**/.028	.390/.025	.385/.039	.391/.038	.393/.019	.399/.037
.925	**.357**/.030	.397/.031	.387/.033	.392/.037	.403/.027	.396/.042
.95	**.330**/.029	.422/.015	.389/.037	.385/.022	.394/.021	.389/.023

(a) Unstemmed and TF-Idf weighted.

.6	.374/.041	.379/.024	.372/.029	.383/.030	.429/.021	.418/.046
.7	**.372**/.032	.380/.034	.375/.036	.382/.030	.438/.030	.409/.038
.8	**.369**/.025	.386/.031	.371/.057	.390/.029	.410/.041	.406/.046
.9	**.351**/.037	.407/.035	.381/.040	.388/.038	.403/.028	.395/.019
.925	**.344**/.020	.411/.024	.391/.029	.396/.050	.407/.044	.398/.036
.95	**.309**/.027	.409/.034	.393/.013	.401/.046	.407/.049	.410/.020

(b) Stemmed and TF-Idf weighted.

.6	.372/.035	.370/.029	.370/.042	.373/.029	.396/.042	.372/.029
.7	**.370**/.040	.377/.039	.370/.044	.374/.026	.403/.028	.376/.017
.8	**.360**/.028	.387/.039	.370/.025	.372/.027	.392/.041	.379/.024
.9	**.346**/.026	.450/.063	.371/.028	.376/.033	.400/.027	.392/.051
.925	**.349**/.029	.485/.045	.379/.017	.375/.039	.395/.038	.408/.045
.95	**.329**/.039	.451/.054	.383/.033	.384/.037	.391/.032	.390/.029

(c) Unstemmed and Log-Idf weighted.

.6	.373/.032	.384/.026	.371/.034	.371/.040	.416/.037	.389/.052
.7	**.365**/.029	.379/.025	.369/.052	.371/.036	.414/.033	.389/.027
.8	**.359**/.039	.415/.041	.368/.044	.374/.026	.396/.022	.390/.022
.9	**.346**/.028	.460/.062	.367/.038	.382/.041	.403/.025	.384/.045
.925	**.337**/.029	.443/.054	.382/.032	.389/.033	.394/.029	.400/.036
.95	**.317**/.035	.496/.048	.382/.040	.384/.024	.391/.029	.385/.017

(d) Stemmed and Log-Idf weighted.

Table 7.1: Cross-validation errors of the supervised learning algorithms of Section 6.1 and Section 6.2. The row gives the sparsity value, the column the algorithm. The first number within the table gives the cross-validation error of formula (7.1) on page 101, the second number the corresponding standard deviation of the estimation as a measure of precision. The Tf-Idf weighting follows formula (5.4), the Log-Idf weighting formula (5.5) on page 82.

Interpreting the Cross-Validation errors When inspecting Table 7.1 on the previous page, the following findings emerge:

1. It holds for all four tables, and all levels of sparsity except the lowest level of 0.6, that the multinomial regression (MNR) and the stabilized linear discriminant analysis (SLDA) return the smallest cross-validation errors over all considered algorithms.

   It holds further that the MNR algorithm is superior to the SLDA algorithm on high levels of sparsity, while the effect weakens on lower levels. The minimal cross-validation errors of the MNR algorithm in Table 7.1 are bold marked. The cross validation errors of the SLDA algorithm are italic marked.

2. Within the class of non-meta algorithms the MNR algorithm and the SLDA algorithm clearly dominate the single-hidden-layer neural networks (NN).

   Within the class of ensemble learning algorithms the boosting (BOO) algorithm dominates both, the bagging (BGG) and the random forests (RF) algorithm. The domination, however, seems to be too weak to assume the BOO algorithm to be superior.

   Further analysis, accounting not only for the cross-validation errors, but also for the standard deviations of the error estimates, is hence required.

3. Unfortunately, no clear picture emerges in an analysis of the stemming effects. On one hand, a term-document-matrix stemming seems to improve the results of the MNR algorithm on high levels of sparsity. On the other hand, however, stemming the term-document-matrix seems to be of no effect on all the other considered algorithms, especially when inspecting the Tf-Idf weighting and the Log-Idf weighting for identical findings.

4. But, a clear picture emerges in an analysis of the weighting effect, given the two considered weightings Tf-Idf and Log-Idf.

   The proportional scaling Tf-Idf weighting dominates the comprise of a proportional and binary scaling Log-Idf weighting in two cases: For the NN algorithm and on high levels of sparsity also for the RF algorithm.

   For all other cases, however, the Log-Idf weighting clearly dominates the Tf-Idf weighting. It seems therefore to be advisable to make use of the comprise of proportional and binary scaling Log-Idf weighting.

A comparison of the errors between the regarded algorithms will uncover the best fitting algorithm on the given data set, but will not give an indication of the degree of improvement, compared with a minimal baseline. Two baselines should therefore be considered:

Chance Baseline Firstly, the chance baseline, which is in a binary classification 0.50, both in accuracy and error rates, or generally in a l-labels classification in terms of errors 1-1/l. The central idea is to assume, because of a lack of frequency knowledge, that all 4 labels are identically distributed. A classifier that predicts only one of these 4 labels will in this case correctly predict 25% of the labels. The chance error baseline is hence 0.75.

Frequency Baseline Secondly, the frequency baseline, accounting also for asymmetric samples. The frequency baseline is in error rates 1-max(f), where f is the percentage of considered instances. For example, assume label 1 corresponds to 70% of all labels, and the labels 2, 3, and 4 to the remaining 30%. Then a classifier that predicts only label 1 will correctly predict 70% of all labels. The frequency error baseline is hence 0.30.

Baseline interpretation of errors The proportion of shocks and non-shocks in the classification task of this thesis depends on (1) the sampling scheme, (2) ask or bid quotes, (3) the volatility estimator, and (4) the significance level α of the applied Wald test in formula (5.2) on page 74. The ratio of shocks of the transaction time sampled asset quotes used in this thesis, is reported in Table 8.1 on page 125.

Taking, for example, the area-adjusted TSRV estimator of ask quotes and α=1e-02 gives a shock to non-shock ratio of 0.446. That means, the remaining 0.554 of the incidents under analysis hold the null hypothesis of the applied Wald test and can not been assumed to cause a shock. The frequency error baseline in this example is therefore 0.446. This configuration is also used for the computations in Table 7.1.

Inspecting Table 7.1, that means, that the maximum suitable error rate to break the frequency baseline is 0.446. Except the NN algorithm manage all other algorithms to break the frequency error baseline. The NN algorithm breaks the frequency error baseline for the Tf-Idf weighting, or using the Log-Idf weighting on low levels of sparsity. A clear out-performance is given for the MNR algorithm on high levels of sparsity.

Please note, that the frequency error rate is always lower or equal to the chance error rate, which is independent of the labels distribution. For example, assume again the constellation of the area-adjusted TSRV estimator applied on ask quotes, then hold the following (in Table 7.2 on the next page) reported chance and frequency error baselines:

α	Chance	Frequency	Dominating label
2e-01	.500	.380	Shocks
1e-01	.500	.436	Shocks
1e-02	.500	.446	Non-shocks
1e-03	.500	.369	Non-shocks

Table 7.2: Chance and frequency error baselines of the area-adjusted TSRV estimates applied on ask quotes. A full table separating for ask and bid quotes and for the different integrated volatility estimators discussed in Section 3.2 is given in Table 8.1 on page 125.

The presented results hold for all 4 errors of the first kind α of the applied Wald test reported in Table 7.2. But, an analysis of the cross-validation error rates alone does not seem to be recommendable to receive a suited decision basis in order to determine dominant supervised classification algorithms. Therefore, the so far investigated descriptive analysis of the cross-validation errors is extended to test for the best fitting algorithm, taking into account not only the errors, but also the standard deviations of the errors estimates.

Implementation Some support for the computation of the cross-validation errors was again given by the RTextTools library. Further noteworthy is the required main memory to compute the cross-validation errors, which ranges from approximately 1 GB for a 0.6 to approximately 32 GB for the 0.95 sparsity level.

7.1.3 *Testing for the Best Fitting Algorithms*

Two canonical candidates to compare different classifiers are (1) the dependent t-test for paired samples and (2) the Wilcoxon sign rank test. Both tests are given in detail in Sheskin (2000).

It is recommendable to compute both tests and to compare the test outcomes. Moreover, the t-test for paired samples is generally more powerful than the Wilcoxon sign rank test, given the necessary assumption of population normality holds, but less powerful, if the population normality is violated, see Demšar (2006). The following calculations are therefore done for both, the dependent t-test for paired samples and the Wilcoxon sign rank test.

Dependent t-test for paired samples The dependent t-test for paired samples assumes the population to be normally distributed, or to be applied on at least 30 independent observations, which are given in all applications of this thesis.

The test accounts for dependency, which is given if the test is applied on two paired samples.

To apply the test on the cross-validation errors, let n denote the sample size, and $x_{1,i}$ respectively $x_{2,i}$, with $i = 1, \dots, n$, denote the cross-validation errors of two supervised learning algorithms. The mean of x_1 is $\overline{x}_1$, the mean of x_2 is $\overline{x}_2$. The variance of the difference of x_1 and x_2 is denoted by $\sigma^2_{x_1 - x_2}$.

The hypotheses of the (1) left- and (2) right-sided paired t-test are:

$$\begin{aligned} &(1) \quad H_0 : \overline{x}_1 \geqslant \overline{x}_2 \text{ vs. } H_1 : \overline{x}_1 < \overline{x}_2, \\ &(2) \quad H_0 : \overline{x}_1 \leqslant \overline{x}_2 \text{ vs. } H_1 : \overline{x}_1 > \overline{x}_2. \end{aligned}$$

Under the null, follows the test statistic

$$t_{\text{paired}} = \frac{\overline{x}_2 - \overline{x}_1}{\sqrt{\sigma^2_{x_1 - x_2}/n}},$$

a t-distribution with $n - 1$ degrees of freedom. Discard the null, if (1) for the left-sided test $t_{\text{paired}} > t_{\alpha;n-1}$ and (2) for the right-sided test $t_{\text{paired}} < t_{\alpha;n-1}$, where α denotes the significance level. For further details on the paired t-test, see e. g. Sheskin (2000).

A point of criticism of the paired t-test is the sensitivity of the test to outliers, which can skew the test statistic and hence decrease the power of the test arising from increased standard errors. The Wilcoxon sign rank test, however, ignores absolute magnitudes of differences and is hence safer to outliers than the paired t-test, see Demšar (2006).

Wilcoxon Sign Rank Test This non-parametrical statistical test was proposed in Wilcoxon (1945) to assess the difference of two paired random samples through their population *ranks*. The Wilcoxon sign rank test assumes the difference of the sample to be independent and identically distributed (i.i.d.) and to be symmetric.

Let again n denote the sample size, and $x_{1,i}$ respectively $x_{2,i}$, with $i = 1, \dots, n$, denote the cross-validation errors of two algorithms. The median of x_1 is $\tilde{x}_1$, the median of x_2 is $\tilde{x}_2$.

The hypotheses of the (1) left- and (2) right-sided Wilcoxon sign rank test are:

$$\begin{aligned} &(1) \quad H_0 : \tilde{x}_1 \geqslant \tilde{x}_2 \text{ vs. } H_1 : \tilde{x}_1 < \tilde{x}_2, \\ &(2) \quad H_0 : \tilde{x}_1 \leqslant \tilde{x}_2 \text{ vs. } H_1 : \tilde{x}_1 > \tilde{x}_2. \end{aligned}$$

The test statistic W to evaluate the hypotheses is calculated as follows:

1. Calculate the absolute difference of the errors $|x_{2,i} - x_{1,i}|$.

2. Exclude all pairs $x_{2,i} = x_{1,i}$ and reduce the sample size n to n'. Note, that a high number of identical observations indicates the validation of H_0.

3. Order the remaining n' differences $|x_{2,i} - x_{1,i}|$ from small to large.

4. Rank the ordered differences, beginning with 1 for the smallest difference, 2 for the next smallest difference and average values for ties. Let R_i for $i = 1, \ldots, n'$ denote the ranks.

5. Calculate the test statistic W_+ and W_-, with I the indicator function, as:

$$W_+ = \sum_{i=1}^{n'} I(x_{2,i} - x_{1,i} > 0) \cdot R_i,$$
$$W_- = \sum_{i=1}^{n'} I(x_{2,i} - x_{1,i} < 0) \cdot R_i,$$

with

$$W = \min\{W_+, W_-\}. \tag{7.2}$$

A significantly greater value of W_+ than of W_- would indicate that with a high likelihood the sample is from a population having a median larger than the hypothesized median. A significant greater value of W_- than of W_+ on the other hand would indicate that the sample is from a population with a median less than the hypothesized median, see Sheskin (2000, p.116).

Support for the alternative hypothesis of the left-sided Wilcoxon test (1) is given if $W_- > W_+$. The right-sided Wilcoxon test (2) is supported if $W_+ > W_-$.

For n' tending to infinity, W is further asymptotic normally distributed. To correct for the continuity of the normal distribution, a factor of 0.5 needs to be subtracted from the test statistic (7.2). The continuity corrected and z-score transformed normal approximation of the Wilcoxon test statistic is then given as, see Sheskin (2000, p.120):

$$z = \frac{|W - \frac{1}{4}n(n+1)| - 0.5}{\sqrt{\frac{1}{24}n(n+1)(2n+1)}} \sim N(0,1). \tag{7.3}$$

Note that the absolute transformation of the numerator in (7.3) yields always in a positive numerator and therefore in a positive value of z.

Which of the alternative hypothesis is supported depends on the values of W_+ and W_-. If $W_+ > W_-$, the right-sided test is supported whereas if

$W_- > W_+$, the left-sided test is supported. The null hypothesis of the supported directional test can be rejected if $z > z_{1-\alpha}$.

The critical values are tabulated for $n \leqslant 50$ in the Wilcoxon rank sum table. For $n > 50$, use the normal approximation (7.3). For a detailed description of the Wilcoxon sign rank test and the Wilcoxon rank sum table, see Sheskin (2000).

Both, the left-sided (first number above the diagonal) and the right-sided (first number below the diagonal) Wilcoxon sign rank test and the left-sided (second number above the diagonal) and the right-sided (second number below the diagonal) dependent t-test for paired samples are reported in Table 7.3 on the next page. All results are based on the calculations of Table 7.1c on page 102, using a Log-Idf weighted and unstemmed term-document-matrix.

To give an example of the interpretation of the table, consider the following test: Let the object of interest be the left-sided test of the MNR versus the SLDA algorithm on a 90% sparsity level, that is H_0 : MNR $\geqslant$ SLDA versus H_1 : MNR $<$ SLDA. When inspecting Table 7.3 it holds, that the null hypotheses is discarded for a 1.9% p-value using the Wilcoxon sign rank test, and for a 2.2% p-value using the paired t-test for depending samples. Therefore, it can be concluded, that the MNR algorithm is superior to the SLDA algorithm on a 5% significance level. The corresponding numbers in Table 7.3c are bold and italic marked.

Interpreting the Cross-Validation Errors Testing The results of Table 7.3 should mirror the findings of Table 7.1 on page 102. When inspecting Table 7.3, the following findings emerge:

1. The MNR algorithm dominates in regard to each other algorithm on a 1% significance level given a 95% level of sparsity and also on a 5% significance level given a 90% level of sparsity. The domination holds for both considered tests, but loses effectiveness on low levels of sparsity. The corresponding numbers are bold marked.

2. The evidently superiority of the SLDA algorithm detected in Table 7.1 can not be confirmed when only considering statistical tests instead of error measures. The superiority holds only on low levels of sparsity and only in comparison with BGG.

3. The NN algorithm is clearly dominated by each other considered algorithm for high levels of sparsity, but this effect weakens on low levels of sparsity.

	MNR	NN	SLDA	BOO	BGG	RF
MNR		.181/.135	.385/.493	.161/.375	.032/.051	.278/.350
NN	.853/.865		.577/.645	.385/.600	.097/.086	.312/.537
SLDA	.652/.507	.461/.355		.216/.383	.032/.027	.278/.307
BOO	.862/.625	.652/.400	.812/.617		.010/.015	.216/.427
BGG	.976/.949	.920/.914	.976/.973	.993/.985		.990/.991
RF	.754/.650	.722/.463	.754/.693	.812/.573	.014/.009	

(a) Sparsity 0.7.

MNR		.049/.038	.278/.151	.348/.189	.032/.025	.138/.084
NN	.962/.962		.688/.860	.903/.844	.500/.409	.615/.765
SLDA	.754/.849	.348/.140		.461/.439	.080/.099	.161/.188
BOO	.688/.811	.116/.156	.577/.561		.053/.046	.539/.316
BGG	.976/.975	.539/.591	.935/.901	.958/.954		.754/.748
RF	.884/.916	.423/.235	.862/.812	.500/.684	.278/.252	

(b) Sparsity 0.8.

MNR		**.002/.001**	**.019/.022**	**.032/.027**	**.001/.001**	**.019/.022**
NN	.999/.999		.993/.996	.976/.985	.976/.977	.997/.998
SLDA	.986/.978	.010/.004		.539/.328	.014/.022	.138/.173
BOO	.976/.973	.032/.015	.500/.672		.042/.038	.097/.247
BGG	.999/.999	.032/.023	.990/.978	.968/.962		.862/.663
RF	.986/.978	.005/.002	.884/.827	.920/.753	.161/.337	

(c) Sparsity 0.9.

MNR		**.001/.001**	**.001/.001**	**.002/.001**	**.002/.001**	**.007/.002**
NN	.999/.999		.998/.999	.997/.998	.993/.994	.995/.996
SLDA	.999/.999	.003/.001		.461/.448	.278/.286	.161/.300
BOO	.999/.999	.005/.002	.577/.552		.312/.316	.161/.356
BGG	.999/.999	.010/.006	.754/.714	.722/.684		.688/.573
RF	.995/.998	.007/.004	.862/.700	.862/.644	.348/.427	

(d) Sparsity 0.95.

Table 7.3: Wilcoxon sign rank test and paired t-test of the cross-validation errors. The first number represents the p-values of the Wilcoxon sign rank test. The second number gives the p-values of the paired t-test. The numbers below the diagonal report the right-sided test. The numbers above the diagonal report the left-sided test. The results are based on the Log-Idf weighted and unstemmed term-document-matrix of Table 7.1c on page 102.

4. Differences between the Wilcoxon sign rank test and the paired t-test are recognizable, but in most cases do not change the interpretation. The differences, however, are strong enough to recommend to make use of both tests when comparing different classifiers.

Similar results emerged for bid quotes and any other of the proposed integrated volatility estimators. Variations in the significance level α used for the Wilcoxon sign rank test and the paired t-test change the error rates in Table 7.1, but not the relations between the algorithms in Table 7.3.

7.2 Confusion Analytics

The analysis of error rates is very useful to evaluate the performance of competing predictors. It may be helpful, however, especially in text categorization applications, to consider not only the unidimensional error rate statistics, but also the consequences of classification mistakes measured in costs of wrong predictions.

7.2.1 *Confusion Matrix*

The potential prediction errors of a two-way classification can be summarized in a simple confusion matrix as given in Table 7.4 on the next page, see e. g. Japkowicz and Shah (2011, pp.77-81).

7.2.2 *Fail Forecasts and Economic Scenarios*

Note, that the in this thesis proposed engineering approach assumes per design, that the measured statistical control instruments reflect a real image of the underlying reality. Meaning, that the evaluation of the time series build on the estimates of the latent integrated volatility can be tested for structural breaks in the underlying DGP, to train a supervised learning algorithm on historical incidents in order to predict the expected reaction of the market to the arrival of an unexpected news in form of a volatility shock.

The confusion matrix in Table 7.4, finally, helps to evaluate the costs of wrong predictions. The potential errors in the case of a volatility shock forecast are:

1. False negative errors: The failure to miss to forecast a volatility shock, which will occur.

2. False positive errors: The misleading forecast of a volatility shock, which will not occur.

		predicted class	
		shock	*no shock*
actual class	*shock*	True positive	False negative
	no shock	False positive	True negative

Table 7.4: Confusion matrix of the four classification outcomes of a two-way classification. True positive events (TP) are identified and predicted as volatility shock causing events. True negative events (TN) are identified and predicted as no volatility shock causing events. False positive events (FP) are identified as no volatility shock causing events, but predicted as volatility shock causing events. False negative events (FN) are identified as volatility shock causing events, but predicted as no volatility shock causing events. The statistical proxy of the actual class is the applied Wald test of formula (5.2) on page 74. The predicted class is determined by the supervised learning algorithms of Section 6.1 and Section 6.2.

Scenarios To analyse the absolute costs of a wrong forecast, it is helpful to consider an economic scenario first. In the following, two different scenarios are considered to give an impression on the differing modes of operation:

A. The first scenario may be a trading application, where no investment has been occurred until the moment of the forecast.

   a) In this scenario a false positive forecast will possibly provoke a trade and cause charges, which could be lost when the trade is closed out, assuming all other conjunctures stayed unchanged within the time of the investment.

   b) A false negative forecast, however, will provoke no additional charges and therefore raise no damage. But, the loss of potential profit raises opportunity costs. Opportunity costs, however, are generally not regarded as costs in the sense of cost and activity accounting. They should nevertheless be taken into account.

B. The second scenario may already have an asset position in the portfolio. Please note, that the position can also be an obligation under contract, e. g. the delivery of goods in pre-defined quantities, but under floating prices. This scenario is for example common in gas and electricity markets, and high-quality iron and steal businesses.

a) In this scenario a false positive forecast will cause the costs of an (afterwards) unnecessary hedging-trade. This effect is similar to subcase a) of scenario A.

b) A false negative forecast, however, could induce irrepressible contract obligations, especially in high-frequent markets, and trigger the obligation to deliver goods and products to highly volatile prices, which can be significantly below the production or purchase prices.

More scenarios, and combinations of these two, are potentially thinkable. The given scenarios, however, will give two corners to adapt individual requirements on the predictive text mining task.

7.2.3 *Precision, Recall, F-measure, and AUC*

Precision, recall, F-measure, and AUC form a subset of statistical criteria to measure the goodness of classification. Two further measures, accounting for false alarms, will be considered in Section 8.1. The first two measures, that take into account false positive (FP) and false negative (FN) errors, are *precision* and *recall.* The harmonic mean of precision and recall, which weights precision as important as recall, is the F_1-*measure*, see van Rijsbergen (1979, pp.133-134). For an overview on performance measures to evaluate classifications, see e. g. Japkowicz and Shah (2011).

Each of these measures is embed in the interval [0,1], where 1 is the best and 0 the worst value. Please note, that the following presented measures of formulas (7.4) to (7.7) each use 3 of the 4 cases in the confusion matrix in Table 7.4. The following measurements differ therefore with regard to the referring population and only those cases can be considered, in which (1) a shock or no shock really exists (sum of rows in the confusion matrix), or the cases, in which (2) a document is classified as shock or no shock (sum of columns in the confusion matrix). Asymmetric distributions in the confusion matrix may therefore have massive effects on the evaluation measures, making a penetrative investigation inevitable. Please note, that asymmetries correspond further to asymmetric cost-functions, making an economic evaluation of the both scenarios under analysis essential.

Positive and Negative Prediction The ratio of correct positive predictions to the total number of positive predictions, called the positive prediction value, or precision, is:

$$\text{Precision} = \frac{\text{TP}}{\text{TP} + \text{FP}}. \tag{7.4}$$

Accordingly, the negative prediction value, or *negative* precision, follows the ratio of correct negative predictions to the total number of negative predictions, as:

$$\text{Neg-Precision} = \frac{\text{TN}}{\text{TN} + \text{FN}}. \tag{7.5}$$

Both measures make use of a population determined by the *predicted class*, which is the outcome of the supervised learning algorithms in Section 6.1 and Section 6.2.

The following measures, sensitivity and specificity, make use of a population determined by the *actual class*, see Table 7.4 on page 111, which is in turn determined by the applied Wald test of formula (5.2) on page 74.

Sensitivity and Specificity The sensitivity, that is the ratio of correct positive predictions to the total number of class members, also called true positive rate, hit rate, or recall, is:

$$\text{Recall} = \frac{\text{TP}}{\text{TP} + \text{FN}}. \tag{7.6}$$

Correspondingly, the specificity, also called true negative rate, correct rejection rate, or *negative* recall, is given as:

$$\text{Neg-Recall} = \frac{\text{TN}}{\text{TN} + \text{FP}}. \tag{7.7}$$

Please note, that the two evaluation measures fallout, formula (8.1), and miss rate, formula (8.2), which will be introduced in Section 8.1.3 on page 127, use identical reference values to the negative recall (7.7) and recall (7.6).

Taking particular account for the false negative and false positive errors allows to apply these four performance measures to the economic scenarios under analysis. It turns out, that each scenario accounts primary for two of the four measures. Therefore, the allocation of the performance measures to the economic scenarios is given in Table 7.5 on the next page.

A point of primary interest in practical applications if often to give an asymmetric importance to precision and recall.

F-measure The measure that accounts for those asymmetries is the F_β-measure, which gives the factor β times importance to recall than to precision, see

Scenario & Measure	Interpretation
A, Precision (7.4)	Percentage of correctly predicted shocks, of all predicted shocks
A, Neg-Recall (7.7)	Percentage of true non-shocks, predicted as non-shocks
B, Recall (7.6)	Percentage of true shocks, predicted as shocks
B, Neg-Precision (7.5)	Percentage of correctly predicted non-shocks, of all predicted non-shocks

Table 7.5: Performance measures in the context of the economic scenarios under analysis.

van Rijsbergen (1979, p.133). The $F_{\beta=1}$-measure, which is denoted as F1-measure, gives therefore equal importance to precision and recall:

$$\text{F1} = 2/\left(\frac{1}{\text{Precision}} + \frac{1}{\text{Recall}}\right), \tag{7.8}$$

respectively the negative F1-measure:

$$\text{Neg-F1} = 2/\left(\frac{1}{\text{Neg-Precision}} + \frac{1}{\text{Neg-Recall}}\right). \tag{7.9}$$

The F1-measure, in difference to precision and recall alone, uses all outcomes in the confusion matrix in Table 7.4.

Interpreting Recall, Precision, and F-measure Recall, is the percentage of shocks, predicted as shocks. The negative recall is therefore the percentage of non-shocks, predicted as non-shocks.

Precision is the percentage of correctly predicted shocks, of all predicted shocks. The negative precision is correspondingly the percentage of correctly predicted non-shocks, of all predicted non-shocks.

This makes recall a measure of detection, and precision a measure of system accurateness, giving an indication about the ability to discard relevant from irrelevant documents. The F1-measure gives a single numeric performance to evaluate the classification algorithms in terms of precision and recall.

For example, the interpretation of a high precision, but at the same time low recall, would be, that a document classified as a shock triggering incident usually causes a shock (high precision), but many of the documents triggering a shock are wrongly labelled as no shock (low recall). Any increase in precision usually lowers the recall. This trade-off can be used to control the precision /

recall interaction using variations in the classifier's arguments, and to fit the algorithms best to the corresponding economic scenario, as indicated in Table 7.5, see Weiss et al. (2010, pp.68-69).

The maybe most critical actuating variable, however, is the significance level α of the applied Wald test in formula (5.2) on page 74, which determines the pre-label of the training set, and dominates the ability of supervised classification. The comparison of the performance measures in dependency of the significance level illustrates the effect of more or less restrictive pre-labellings on precision, recall, and the F1-measure.

For this purpose Table 7.6 on the next page illustrates the performance measures recall, precision, and F1-measures plus the corresponding negative measures at different significance levels α of the applied Wald test. The reported values are calculated for the area-adjusted TSRV estimates of the ask quotes and, following the findings of Table 7.1, on a Log-Idf weighted, unstemmed and for the sparsity level of 0.9 reduced term-document-matrix.

An evaluation of the classification goodness by the F1-measure would suggest using a high significance level α, while an evaluation based on the negative F1-measure would suggest using a low significance level and therefore a restrictive pre-labelling. Note however, that neither the negative F1-measure nor the F1-measure account for asymmetries in the proportions of true positive and true negative values. But, on the other hand, any restrictive pre-labelling will also induce an asymmetry that holds disproportionately high the null hypotheses of no shock.

Discussion When applying the consolidated findings on the presented scenarios, discriminate between scenario A, the trading application, and scenario B, the risk-controlling application:

1. Start with an analysis under scenario A, the trading application, not invested in the underlying asset in the moment of the forecast: Any false negative (FN) error, scenario A sub-case b), will provoke no additional costs, except from opportunity costs, making the false positive (FP) forecast the error measure of interest. The measures including the FP error are precision (7.4) and negative recall (7.7).

   The best would be a high precision, which means those who are classified as shocks will cause a shock, and a high negative recall, non-shock causing documents are not wrongly classified as shock causing documents. Inspecting Table 7.6 for high precision and simultaneously high negative recall statistics clearly shows, that the F1-measure inspection alone, which would suggest to prefer a high alpha, is not suitable to consider the characteristics of scenario A. Instead, the maximized (weighted) combination

	MNR	NN	SLDA	BOO	BGG	RF
Neg-/Precision	.70/.48	.67/.62	.67/.62	.66/.35	.67/.38	.67/.42
Neg-/Recall	.83/.30	.97/.09	.97/.09	.92/.09	.83/.21	.91/.13
Neg-/F1	.76/.37	.79/.16	.79/.16	.77/.14	.74/.27	.77/.20

(a) Alpha 1e-03.

Neg-/Precision	.67/.49	.56/.37	.64/.49	.62/.55	.65/.48	.65/.50
Neg-/Recall	.62/.54	.43/.50	.75/.35	.92/.14	.69/.43	.73/.41
Neg-/F1	.64/.51	.49/.43	.69/.41	.74/.22	.67/.45	.69/.45

(b) Alpha 1e-02.

Neg-/Precision	.55/.54	.50/.54	.53/.53	.49/.62	.49/.52	.54/.54
Neg-/Recall	.30/.78	.49/.55	.15/.88	.96/.07	.32/.69	.29/.77
Neg-/F1	.39/.64	.49/.54	.23/.66	.65/.13	.39/.59	.38/.63

(c) Alpha 1e-01.

Neg-/Precision	.50/.61	.47/.63	.56/.59	.43/.67	.49/.60	.54/.60
Neg-/Recall	.29/.80	.48/.62	.08/.95	.91/.12	.25/.82	.15/.91
Neg-/F1	.37/.69	.47/.62	.14/.73	.58/.20	.33/.69	.23/.72

(d) Alpha 2e-01.

Table 7.6: Precision, recall, and F1-measure. The first number in the row reports the negative statistics given with the formulas (7.5), (7.7), and (7.9). The second number in the row gives the statistics of precision (7.4), recall (7.6), and F1-measure (7.8). The Tables 7.6a to 7.6d report for comparison the results for the test alpha values 1e-03, 1e-02, 1e-01, and 2e-01 of the applied Wald test in equation (5.2) on page 74.

of both, the precision and the negative recall seems to be preferable. To evaluate the combination of both, further analysis is required.

2. In scenario B, the risk-controlling application, a significant investment in the underlying asset already exists. A false positive (FP) error will hence induce similar costs as presented in scenario A. Note however, that the main costs of the false positive error will be carried by the transaction costs of the (afterwards) waste hedge. But, transaction costs are normally low. Some theoretical reflections even completely miss to reflect on them. False negative errors (FN), however, have the potential to induce considerable costs. The measures including the FN error are recall (7.6) and negative precision (7.5).

The best, however, is not to maximize the ratio of both errors, but a weighted maximized error, to account for the asymmetric costs comprised in this scenario. Therefore, the statistic of primary interest is recall, giving an indication that upcoming shocks are marked as shocks. A high negative precision will also indicate, that documents that are marked as non-shocks, will not release a shock. Inspecting Table 7.6 for high recall statistics alone, would clearly indicate the use of a high alpha. To evaluate the combination of both, however, further cost- and consequences-analysis is also required in scenario B.

Goodness of Classification The hitherto given results account for the classification errors, but no effort was given to the performance of the competing classifiers.

ROC graphs A useful technique to visualize the performance of competing binary classifiers is the receiver operation characteristic (ROC) graph, that plots the sensitivity, or recall, on the ordinate against 1 minus specificity, or in the here preferred notation 1 minus negative recall, on the abscissa. The value on the abscissa is also called fallout (to be discussed in formula (8.1) in Section 8.1.3 on page 127). ROC graphs are also known as Lorentz diagrams, see Hand (1997, p.132).

A selection of the four best fitting algorithms multinomial regression (MNR), stabilized linear discriminant analysis (SLDA), bagging (BGG), and random forests (RF) is given in the ROC graphic in Figure 7.1 on the next page. The four dotted lines represent the four best fitting algorithms. The dark black line gives the average of the four presented algorithms, where the number within the dark black line gives the ratio of recall to 1 minus negative recall depending on the corresponding cutoff level. The commonly used cutoff level for binary classifications is 0.5. This cutoff level is also used in this thesis.

The dashed bisecting line represents further the random case. Classifications better than random are in the left upper triangle. Classification results worse than random will correspondingly be in the right lower triangle. For an introduction to ROC graphs, see e. g. Fawcett (2006).

The illustrated cutoff levels in the ROC graphic show, that increasing the cutoff level from the 0.5 default value to 1 would also decrease the recall as well as the 1 minus negative recall value, decreasing the cutoff level to 0, however, would increase both values. This finding is subject to further analysis and will be discussed in Section 8.3.1.

Area under curve Instead of the curves, one can also inspect the area under the curves (AUC), see e. g. Bradley (1997). The AUC returns a single number to

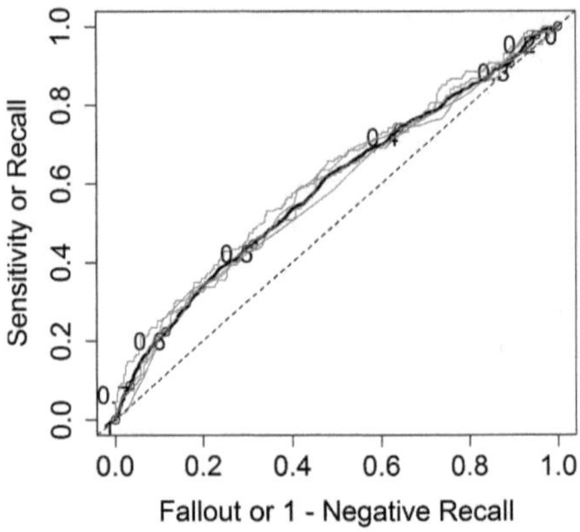

Figure 7.1: Receiver operating characteristic of the supervised learning algorithms. The ordinate gives the sensitivity or recall value, the abscissa gives 1 minus the negative recall, which is also the fallout value (to be discussed in Section 8.1.3 on page 127). The dashed bisecting line gives the random guess. Classifiers better than random are in the left upper triangle, what means that the classifier has a higher sensitivity than fallout value. The grey lines give the results for the four different algorithms multinomial regression (MNR), stabilized linear discriminant analysis (SLDA), bagging (BGG), and random forests (RF). The black line gives the average of these algorithms, where the number in the black line gives additionally the values at the corresponding cutoff level. The cutoff level is the required minimum level of probability for the classifier to predict a shock. The canonical cutoff in a binary classification is 0.5.

each of the competing algorithms which alleviates any direct comparison of the algorithms classification goodness. The AUC is the portion under the curve in the ROC space. This makes the AUC to be between 0 and 1. The AUC of realistic classifiers should not be lower than 0.5, see Hand and Till (2001).

Applying the area-adjusted TSRV estimator on ask quotes and an unstemmed term-document-matrix transformed by the Log-Idf weighting with a 90% level of sparsity, where the significance level α of the applied Wald test is fixed with α=1e-02, emerges the following AUCs:

	MNR	NN	SLDA	BOO	BGG	RF
AUC	.609	.455	.599	.530	.582	.593

Implementation The visualization of the ROC graphics is implemented in the ROCR library by T. Sing, O. Sander, N. Beerenwinkel, and T. Lengauer.

7.3 Random Observations

The consideration of error rates and accuracy measures alone is not sufficient to determine the quality of a new engineering approach. Another important evaluation measure is the ability of the system to uncover potential volatility shocks, provoked through unexpected but observable incidents, in comparison to volatility shocks, that can not been assigned to a single news.

7.3.1 *Request*

The request of the task to benchmark the so far proposed engineering approach, consisting of

1. a sequence of competing models to measure and to calculate the unobservable volatility,
2. a new two-state Markov switching mixture model for continuous and zero-inflated time-series to estimate the latent data generation process and
3. a selection of competing pattern recognition algorithms to classify the potential information embedded in unexpected, but public observable text data in shock and non-shock information,

is, to find an answer to the following questions:

1. What is the effect of a single and unexpected ad-hoc news on the latent asset volatility, measured by a shock or non-shock decision and determined by a time-series analysis?
2. How do the incidents identified by the ad-hoc news monitoring system differ from the as non-shocks identified incidents?
3. Do the classification errors of false classified shock triggering incidents and the classification errors of false classified non-shock incidents differ?

A detailed investigation of these questions is part of Chapter 8. The first step in order to investigate these questions, is to select a sample of pure random observations, not correlated with the observed observations, and to compute the benchmark values to calibrate the monitor.

In contrast to (1) the benchmarking of competing supervised learning algorithms, discussed in Section 7.1 in a statistical analysis of the classification errors, and in Section 7.2 in a confusion analysis of scenario depending costs, is (2) the use of random observations to benchmark the system intrinsic qualification to measure the effect of ad-hoc news arrivals in comparison to a natural occurrence of volatility shocks.

7.3.2 *Choosing Random Sample*

The required random sample has to be related to the proposed system, the sample should therefore match with the characteristics of the ad-hoc news under analysis. These are:

1. The considered asset should be listed in one of the prime standard indices DAX, MDAX, SDAX, or TecDAX.

2. The full time under analysis, which is in the proposed approach four hours, should not overlap with the four hour windows surrounding any of the ad-hoc news given in the sample of Section 5.1.1 on page 66.

3. Beside the ad-hoc news, avoid further a four hour window surrounding any macroeconomic news, for example the publishing of unemployment figures. This type of news is not assigned to a single asset, but can nevertheless have a significant effect on the asset under analysis.

4. The full four hour time window should be within a single day to avoid overnight effects.

The central idea is therefore to analyse the reaction of the proposed system on a time series, that has not been infected by the arrival of an unexpected news.

Because of the lack of an underlying news, the analysis is restricted to the findings of the time series analysis, which is in this thesis primarily the effect on the applied Wald test of formula (5.2) on the volatility estimates of a random asset. The two main questions answered by this analysis are:

1. Does the applied Wald test hold the test level? That means, is the proportion of identified shocks equal or higher the chosen significance level?

2. To what extent is the applied Wald test a proxy to identify volatility shock causing news?

7.3.3 *Determining the Monitoring Benchmark*

Therefore, 1,000 random time points were selected and unambiguously assigned to one of the considered prime standard assets. The selected times are chosen in such a way, that they are uncorrelated with the time windows of the 1,938 incidents under analysis. But no extra effort was given to analyse the arrival of further macroeconomic news, which means that the arrival of unobserved news within the time windows can not be ruled out.

The asset quotes surrounding the random time point were

- recorded in transaction time and pre-processed according to Section 2.3,
- used to estimate the integrated volatility according to Section 3.2,
- tailored to intraday periodicities according to Section 3.3, and
- applied to the Markov switching mixture model for zero-inflated and autocorrelated time series according to Section 4.3,
- which is tested for structural changes in the latent data-generation process according to Section 5.1.

Because of the randomness of the selected time points and the preliminary work to choose time points independently from the hitherto considered incidents, no text mining procedures were applied.

The analysis of the sensitivity of the proposed shock identification system applied on random time series in comparison with the time series surrounding ad-hoc news, is part of Section 8.1.1.

8 Monitoring

A frequently occurring request to an engineering approach is to specify a "good practise roadway", how to apply the proposed approach on a practical application.

The good practise roadway in the context of this thesis, however, demands beyond the system intrinsic evaluation of (1) the best volatility estimator, (2) the best data describing model, (3) the best classification algorithm, and (4) in each step the best setting of all adjustable screws, also (5) an outside standing regular assessment, or monitoring, to evaluate the engineering approach in total.

Monitoring as a concept is an umbrella term and means the systematic observation of a process. The economic monitoring considered here distinguishs further between three different comparisons, see Küsters et al. (2012):

1. Plan versus forecast,
2. Plan versus actual, and
3. Forecast versus actual.

The first two concepts, (1) plan versus forecast and (2) plan versus actual, are primarily used in controlling. The monitoring concept that is used in this thesis is (3) forecast versus actual, which is also called statistical monitoring. This type of monitoring refers primarily to outlier diagnostics, see e. g. Kruger and Xie (2012) for a general reference.

The monitor of this thesis is hence twofold: First, the systematic observation of ad-hoc news disclosures and the estimation of the integrated volatility (this is the process monitoring) and second, the comparison of the forecasted with the actual effect of the news disclosure on the corresponding volatility estimates (this is the outlier diagnostic).

The missing point is, the evaluation of the difference between forecast and actual. The content of this chapter is therefore: In Section 8.1, the extended analysis of the systems power to forecast latent volatility jumps. In Section 8.2, the analysis of the different effects of ask and bid quotes, the different effects of the volatility estimators, and the advanced analysis of the different classification algorithms. In Section 8.3 the evaluation of the monitoring system under taking special attention to the trading scenario A and the risk managing scenario B.

8.1 System Evaluation

The investigation of the questions asked in Section 7.3.1 on page 119, requires to analyse

1. the sensitivity of the proposed Markov switching mixture model to map volatility shock causing incidents, this is treated in Section 8.1.1,
2. the difference between volatility shock causing events and non-shock causing events, this is treated in Section 8.1.2, and
3. the classification errors of wrongly classified shock causing and wrongly classified non-shock causing incidents, this is treated in Section 8.1.3.

8.1.1 *Effect of Ad-Hoc News*

The presented monitoring system is built-up on the economic utilisation of ad-hoc news, which represent new and unexpected but publicly observable information.

The discrimination of news announcements from random benchmark fluctuations therefore determines the additional effect of ad-hoc news, and accounts hence for the first question:

Question 1 *What is the effect of a single and unexpected ad-hoc news on the latent asset volatility?*

The influence of public information on intraday stock returns is well-known in financial econometrics, see e. g. Kalev et al. (2004) for an analysis of news arrival rates on the conditional volatility of intraday stock returns, and e. g. Muntermann and Guettler (2007) for an analysis of ad-hoc disclosures on intraday stock prices on the German market.

In line with the results of the above mentioned authors, Table 8.1 on the next page shows, that the analysis of structural breaks in the latent DGP uncover more breaks along ad-hoc disclosures than along the random benchmark. Please note, that the benchmark windows can also surround unobserved events, e. g. the publishing of macroeconomic news. It is therefore recommendable to also assume random structural breaks that can not be assigned to a single news.

Answering Question 1 The analysis performed in this thesis is contrary to the analysis in Muntermann and Guettler (2007) restricted to ad-hoc disclosures appearing at the earliest two hours after opening and at the latest two hours

	RV can	RV avg	TSRV cla	TSRV adj	TSRV aa
ask	.397/.359	.421/.338	.385/.353	.398/.360	.369/.357
bid	.393/.378	.371/.337	.389/.325	.392/.333	.382/.351

(a) Alpha 1e-03.

ask	.483/.434	.499/.416	.455/.421	.474/.439	.446/.446
bid	.478/.459	.450/.398	.460/.416	.471/.392	.452/.418

(b) Alpha 1e-02.

ask	.614/.562	.611/.531	.560/.531	.595/.559	.564/.559
bid	.591/.576	.562/.522	.573/.503	.589/.515	.584/.521

(c) Alpha 1e-01.

ask	.666/.618	.650/.584	.618/.586	.639/.612	.620/.603
bid	.635/.624	.616/.576	.623/.584	.630/.587	.628/.586

(d) Alpha 2e-01.

Table 8.1: Sensitivity of the Markov switching mixture model to map volatility shocks. The table reports for this purpose the percentage of as shocks labelled time series. The first number gives the percentage of shocks along the recorded ad-hoc news. The second number gives the percentage of shocks at random time points according to Section 7.3. The rows differentiate the analysis of ask and bid quotes, both measured in transaction time, the columns the integrated volatility estimators discussed in Section 3.2. Table 8.1a to Table 8.1d differentiate further different significance levels α of the applied Wald test in formula (5.2) on page 74.

before closing. This excludes all ad-hoc disclosures appearing in the morning, when traders start to build-up their portfolios, and in the evening, when the traders sell their positions to clear the portfolio before closing. Over-night effects are thereby avoided and the results account for pure unexpected at-the-day effects.

A significant number of ad-hoc disclosures however, are reported from 7:00 a.m. to 9:00 a.m., see Muntermann and Guettler (2007), which is one reason for the increased volatility shortly after opening (see also Figure 5.1 on page 67). But, this is no decisive factor as the sample size is sufficiently large with 1,938 ad-hoc news for the requirements of this thesis.

Nevertheless, it seems to be critical that Muntermann and Guettler (2007) did not explicitly account for a start-of-the-day asset typical volatility. In line with the results of Muntermann and Guettler (2007), however, Table 8.1 shows that ad-hoc disclosures increase the rate of shock reports for all volatility estimators and for ask as well as bid quotes. The effect, however, is small but sufficiently large to discriminate the effect of shocks caused by ad-hoc news disclosures from the general market fuzziness.

8.1.2 *Discriminating Shocks from Non-Shocks*

The discrimination of shocks from non-shocks accounts for the second question:

Question 2 *How do the incidents identified by the ad-hoc news monitoring system differ from the as non-shocks identified incidents?*

The difference is in the words used in the texts and published as ad-hoc news documents. Note the simple fundamental idea behind this approach. Each statement knows only a tight vocabulary to express central information. According to the fact that repeated messages, e. g. profit warnings or offers for takeovers, or in general most of the information appearing in ad-hoc news, is built-up on continuously repeated words, most of the shock triggering incidents also exhibit identical words, while the non-shock incidents do not, or only sporadically. It is therefore the content of the news, that discriminates shock triggering from non-shock triggering news, and the used proxy to determine the content, are the words used in the news.

If the difference between the incidents is in the number of words, then the difference is also part of the term-document-matrix. For comparison purposes are therefore two heat maps illustrated in Figure 8.1 on page 128. Heat maps are used to illustrate a third dimension in a two dimensional diagram, where the third dimension is mapped by the colour-coding. In the given figure a platinum-white colour represents, that the value in the corresponding cell within the term-document-matrix is close to zero, while a deep black colour represents the highest of all observed values. A word occurring very often (row) will therefore get a deep black colour in the corresponding document (column). Figure 8.1a illustrates the words used in the documents marked as volatility shock triggering incidents, Figure 8.1b illustrates the identical words, but for the as non-volatility shock labelled incidents. Note, that the words and the documents only represent a random sample of the hole term-document-matrix.

Both heat maps are based on news, that were tested to be volatility shock causing using the applied Wald test of formula (5.2) on page 74 with a significance level of α=1e-02. The corresponding time series of integrated volatilities is estimated using the area adjusted TSRV estimator and the sparsity level of the document pre-processing fixed with 0.9. The used term-document-matrix is unstemmed and weighted using the Log-Idf weighting scheme. The heat map is determined on the test data. Using stemmed instead of unstemmed words returns similar results.

Answering Question 2 The importance of single words for the approach used in this thesis to discriminate volatility shock causing from non-shock incidents is obvious, when inspecting the heat maps in Figure 8.1.

But, further attention should be given to some single words, e. g. word 1 and word 22 in the heat map of shock triggering incidents. These words correspond to word 4 and word 100 in the heat map of non-shock triggering incidents. The first word, this is word 1 in Figure 8.1a and word 4 in Figure 8.1b seems to appear rarely in non-shock documents, but very often in shock causing documents. This word has therefore a high contribution to the discriminating power of shock causing from non-shock causing incidents. Word 22 in Figure 8.1a, corresponding to word 100 in Figure 8.1b, however, seems to appear regularly in both types of documents. The contribution of this word is hence questionable and it is suggested for future research, to analyse the discriminating power of the supervised learning algorithms, when adding these words to a stoplist first.

Note, that the number of words used for the discrimination of ad-hoc news in shock causing and non-shock causing, is primarily determined by the sparsity value fixed in the document pre-processing. Compare in this context also Table 6.1 on page 95.

Implementation The heat map is mainly built using the ggplot2 library. Some support was further given by the reshape2 library of H. Wickham to restructure and aggregate the words of the term-document-matrix.

8.1.3 *Errors of Shocks and Errors of Non-Shocks*

Fallout and miss rate, two further performance measures to evaluate classification outcomes, give the errors of non-identified shocks and the errors of wrongly marked non-shocks. These measures account therefore for the third question:

Question 3 *Do the classification errors of false classified shock triggering incidents and the classification errors of false classified non-shock incidents differ?*

False positive rate The first performance measure is fallout, which is interpreted as the error of non-identified non-shocks. This is the proportion of shock predictions, that are non-shocks. This measure is almost already defined, when

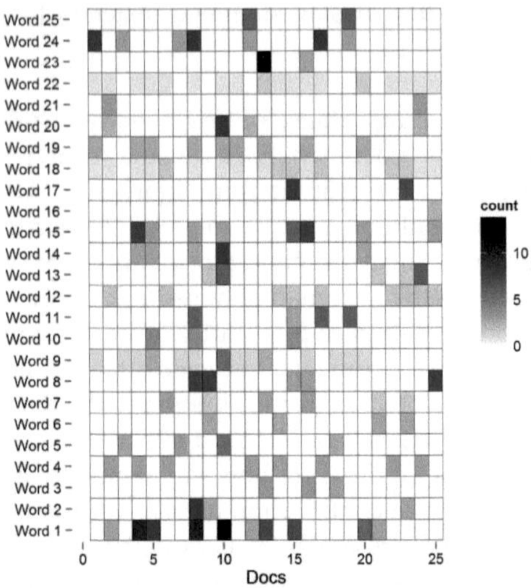

(a) Shock triggering.

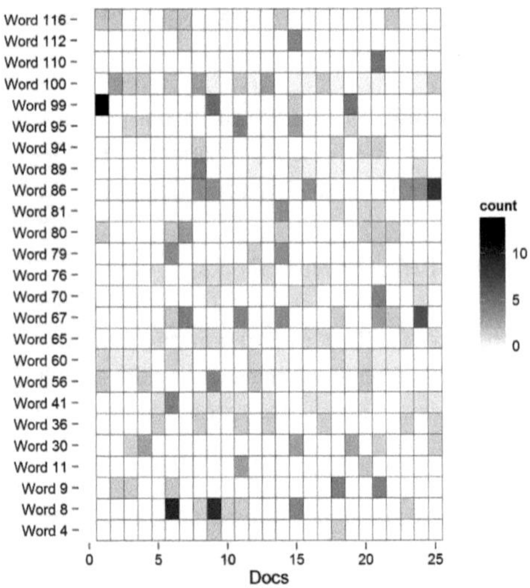

(b) Non-shock triggering.

Figure 8.1: Exemplary heat maps of shock causing and non-shock causing incidents. Figure 8.1a presents the heat map of documents, marked as shock triggering while Figure 8.1b presents the heat map of documents, marked as non-shock triggering. Both figures present the heat maps of identical words. For example, word 1 in Figure 8.1a corresponds to word 4 in Figure 8.1b, word 2 corresponds to word 8.

using the definition of the negative recall in formula (7.7) on page 113, but subtracting the value from 1, that is 1 minus the negative recall, or:

$$\text{Fallout} = \frac{\text{FP}}{\text{TN} + \text{FP}}. \tag{8.1}$$

False negative rate The second performance measure is the miss rate, which is interpreted as the error of non-identified shocks. This is the proportion of non-shock predictions, that are shocks. This measure is again already defined, when using the definition of recall in formula (7.6) on page 113, but subtracting the value from 1, that is 1 minus recall, or:

$$\text{Miss rate} = \frac{\text{FN}}{\text{TP} + \text{FN}}. \tag{8.2}$$

Table 8.2 on the next page gives the fallout and the miss rate of the classification outcomes for each of the supervised learning algorithms presented in Section 6.1 and Section 6.2. The volatility is again estimated with the area-adjusted TSRV estimator applied on ask quotes. The term-document-matrix was again transformed by the Log-Idf weighting were the terms are unstemmed. The results vary for the different volatility estimators as well as for separated analysis of ask and bid quotes, which will be discussed in detail in Section 8.2.1, but the main findings remain unchanged.

Answering Question 3 Inspecting Table 8.2, the following general findings emerge:

1. The errors fallout and miss rate tend in opposite directions. An increase in the significance level α of the applied Wald test in formula (5.2) will increase the fallout, but simultaneously decrease the miss rate. This is not surprising, when interpreting the confusion matrix in Table 7.4 on page 111 as a decision table. Then corresponds (1) the false positive error, which is part of the fallout measure, with the alpha error, and (2) the false negative error, which is part of the miss rate measure, with the beta error.

2. The two algorithms SLDA and BOO switch from close to zero fallout rates and close to one miss rates for low significance levels α to the exact converse for high significance levels. The transition, however, should be considerably smooth for uniformly increased significance levels. It is therefore recommendable to set these both algorithms as second-tier in any ensemble analytics using a combination of supervised learning algorithms.

3. The effect of the sparsity level on the classification errors can be seen clearly, anyway, the classification errors are not consistent. An increased

	MNR	NN	SLDA	BOO	BGG	RF
.6	.01/.99	.04/.94	.01/.99	.02/.98	.12/.84	.02/.99
.7	.02/.98	.01/.99	.01/.99	.01/.99	.09/.93	.04/.97
.8	.04/.92	.01/.99	.01/.99	.01/.99	.20/.75	.07/.91
.9	**.17/.70**	**.03/.91**	**.03/.91**	**.08/.91**	**.17/.79**	**.09/.87**
.95	.22/.74	.23/.70	.04/.90	.10/.87	.11/.83	.05/.90

(a) Alpha 1e-03.

.6	.23/.71	.65/.39	.10/.89	.01/.99	.19/.77	.21/.81
.7	.27/.63	.13/.84	.09/.87	.01/.99	.25/.71	.18/.78
.8	.23/.62	.19/.69	.10/.88	.05/.96	.36/.64	.28/.66
.9	**.38/.46**	**.57/.50**	**.25/.65**	**.08/.86**	**.31/.57**	**.27/.59**
.95	.33/.50	.44/.63	.32/.66	.12/.85	.39/.50	.26/.62

(b) Alpha 1e-02.

.6	.91/.07	.90/.09	.99/.01	.99/.01	.75/.22	.84/.14
.7	.87/.12	.77/.22	.99/.01	.01/.99	.62/.32	.78/.20
.8	.87/.10	.90/.11	.99/.01	.04/.99	.58/.33	.81/.17
.9	**.70/.22**	**.51/.45**	**.85/.12**	**.04/.93**	**.68/.31**	**.71/.23**
.95	.56/.33	.45/.44	.79/.16	.07/.95	.73/.26	.78/.20

(c) Alpha 1e-01.

.6	.95/.06	.99/.01	.99/.01	.98/.03	.75/.23	.89/.10
.7	.93/.11	.99/.01	.99/.01	.99/.01	.75/.21	.88/.11
.8	.88/.04	.99/.01	.99/.01	.99/.01	.73/.23	.85/.12
.9	**.71/.20**	**.52/.38**	**.92/.05**	**.09/.88**	**.75/.18**	**.85/.09**
.95	.62/.27	.99/.01	.86/.07	.17/.75	.82/.11	.86/.11

(d) Alpha 2e-01.

Table 8.2: Fallout and miss rate of the supervised learning algorithms applied on the volatility estimates of ask quotes using the area-adjusted TSRV estimator of Section 3.2.5. The first number gives the fallout of formula (8.1). This is the error of non-shocks predicted as shocks. The second number gives the miss rate of formula (8.2). This is the error of shocks predicted as non-shocks. The rows give the level of sparsity and the column the corresponding classification algorithm according to Section 6.1 and Section 6.2. Table 8.2a to Table 8.2d differentiate further various significance levels α of the applied Wald test in formula (5.2) on page 74. Note, that the bold marked numbers are 1 minus the corresponding Neg-/Recall line in Table 7.6 on page 116.

sparsity level for a fixed α increases the fallout but reduces the miss rate and vice versa, given the significance level is low with α = 1e-03 or α = 1e-02. However, this effect is inverted on the high significance levels α = 1e-01 and α = 2e-01. Here, an increase in sparsity reduces the fallout, but increases the miss rate.

The explanation of this effect is simple: The less terms are taken into account (low sparsity level), the more probably is a classification for the set, that has a majority in the number of documents. For this purpose, please note Table 8.1 on page 125, illustrating the 50% switch between the two significance levels α=1e-02 and α=1e-01. An increase in the number of terms (high sparsity level), will therefore also increase the probability to classify for the set that is in minority and hence also the probability of a misclassification.

4. The meta learning algorithms BOO, BGG, and RF seem to be more robust to variations in the sparsity level than the ordinary learning algorithms MNR, NN, and SLDA. That means, that meta learning algorithms seem to be less sensitive to the effect of single words than the ordinary learning algorithms.

The false positive and false negative errors of the given classification algorithms are therefore of (1) opposing trend, (2) depend massively on the pre-classification of the training data and (3) depend on the level of sparsity and therefore also from the stopword list and stemming facility.

Hence, further analysis is required that explicitly takes the costs of both into account, false positive and false negative errors. This analysis, that depends also on the considered scenario, is part of Section 8.3.

8.2 Variation in Identification

The efforts given so far have shown, that the proposed system to forecast unexpected volatility shocks in the latent DGP can (1) measure the additional effect of ad-hoc disclosures, (2) discriminate harmless from risky disclosures, and (3) discriminate false positive and false negative classification errors, which accounts for the considered economic scenarios. A general finding of the results given so far was, that the monitoring strategy needs to be conform with the economic scenario and that no single statement, how to do it "best", could hitherto be given. Therefore, it seems also to be of interest, which effect ask and bid quotes (Section 2.3.2), the presented volatility estimators (Section 3.2) and the presented classification algorithms (Section 6.1 and Section 6.2) have on the final forecast.

8.2.1 *Ask and Bid Quotes*

A remarkable proportion of financial analysis is build-up on mid-quotes, which is simply the mean of ask and bid quotes. But less effort, e. g. Hasbrouck (1999); Escribano and Pascual (2005); Zhang et al. (2008), was given to discriminate the effects of ask quotes (which are of primary interest for purchasers), and bid quotes (which are contrarily mostly of interest for sellers). The question is therefore:

Question 4 *What is the effect of a scenario depending discrimination of ask and bid quotes on the classification errors, which would be impossible to analyse when using mid quotes only?*

The fallout and miss rate computed on ask quotes as well as on bid quotes are given in Table 8.3 on the next page. The used supervised learning algorithm is the multinomial regression of Section 6.1.1 on page 88 due to the minimal cross-validation errors reported in Table 7.1 on page 102 which is confirmed by the Wilcoxon sign rank test and the paired t-test in Table 7.3 on page 109.

The underlying control parameters are, if not subject of analysis, unchanged. The term-document-matrix is again unstemmed and Log-Idf weighted. The sparsity level is fixed with 0.9. The number of documents is due to the test data 438. The proposed estimators of the integrated volatility are given in the columns, while the separation of ask and bid quotes is given in the rows. Please note, that the errors based on the area-adjusted TSRV estimates of ask quotes in Table 8.3 (bold marked) correspond to the first column in Table 8.2 on page 130 for the sparsity level 0.9.

Answering Question 4 Inspecting Table 8.3 and comparing the results for ask and bid quotes, it clearly emerges that the errors on ask quotes differ clearly in comparison with the errors on bid quotes, albeit both series cross over one identical news disclosure. The often applied method to use mid quotes instead of the separate use of ask and bid quotes seems hence to be inappropriate. Instead, it seems to be meaningful to use the series corresponding to the investors economic scenario, and the error measure, accounting for the baneful errors in the given investment.

Discussion Simply expressed, in terms of the economic scenarios under consideration, see Section 7.2.2 on page 110:

1. In scenario A, the trading application, the trader is interested in building up a long position in an asset before the market has had time to react on the news disclosure. Holding actually no position in the asset makes the

	RV can	RV avg	TSRV cla	TSRV adj	TSRV aa
Ask	.25/.73	.27/.69	.28/.78	.31/.64	**.17/.70**
Bid	.17/.77	.20/.78	.24/.78	.34/.69	.24/.76
(a) Alpha 1e-03.					
Ask	.45/.41	.47/.52	.41/.63	.50/.47	**.38/.46**
Bid	.42/.53	.35/.69	.39/.60	.49/.52	.37/.61
(b) Alpha 1e-02.					
Ask	.76/.14	.78/.24	.68/.38	.86/.14	**.70/.22**
Bid	.65/.35	.69/.34	.74/.33	.75/.25	.64/.30
(c) Alpha 1e-01.					
Ask	.84/.11	.81/.18	.83/.24	.87/.15	**.71/.20**
Bid	.77/.25	.83/.18	.76/.25	.83/.20	.72/.24
(d) Alpha 2e-01.					

Table 8.3: Fallout and miss rate separated for ask and bid quotes in the rows and for the different volatility estimators of Section 3.2 in the columns. The first number gives the fallout of formula (8.1). This is the error of non-shocks predicted as shocks. The second number gives the miss rate of formula (8.2). This is the error of shocks predicted as non-shocks. Note, that the errors based on the area-adjusted TSRV estimates of ask quotes (bold marked) correspond to the first column in Table 8.2 on page 130 for the sparsity level 0.9. The used supervised learning algorithm is the multinomial regression of Section 6.1.1 on page 88.

investor currently be interested in the ask prices. However, after the trade, the investor holds a long position making the investor suddenly interested in the *bid* prices. The primary error measure of interest for the trader is hence the fallout on bid quotes, which corresponds to the error of falsely as shock triggering classified non-shock disclosures.

Please note, that (a) when accounting for opportunity costs in form of missed potential profits the investor would simultaneously be interested in the miss rate and (b) in the end, it is the corresponding volatility derivative that determines the profit of the trade. Note in this context that a discussion of error rates is not an evaluation of a trading strategy which would for example make use of volatility derivatives as discussed in Section 1.1 on page 1. A full deployed trading strategy as well as the corresponding evaluation of the strategy is not part of this thesis.

2. In scenario B, the risk management application where the investor is already long in the asset, the risk manager is right from the start be interested in the *bid* prices to (a) close out the position or to (b) hedge the position before the prices shift on new levels. The error measure of interest for the risk manager is primary the miss rate which corresponds to shocks that were not previously recognized.

   Note, that in the same manner as in scenario A, the risk-manager will (a) take into account the transaction costs of afterwards unnecessary hedging-trades and therefore also account for the fallout and (b) in the end, it is for example a contract obligation that determines the profitability of an investment, where the underlying of the contract is the asset under analysis. For example: Assume the situation of an intermediary, that has on one hand one long-term supply contract with a fixed price, and on the other hand, multiple short-term delivery obligations where the delivery price depends on the day-usual exchange price. A price shock in the wrong direction, which is forecasted in this thesis using the resulting volatility shock, could obligate the intermediary to delivery the goods to day actual prices below the purchase price. The counter-party will usually use all possibilities of the contract in this situation.

8.2.2 *Volatility Estimators*

The theoretical consideration of the selected volatility estimators would suppose to use the adjusted TSRV estimator of Section 3.2.4, or on small samples the area-adjusted TSRV estimator of Section 3.2.5. Both estimators inherit the properties to be unbiased and consistent from the classical TSRV estimator, but weaken additionally the i.i.d. assumption on the microstructure noise. The TSRV estimators should hence dominate the RV estimators on ultra-high-frequency sampled data and the average RV estimator should return lower errors than the canonical RV estimator as well as the area-adjusted and the adjusted estimator should return lower errors than the classic TSRV estimator. The corresponding question is:

Question 5 *What is the effect of the integrated volatility estimator on the classification errors?*

Answering Question 5 When inspecting Table 8.3 on the previous page and discriminating the results for the individual volatility estimators (columns 1 to 5), no clear picture emerges. In some cases (but not all), the fallout is lowest or near lowest for the area-adjusted TSRV estimator. This supports the assumption that the awareness of microstructure noise in volatility estimations improves the results in economic applications. A similar result for the miss rate, however, can not be observed for the area-adjusted TSRV estimator, but for the adjusted TSRV estimator. A simple RV estimation, however, seems to be adequate enough for the analysis in this thesis on high-frequency text forecasting, where the pattern recognition task evaluates the integrated volatility estimator. Note, that the volatility estimates may differ, but the text news based classification outcomes are nevertheless nearly identical.

8.2.3 *Coinciding Classification Algorithms*

It was recently shown by Collingwood and Wilkerson (2012), that the consideration of a set of supervised learning algorithms that coincide in the classification outcome, can improve the recall and precision values in comparison with a single supervised learning algorithm. The question is therefore:

Question 6 *What is the effect of a concordance of a majority of supervised learning algorithms on the misclassification errors in comparison to a single supervised learning algorithm?*

For this purpose Table 8.4 on the next page reports the two errors of interest fallout and miss rate. Note, that at least 4 supervised learning algorithms need to coincide in a binary classification to talk of a majority when considering 6 algorithms in total. For example, $n \geqslant 4$ means, that 4, 5, or 6 of the 6 considered supervised learning algorithms return an identical classification outcome. Which of the algorithms coincide, is in this consideration irrelevant. The underlying term-document-matrix is in line with the so far considered results again unstemmed and Log-Idf weighted. The calculation is on the ask quotes. The sparsity level is 0.9.

Answering Question 6 In a direct comparison of Table 8.3 on page 133 to Table 8.4 on the next page, it clearly emerges that a majority of coinciding classification algorithms can remarkably decrease the fallout, but for the costs of an increased miss rate. This supports the findings of Collingwood and Wilkerson (2012) who report similar results. But no effort is given in Collingwood and Wilkerson to consider further the negative recall, which must increase as the fallout decreases. These findings demand to consider not only the error rates but the investment scenario conditional economic costs:

1. In scenario A, the trading application, is the fallout the error measure of primary interest. Investors will therefore be interested in reducing the fall-

	RV can	RV avg	TSRV cla	TSRV adj	TSRV aa
$n \geqslant 4$	.05/.84	.03/.98	.01/.99	.14/.86	.02/.92
$n \geqslant 5$	.03/.98	.01/.99	.01/.99	.07/.93	.01/.97
$n = 6$	.01/.99	.01/.99	.01/.99	.03/.99	.01/.99

(a) Alpha 1e-03.

$n \geqslant 4$	.28/.56	.21/.79	.14/.81	.22/.78	.15/.71
$n \geqslant 5$	.12/.77	.07/.93	.05/.91	.10/.92	.06/.86
$n = 6$	.01/.99	.01/.99	.01/.99	.01/.99	.02/.96

(b) Alpha 1e-02.

$n \geqslant 4$	.72/.16	.73/.29	.56/.43	.88/.16	.53/.38
$n \geqslant 5$	.50/.48	.46/.56	.29/.72	.64/.33	.35/.63
$n = 6$	.04/.92	.03/.98	.03/.99	.14/.89	.01/.95

(c) Alpha 1e-01.

$n \geqslant 4$	.85/.12	.81/.21	.72/.31	.88/.16	.63/.26
$n \geqslant 5$	.54/.40	.54/.42	.53/.53	.73/.30	.38/.50
$n = 6$	.10/.79	.05/.95	.07/.97	.08/.92	.07/.92

(d) Alpha 2e-01.

Table 8.4: Fallout and miss rate of a concordance classification. The row gives the number of supervised learning algorithms that coincide in the classification outcome. Note, that at least 4 supervised learning algorithms need to coincide in a binary classification to talk of a majority when considering 6 algorithms in total. For example, $n \geqslant 4$ means, that 4, 5, or 6 of the 6 considered supervised learning algorithms return an identical classification outcome. Which of the algorithms coincide, is in this consideration irrelevant. The column gives the different volatility estimators of Section 3.2. The first number gives the fallout of formula (8.1). This is the error of non-shocks predicted as shocks. The second number gives the miss rate of formula (8.2). This is the error of shocks predicted as non-shocks. The underlying term-document-matrix is in line with the so far considered results again unstemmed and Log-Idf weighted. The calculation is on the ask quotes. The sparsity level is 0.9.

out. The investors in this scenario will clearly benefit from (a) a set of coinciding classifications and (b) low significance levels of the applied Wald test. Taking into account the opportunity costs of missed profit would require to account also for the miss rate. The trade-off of fallout and miss rate determines further the sparsity level.

2. In scenario B, the risk management application, are the investors primary interested in the miss rate, while the fallout gives the unnecessary transaction costs of wasted hedges. But, a low miss rate to the costs of high fallouts is generally hard to finance due to the transaction costs. The conservative and low cost strategy to classify new ad-hoc disclosures as non-shock triggering news as long as no sufficient evidence is given to classify the disclosure as shock, plays here in the long run against the investors. It can hence not be found, that a set of coinciding classifiers brings additional benefit in contrast to single algorithms in a risk management application. The investors in this scenario will clearly benefit from (a) considering single supervised learning algorithms and (b) high significance levels of the applied Wald test. The trade-off of miss rate and fallout again determines the sparsity level.

8.3 Economic Evaluation

The analysis of the benchmark statistics to evaluate the algorithms performance has shown, that precision, recall, and the F1-measure, which are common statistics in information retrieval, see e. g. Zhang (2008), have the potential to provide scenario depending requirements on evaluation, but do not provide a single statistic to evaluate the different cost structures of the two scenarios under consideration.

Thus, the objective is to provide a combination of the false positive and false negative errors to account for the scenario depending cost structures in order to evaluate different strategies in dependency of the trading or risk managing application.

8.3.1 *Costs of Misclassification*

When taking the intrinsic forecasting error of the monitoring system into account, the following question arises:

Question 7 *What are the total costs of misclassifications?*

To give an answer to this question, analyse the explicit costs when applying the proposed monitor. Figure 8.2 on page 140 and 141 gives on the left side the explicit costs of false negative errors and on the right side the explicit costs of false positive errors for this purpose, according to the confusion matrix of Table 7.4 on page 111. Note, that false negative errors are part of the miss rate of formula (8.2), false positive errors on the other hand are part of the fallout of formula (8.1).

Each line in the figures represents one of three different cost scenarios representing the costs of errors coming with the misclassification of ad-hoc news. The left side of Figure 8.2 gives the costs of not predicted shocks, the right side the costs of erroneously shock predictions. The costs of false positive respectively false negative errors are in both cases normed to be 5, 3, or 1 unit(s). A unit could for example be 1 Euro. The lowest costs in Figure 8.2 represent 1 unit while the highest costs correspond to 5 units.

The cutoff on the abscissa gives further the required minimum level of probability of the supervised learning algorithm to predict a shock. The hitherto given results were all for the default cutoff of 0.5, giving both outcomes the identical probability. Meaning that if the classification algorithm returns a probability in the interval [0, 0.5], then the classifier will forecast no shock, but the classification algorithm will forecast a shock if the probability is in the interval (0.5, 1]. Please note, that a cutoff of 1 would classify all news as non-shocks, while a cutoff of 0 would correspondingly classify all news as shocks.

The exact cost function depends on the supervised learning algorithm and the corresponding classification outcome. For this purpose, Figure 8.2 gives one boxplot for each cutoff level, representing the variation of the cost function in dependence of the four used supervised learning algorithms multinomial regression (MNR), stabilized linear discriminant analysis (SLDA), bagging (BGG), and random forests (RF), as they are given in the ROC graphic in Figure 7.1 on page 118.

The costs are calculated in accordance with the so far presented results for the area-adjusted TSRV estimates of ask quotes using a Log-Idf weighted and unstemmed term-document-matrix. Similar results emerged for bid quotes and different volatility estimators.

Answering Question 7 Inspect for example Figure 8.2a. According to Table 8.1 on page 125 approximately 40% of all news are classified as shock triggering, given the significance level α of the applied Wald test is 1e-03. A cutoff of 1.0 will classify all news as non-shocks. The proportion of wrongly classified news using a cutoff of 1.0 is therefore 40%, which is exactly the value of the for 1 unit normed lowest line at the cutoff 1.0 in Figure 8.2a. Inspect now Figure 8.2b, which has for a cutoff of 1.0 zero costs. That is, because all news are classified as non-shocks, what means also a false positive error of zero. However, the cutoff 0.0 will all news classify as shocks, and 60% of non-shocks wrongly classify. This is exactly the value of the for 1 unit normed lowest line at the cutoff 0.0. Taken together, the value for the cutoff 1.0 in Figure 8.2a plus the value for the cutoff 0.0 in Figure 8.2b sum to 1, 3, and 5, which are exactly the given cost scenarios. This finding holds for all significance levels α.

The total costs of misclassifications depend therefore of

1. The true proportion of shock and non-shock triggering ad-hoc news.

   This is a question about measuring, and the control instrument to separate shock causing from non-shock causing news is the significance level of the applied Wald test. The underlying quantity is the volatility estimate of ask or bid quotes.

2. The automatism using the pre-labelled ad-hoc news to split shock from non-shock causing incidents.

   The control instrument of the automatism is the cutoff level of the supervised learning algorithms. The underlying quantity is the pre-labelled ad-hoc news.

3. The costs of false negative and false positive errors.

   The relationship of false negative to false positive errors depends on the economic scenario under consideration. While it is in (a) the trading application mostly of interest to minimize the false positive errors, it is on the other hand in (b) the risk management application mostly of interest to minimize the false negative errors.

All in all, this means that further analysis for a scenario depending evaluation is required. The evaluation of the trading application is discussed in Section 8.3.2, the evaluation of the risk managing application in Section 8.3.3.

Implementation Some support for the visualization of the cost curve graphics was given by the ROCR library.

8.3.2 *Evaluating the Trading Scenario*

The main error measure of interest in the trading scenario, this is scenario A in Section 7.2.2 on page 110, is the false positive error, which is also part of the fallout. A false negative error does add no strictly accounting costs, but can nevertheless be interpreted as opportunity costs. The main question in this scenario is therefore:

Question 8 How will overall costs in the investment scenario develop?

The explicit costs primarily result from misleadingly predictions of volatility shocks, that will not occur. Figure 8.3 on page 143 gives therefore the explicit

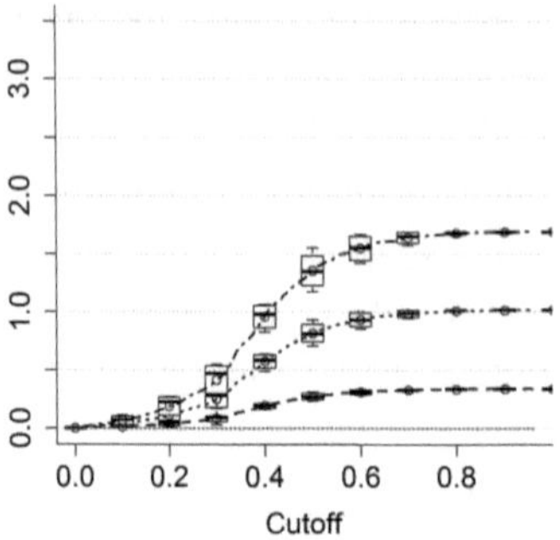

(a) False negative, α = 1e-03.

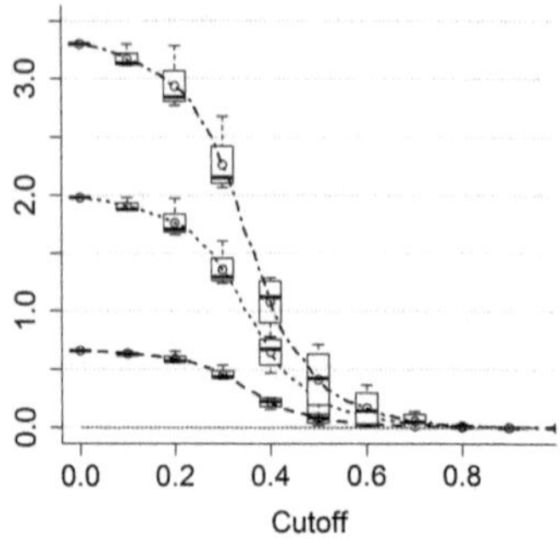

(b) False positive, α = 1e-03.

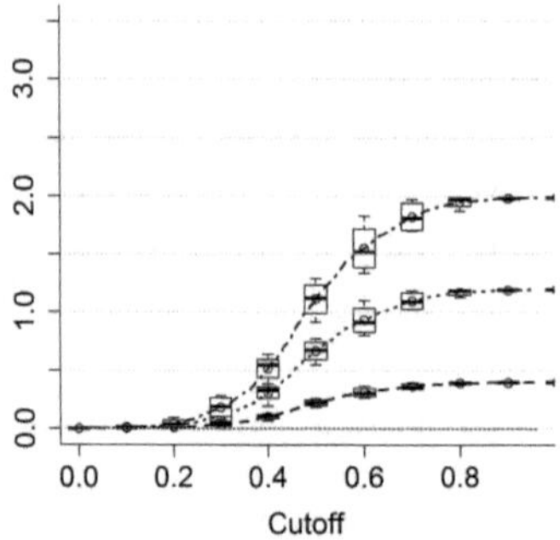

(c) False negative, α = 1e-02.

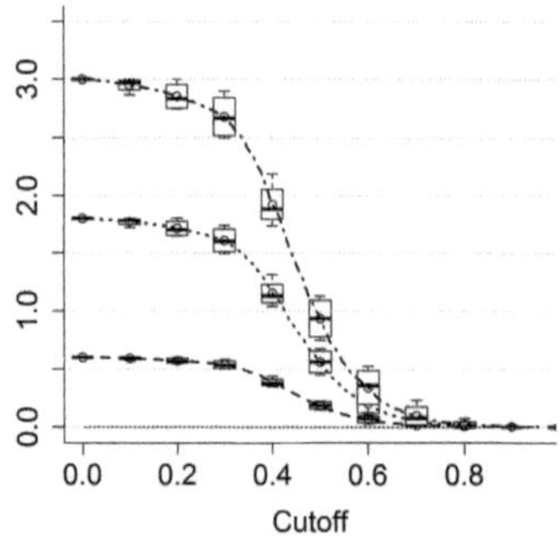

(d) False positive, α = 1e-02.

Figure 8.2: Costs of misclassification. The functions give on the left side the explicit costs of false negative errors and on the right side the explicit costs of false positive errors, according to the confusion matrix of Table 7.4 on page 111. Each line in the figures represents one of three different cost scenarios representing the costs of errors coming with the misclassification of ad-hoc news. The costs of false positive respectively false negative errors are in both cases normed to be 5, 3, or 1 unit(s). The highest line gives the 5 units, the lowest line the 1 unit case. The abscissa gives further the costs to the corresponding cutoff levels. The boxplots for each cutoff level represent the variation of the cost function in dependency of the four used supervised learning algorithms multinomial regression (MNR), stabilized linear discriminant analysis (SLDA), bagging (BGG), and random forests (RF). The connecting line cuts always the middle of the corresponding box. The α value corresponds to the applied Wald test of formula (5.2) on page 74. The results are for area-adjusted TSRV estimates of ask quotes using a Log-Idf weighted and unstemmed term-document-matrix.

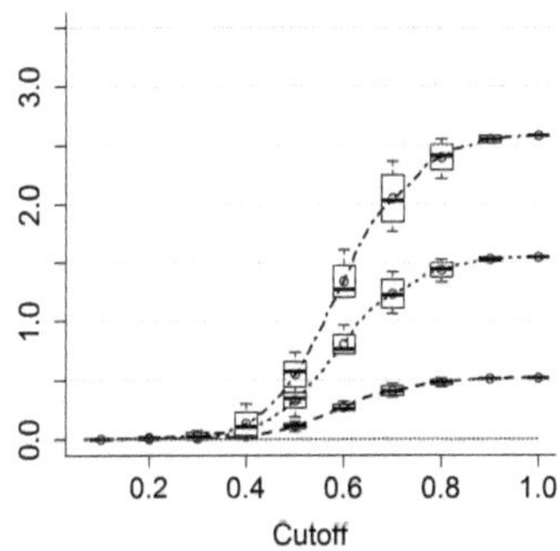

(e) False negative, α = 1e-01.

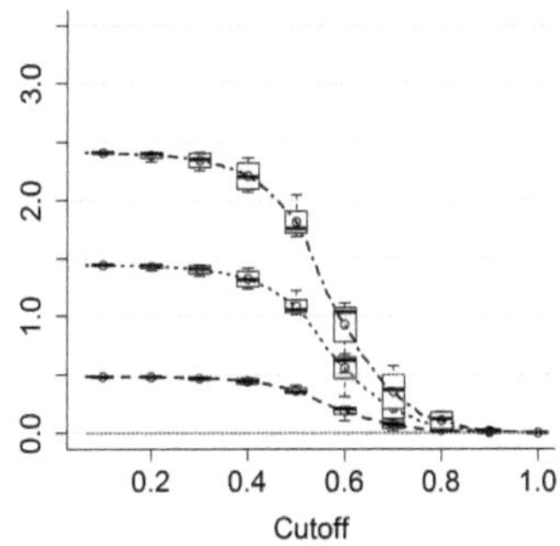

(f) False positive, α = 1e-01.

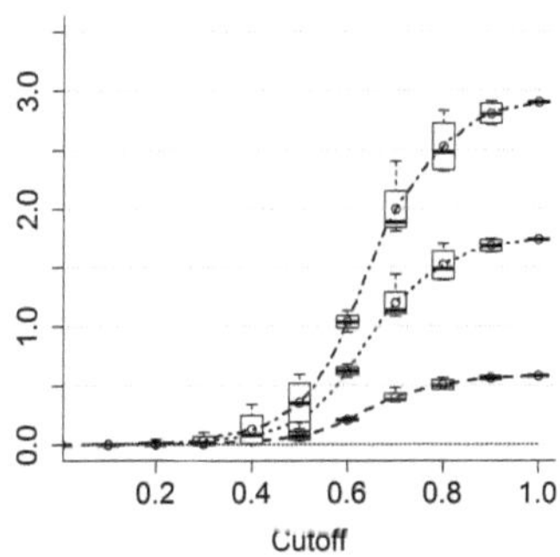

(g) False negative, α = 2e-01.

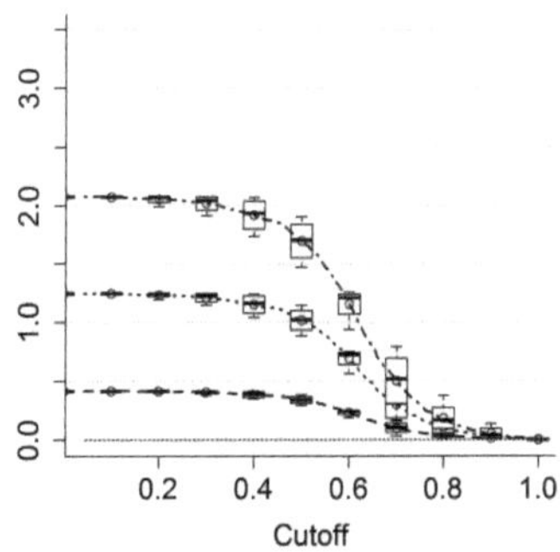

(h) False positive, α = 2e-01.

costs for the four different cutoff levels 0.4, 0.5, 0.6, and 0.7 if false negative errors provoke costs of 1 unit to account also for opportunity costs, but false positive errors provoke costs of 0, 1, 3, or 5 units to account for misleadingly predictions of volatility shocks. Please note, that the costs of false negative errors (FN) and false positive errors (FP) can be interpreted as proportions of costs. For example, 1 (FN) to 5 (FP) costs is to be understood, that the costs of false positive errors are 5 times as much as the costs of false negative errors.

The results are again for area-adjusted TSRV estimates of ask quotes using a Log-Idf weighted and unstemmed term-document-matrix.

Answering Question 8 Inspecting Figure 8.3, three main findings emerge:

1. An increase of the cutoff level in the area from 0.4 to 0.7 will decrease the costs.

   This effect is not surprising, as an increased cutoff level will mark only those disclosures as a shock, for which the classification algorithms return a probability above the cutoff. The set of shock predictions becomes smaller the higher the cutoff level is. Thus, the number of false positive predictions will also decrease and hence the overall costs of wrong predictions.

2. Except the case of 0 FP costs, the lowest of the considered significance levels 1e-03, 1e-02, 1e-01, and 2e-02 gives also the lowest costs.

   A low significance level in the applied Wald test that is used to discriminate shock from non-shock incidents on the basis of volatility estimates will label only those news as volatility shock triggering, that can significantly decline the null hypothesis of no shock to the given significance level α. The restrictive pre-labelling further reduces the number of false positive predictions and hence the total costs of wrong predictions.

3. The cost trend can topple. While an increase of the significance level α will in general also increase the overall costs, can nevertheless a turning point be reached, as it is given in Figure 8.3a for the combination 1 FN to 1, 3, or 5 FP costs.

   This effect is caused by the extensive labelling of ad-hoc news as shock triggering news, when using a disproportionately high significance level α. Note, that a high significance level pre-labels many of the documents as shock triggering, that could also be labelled as non-shock triggering.

   In combination with a low cutoff level of the supervised learning algorithms, however, the effect is, that new ad-hoc news seem to be more similar with historical shock causing news, than with non-shock causing news. This shock triggering label in turn will disproportionately often be confirmed by the high significance level of the applied Wald test. The overall costs will therefore decrease. This effect, however, is based on irrational control parameters and should not be considered.

Final remarks The effects of (1) and (2) are similar, as increased cutoff levels and decreased significance levels will reduce the risk and err the investor on

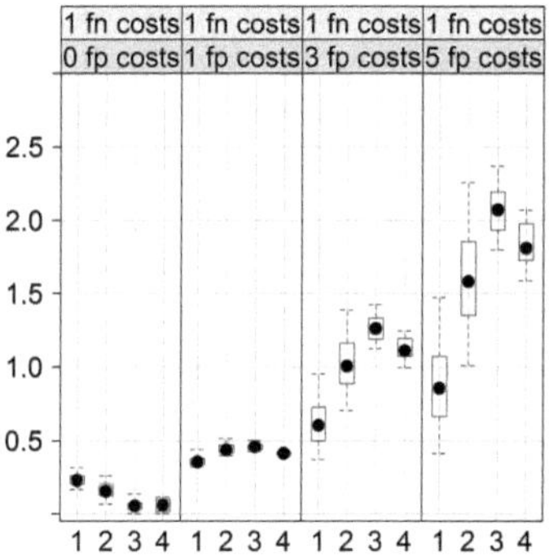

(a) Cutoff = 0.4.

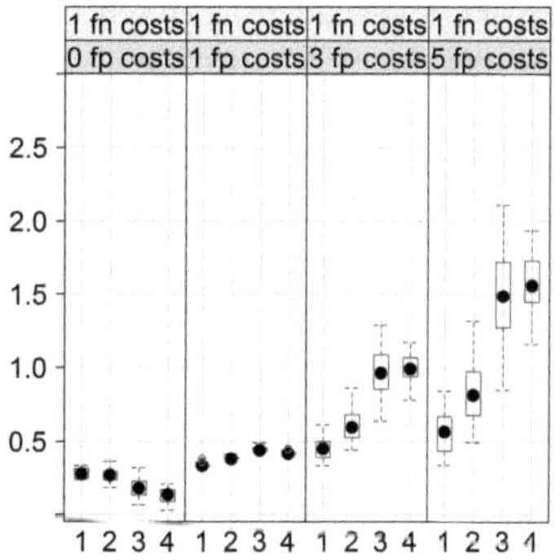

(b) Cutoff = 0.5.

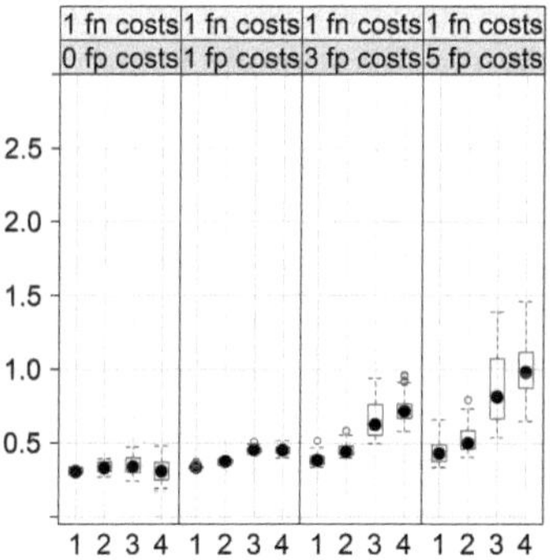

(c) Cutoff = 0.6.

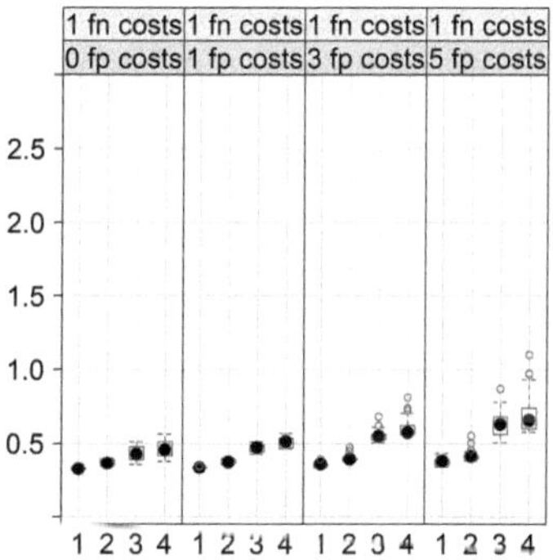

(d) Cutoff = 0.7.

Figure 8.3: Explicit costs of scenario A, a trading application. The costs of false negative errors (FN) are fixed with 1 unit, accounting for opportunity costs, while the costs of false positive errors (FP) are given for 0, 1, 3, and 5 units. The ordinate gives the explicit costs, the abscissa the significance level of the Wald test in formula (5.2) on page 74, which is for 1: 1e-03, 2: 1e-02, 3: 1e-01, and 4: 2e-01. Figure 8.3a to 8.3d discriminate further the cutoff level used in the supervised learning algorithms from 0.4 to 0.7. The boxplots for each α represent the variation of the cost function in dependence of the four used supervised learning algorithms multinomial regression (MNR), stabilized linear discriminant analysis (SLDA), bagging (BGG), and random forests (RF). Note, that the costs of false negative errors (FN) and false positive errors (FP) can be interpreted as proportions of costs. For example, 1 (FN) to 5 (FP) costs is to be understood, that the costs of false positive errors are 5 times as much as the costs of false negative errors. The results are for area-adjusted TSRV estimates of ask quotes using a Log-Idf weighted and unstemmed term-document-matrix.

the side of conservatism. The recommendation for scenario A investors is hence to make use of high cutoff levels and simultaneously low significance levels. This will on the one hand considerably reduce the number of signals, but on the other hand reduce the costs of errors. Whether the monitoring system is profitable, depends on the revenues gained with the correct prediction of the shocks. Therefore, since the costs of the monitoring system are estimable, this is finally a question of contract terms. The insight of (3) admonishes, to make use of reasonable control parameters, which could be a significance level α of 1e-02 and a cutoff of 0.5.

8.3.3 *Evaluating the Risk Management Scenario*

The main error measure of interest in the risk managing scenario, that is scenario B in Section 7.2.2 on page 110, is the false negative error, which is also part of the miss rate. A false positive error will cause the costs of an (afterwards) unnecessary hedging-trade. The main question in this scenario is therefore:

Question 9 How will overall costs in the risk management scenario develop?

In scenario B a false positive error will cause the costs of an unnecessary hedging-trade. A false negative prediction, however, could induce immense contract obligations. Figure 8.4 on the next page gives therefore the explicit costs of the four different cutoff levels 0.4, 0.5, 0.6, and 0.7 if false positive errors provoke one unit of costs, but false negative errors provoke costs for 0, 1, 3, or 5 units.

Answering Question 9 Inspecting Figure 8.4, again three main findings emerge:

1. Increasing the cutoff level in the area from 0.4 to 0.7 will also increase the costs, provided the costs of false negative errors exceed the costs of false positive errors.

   As it was argued before, the set of shock predictions becomes smaller when the cutoff level increases, which will also increase the costs of false negative errors, missing to predict potential shocks.

2. A low significance level will not necessarily reduce the costs. This holds on the high cutoff level 0.7, but not on the low cutoff levels 0.4 and 0.5.

   A high cutoff level in combination with a low significance level will classify those news as shock triggering, that have a high degree of conformity in the words used in the ad-hoc news (high cutoff level), but also in the measured effect of the time series of volatility estimates (low significance

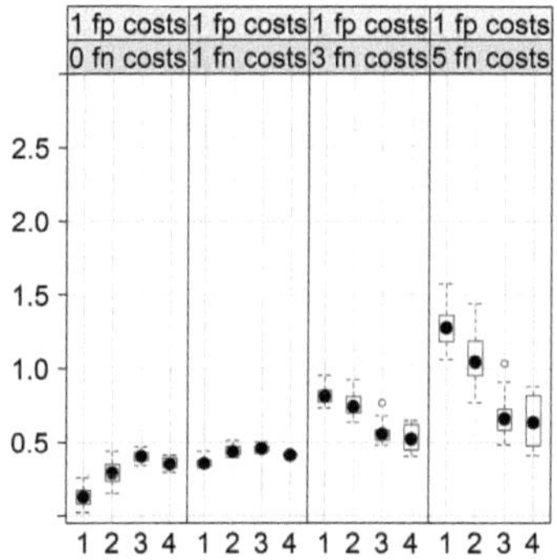

(a) Cutoff = 0.4.

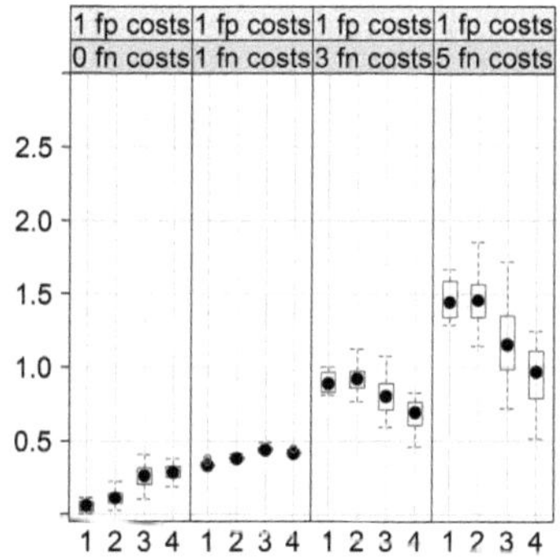

(b) Cutoff = 0.5.

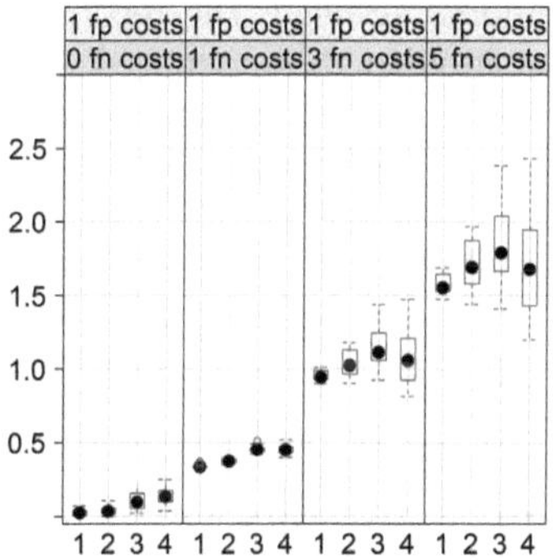

(c) Cutoff = 0.6.

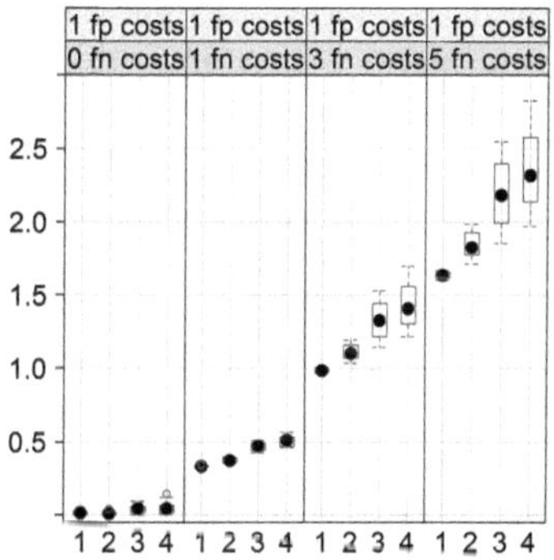

(d) Cutoff = 0.7.

Figure 8.4: Explicit costs of scenario B, a risk-management application. The costs of false positive errors (FP) are fixed with 1 unit, accounting for the afterwards unnecessary hedging trade, while the costs of false negative errors (FN) are given for 0, 1, 3, and 5 units. The rest is identical to Figure 8.3 on page 143. The ordinate gives the explicit costs, the abscissa the significance level of the Wald test in formula (5.2) on page 74, which is for 1: 1e-03, 2: 1e-02, 3: 1e-01, and 4: 2e-01. Figure 8.4a to 8.4d discriminate further the cutoff level used in the supervised learning algorithms from 0.4 to 0.7. The boxplots for each α represent the variation of the cost function in dependence of the four used supervised learning algorithms multinomial regression (MNR), stabilized linear discriminant analysis (SLDA), bagging (BGG), and random forests (RF). The results are for area-adjusted TSRV estimates of ask quotes using a Log-Idf weighted and unstemmed term-document-matrix.

level). This restrictive classification of news as shock triggering will massively increase the costs of missed shock predictions. A low cutoff level in combination with a high significance level on the other hand, would classify too many news as shock triggering, but to the low costs of unnecessary hedges.

3. The cost trend can also toggle in analogy to scenario A in scenario B.

   In contrast to scenario A, however, the extensive labelling of ad-hoc news as shock triggering news is desirable in scenario B. The effect is, that a low cutoff level in combination with a high significance level α will classify too many news as shock triggering. This will avoid high costs of contract obligations to low costs of afterwards unnecessary hedging trades.

Final Remarks The non-consistent effects of different cutoff levels, significance levels, and cost levels call for a risk conditional strategy. The recommendation for scenario B investors, holding a position in the monitored asset, is hence to make use of a low cutoff level and a moderate significance level. These are within the class of the observed significance levels α = 1e-01 and α = 2e-01 for the cutoff level 0.4 or 0.5.

Note, that if the costs of a non-hedged volatility shock are lower or equal to the costs of a superfluous hedge, then it is recommendable for the investor to make use of a high cutoff level and a low significance level. This corresponds to the situation given in scenario A.

Summary The two scenarios of Section 7.2.2 on page 110 constitute two economic situations that should be considered separately. It was found, that (1) a single evaluation measure like the F1-measure is unsuitable to account for the characteristics of the given scenarios and that (2) an explicit cost evaluation of the false positive errors and the false negative errors can be used to determine the control parameters of the monitoring system. Finally, the proposed monitoring system is an instrument to measure the profitability of any desired strategy that depends on the forecasts of volatility shocks.

9 Conclusion

The aim of this dissertation has been to provide an analytical real-time monitoring system to forecast high-frequency volatility shocks. Therefore, the system made use of quantitative and qualitative mass data where price changes in tick-time served for the quantitative data, while ad-hoc news disclosures were used for the qualitative data. The principle idea to make use of not only quantitative but also qualitative mass data was to forecast changes in the latent DGP that can not be predicted by quantitative data alone.

The main problems of this task were:

1. The measuring problem of the latent integrated volatility, which has been implemented by five competing realized volatility estimators.
2. The identification problem of the latent data generation process (DGP), which has been considered by the new Markov switching mixture model of Kömm and Küsters (2015).
3. The problem to forecast the effect of a new and unexpected ad-hoc disclosure on the measured volatility, which has been accounted for by the prediction of six competing supervised learning algorithms.
4. The evaluation problem of the proposed monitoring system, which has been specialized in an evaluation of the economic scenario under consideration.

The closure of this thesis is separated as follows: Section 9.1 will give a resume of the primary results of this thesis adjusted to the four main problems. Section 9.2 will constitute the limitations of the proposed monitor. Section 9.3, finally, will give proposals to future research in the area of text-based high-frequency volatility forecasting.

9.1 Primary Findings

The primary findings of this thesis are adjusted to the four main problems:

Problem 1 The measuring problem of the latent integrated volatility. This problem is addressed to the underlying asset prices and to the used integrated volatility estimator.

1. The influence of ask, bid, and mid quotes:

   The time series under analysis can either be the time series of mid quotes, or the separated inspection of ask and bid quotes. It was found that the usage of mid quotes will reduce the discrimination effect in the classification tasks and therefore increase the corresponding classification errors. It can hence not be advised to only make use of mid quotes. Instead, the time series relevant for the economic application should be used in any high frequency application.

2. The influence of the volatility estimator on the classification task:

   In a separate inspection of the error rates of five different volatility estimators, no evidence could be found that a simple RV estimation will not be adequate enough for the scenario of high-frequency text monitoring. The theoretical aspects to account for microstructure noise and to weaken i.i.d. assumptions of the volatility estimators, seem therefore to be of primary interest in theoretical considerations, but no evidence was found in this thesis that specialized volatility estimators give a significant advantage in the economic scenario under analysis.

Problem 2 The identification problem of the latent data generation process. This problem refers to the sampling scheme as well as to the identification of the latent DGP.

1. The influence of ultra-high frequency sampling:

   Ultra-high frequency samplings of asset quotes in transaction time generally lead to zero-inflated time series of returns. Accordingly, any estimation of the latent integrated volatility will compulsorily inherit this non-negligible characteristic. It was further found that the proportion of zeros in the estimated volatility series will rise, even if the trading frequency of the considered asset tends to be low.

2. The search for the data generation process (DGP) describing model:

   The dominating model that best describes the estimated volatility series was necessarily found to be the model that accounts explicitly for zero-inflation and autocorrelation. The used pragmatism in this context was, to estimate a sequence of nested sub-models accounting for different combinations of zero-inflation, autocorrelation, and constant terms and to determine the model as winner that best describes the latent DGP, measured by the minimal information criteria AIC. Models, that do not explicitly account for zero-inflation and autocorrelation therefore seem to be inappropriate in the given task to this thesis.

Problem 3 The problem to forecast the effect of a new and unexpected ad-hoc disclosure on the measured volatility. This problem is addressed to the text mining specifications and to the supervised learning algorithms.

1. The influence of text mining specifications: Three aspects have been found:
   a) Stemming: In accordance to the current literature it could not be found that stemming provable and systematically reduced the classification errors.
   b) Weighting schemes: Here again in accordance to the current literature it can be confirmed, that the choice of a suitable weighting scheme can reduce the classification errors. But also, that the dominating weighting scheme depends on the classification algorithm.
   c) Sparsity level: A too low level of sparsity is accompanied with too less words in the term-document-matrix, what will reduce the discriminating power of the supervised learning algorithms.
2. The dominating supervised learning algorithm:

   It was found, that all considered algorithms beat the baseline in terms of cross-validation errors, and that the multinomial regression (MNR) and the stabilized linear discriminant analysis (SLDA) return the smallest errors. The dominance of the MNR algorithm was further confirmed by statistical tests on high levels of sparsity. The calculation of the area under the curve (AUC) confirmed 5 of the 6 considered algorithms. The highest AUC values were found for the MNR and SLDA algorithms, confirming the findings of the analysis of the cross-validation errors. These two statistical algorithms are therefore advisable in the given context of this thesis.

Problem 4 The evaluation problem of the proposed monitoring system. On the one hand, this problem is addressed to the proposed monitor as a whole, but on the other hand also to the economic scenario under consideration.

1. The benefit of the proposed monitoring system.

   The evaluation of the monitoring system as a whole in combination with the evaluation of the economic scenarios under consideration showed, that the proposed system designed to forecast unexpected volatility shocks in the latent DGP, see Figure 1.2 on page 9 for the full architectural plan, can measure the additional effect of ad-hoc disclosures, discriminate harmless from risky disclosures, and discriminate the source of error to account for the considered economic scenario. It was further shown, that the discriminating power of shock causing incidents and non-shock causing incidents is in the use of words. Shock causing incidents published by ad-hoc news are clearly communicated by a vocabulary, different from the portfolio of words used to express non-shock causing ad-hoc news.

2. The necessary distinction of the economic scenario: Discriminate the scenarios A and B:

   a) It was found that investors in the simulated scenario of a trading application, this is scenario A, will benefit from sets of coinciding classifications, high cutoff levels and simultaneously low significance levels of the applied Wald test.

   b) But, in a risk management application, this is scenario B, no evidence was found that a set of coinciding classifiers brings additional benefit in contrast to a single supervised learning algorithm. The investor in a risk management scenario, however, will benefit from low cutoff levels and simultaneously high significance levels of the applied Wald test.

   All in all it was found, that a single evaluation measure as the F1-measure is not suitable to evaluate the performance of competitive supervised learning algorithms in the context of the economic scenarios presented in this thesis. Instead, it is recommendable to evaluate the scenario depending total costs of false positive and false negative errors, which depend on the control parameters (1) used supervised learning algorithm, (2) cutoff levels of the algorithms, (3) the significance level of the applied Wald test determining the labelling of the data, and (4) the sparsity level, which can be determined from the best fitting combination of the parameters (1) to (3).

9.2 Weaknesses and Limitations

However, the given list of findings can not cover the weaknesses and limitations of the proposed engineering approach. These are:

1. *The effect of ad-hoc news on the volatility shock detection rate of the proposed monitoring system is measurable, but weak.*

   The comparison of the percentages of shock reports along the recorded ad-hoc news in comparison with the percentage of shock reports along random time points in Table 8.1 on page 125 clearly shows, that the discrimination of the effect of additional ad-hoc news is possible, but in general difficult to apply.

2. *The proposed monitoring system discriminates shock causing from non-shock causing news on the basis of used words and word frequencies, but the measured differences are weak.*

   The final classification performance is better than random for most of the algorithms, but not overwhelming. The ROC graphic in Figure 7.1 on page 118 is a very fine example of this weak effect. An error-free classification would be illustrated by a graph close to the top left corner, from which the given graphs are currently far away.

   This result is not surprising. The large number of overlapping words that are used in non-shock causing as well as shock causing news, as it is illustrated in Figure 8.1 on page 128, complicates the classification task of supervised learning algorithms.

3. *The intrinsic evaluation of the costs arising from false positive and false negative errors lacks to evaluate the potential profits.*

   It was shown, that the final prediction errors can be scenario dependently minimized, but the benefit of the strategy depends not only on the costs, but also on the profit of the classification hits. The profit, however, is not evaluated in this thesis. The given evaluation is only built on the system intrinsic costs of errors. There is a good reason for this proceeding: It can not be evaluated which profit for example a volatility swap will have in the presented trading scenario, since no data is available in this analysis for the over the-counter traded volatility swaps. The same argument applies to the risk-management scenario, where the profit is to avoid losses and where the scale of the losses depends on the internal company contracts.

9.3 Proposals to Future Research

The following proposals to future research can be given:

1. *Proposals to the estimation of the integrated volatility.*

   a) An interesting approach is given with the jump robust RTSRV estimator proposed by Boudt and Zhang (2010). The estimator is designed to remove returns that exceed a user specified threshold of the returns distribution under the assumption of no jumps, see Boudt and Zhang (2010). The effect on the volatility estimation is, that a single jump in the return series will not increase the corresponding volatility estimate. The object of interest would hence be, how the jump robust RTSRV estimator effects the discrimination goodness of the overall monitoring system in competition to the presented integrated volatility estimators.

Note, that this jump robust RTSRV estimator assumes the underlying price process to follow a diffusion of the form of formula (3.10) on page 40, which was solely used to estimate the interday periodicity in this thesis. The five used integrated volatility estimators in this thesis are contrary to the RTSRV estimator built on the assumption that the price process follows an Itō process of the form (2.7) on page 18.

b) Another primary interest could be to develop new estimators that overcome the problem of missing observations, e. g. caused by non-trading hours. A first approach in this direction could be the method of Hansen and Lunde (2005) for intermittent high-frequency data. In this thesis, however, missing observations did not occur, because of (1) the transaction time sampling of asset returns on a Bloomberg terminal that guaranteed an uninterrupted data acquisition, see Section 2.3.2 on page 21, and (2) the sampling filter that guaranteed that over-night effects did not contaminate the identification of volatility shock causing ad-hoc news, see Section 5.1.1 on page 66.

2. *Proposals to the identification of the latent data generation process (DGP).*

The true data generation process can not be known. The approach used in this thesis to identify best the latent DGP of the time series of integrated volatility estimates was, to train in total a dozen of nested sub-models and to declare the model with the minimal AIC as the DGP describing model, see Section 4.3.2 on page 58. The combination of the DGP describing model with the applied Wald test of formula (5.2) on page 74 allowed the separation of volatility shock causing incidents from non-shock causing incidents.

a) An interesting approach would be, to discriminate volatility shock causing from non-shock causing incidents not by an analysis of structural breaks in the DGP, but by an analysis of an additional jump component $\kappa_t dJ_t$ in the data generation process of the form of formula (3.10) on page 40, see e. g. Andersen et al. (2007) and e. g. Busch et al. (2011) for first approaches in that direction. Note, however, that testing for significant jumps in the continuous model of formula (3.10) would miss to account for the substantial number of discrete zeros which have been observed in the given data, see Section 4.1.3 on page 50, and hence miss to account for the fact of zero-inflation.

b) Furthermore, it could be recommendable to analyse the effects of higher orders of autocorrelation on the identification of the latent DGP, as the proposed engineering approach in this thesis only accounts for first order autocorrelation. It was, however, not to be found that higher order autocorrelation will be significant in ultra-high-frequent transaction time samples. But this finding could be different for samplings in calendar time, business time, or tick time, see Section 2.3.1 on page 20.

3. *Proposals to the classification of ad-hoc news in volatility shock and non-shock triggering incidents.*

   The approach implemented in this thesis makes use of term-document-matrices and hence the total number of words occurring in shock causing and non-shock causing incidents.

   a) This approach could be extended making additional use of sentiment analysis. This opinion mining approach tries to extract subjective information and to determine the overall attitude of the writer to a given text. For example, a simple extension would be to combine a set of pre-defined words with a positive or negative attitude. The frequency of positive or negative terms in the term-documents-matrix could then be used to determine the suspected attitude of the hole document.

      Sentiment analysis could be of special importance when the documents under analysis miss to be clear and unequivocal, for example ironic or sarcastic texts. Ad-hoc news are generally free of these language tools, but a monitoring of, for example an online forum of asset traders, would be quite different. An general introduction to sentiment analysis is for example given in Haddi et al. (2013).

   b) An iterative enlargement of the stop-words list with words, that are identified to appear nearly equally in shock causing and non-shock causing incidents, could further improve the discriminating power of the classification algorithms. An example of this effect is given in the heat map in Figure 8.1 on page 128. Word 22 in Figure 8.1a corresponds to word 100 in Figure 8.1b. This word appeared nearly equally in both, shock causing and non-shock causing documents. The contribution of this word to the discrimination power is therefore in the best case low.

A Software Libraries

A.1 R

The following list reports the author(s), the last requested library version, and the publication date of the used R-libraries in this thesis. All libraries are used in the 64-bit implementation of R-2.15.2. The library RBloomberg was downloaded from http://findata.org/rbloomberg/. The remaining libraries were all downloaded from http://cran.r-project.org/.

Note, that the packages realized and RTAQ were removed from the CRAN repository. But, formerly available versions can normally be obtained from the CRAN archive.

caTools	J. Tuszynski. Several basic utility functions including LogitBoost classifier, 1.16, 2013.
ggplot2	H. Wickham and W. Chang. An implementation of the Grammar of Graphics, 0.9.3.1, 2013.
ipred	A. Peters, T. Hothorn, B. D. Ripley, T. Therneau, and B. Atkinson. Improved predictive models by indirect classification and bagging, 0.9-2, 2013.
lattice	D. Sarkar. High-level data visualization system, 0.20-24, 2013.
MASS	B. Ripley, B. Venables, D. M. Bates, K. Hornik, A. Gebhardt, and D. Firth. Support Functions and Datasets for Venables and Ripley's "Modern Applied Statistics with S", Venables and Ripley (2004), 7.3-29, 2013.
maxLik	O. Toomet and A. Henningsen. Tools for Maximum Likelihood Estimation, 1.2-0, 2013.
maxent	T. P. Jurka and Y. Tsuruoka. Low-memory Multinomial Logistic Regression with Support for Text Classification, 1.3.3.1, 2013.
nnet	B. Ripley. Software for feed-forward neural networks with a single hidden layer, and for multinomial log-linear models, 7.3-7, 2013.

outliers — L. Komsta. A collection of some tests commonly used for identifying outliers, 0.14, 2011.

randomForest — A. Liaw and M. Wiener. Classification and regression based on a forest of trees using random inputs, 4.6-7, 2012.

RBloomberg — A. Nelson. Fetching data from the Bloomberg financial data application, 0.4-144, 2010.

realized — S. Payseur. Realized variance, covariance and correlation estimators, 1.0.1, 2012.

reshape2 — H. Wickham. Flexibly reshape data, 1.4, 2014.

RMySQL — D. A. James and S. DebRoy. Database interface and MySQL driver for R, 0.9-3, 2012.

ROCR — T. Sing, O. Sander, N. Beerenwinkel, and T. Lengauer. Visualizing the performance of scoring classifiers, 1.0-5, 2013.

rpart — T. Therneau, B. Atkinson, and B. Ripley. Recursive partitioning and regression trees, 4.1-3, 2013.

RTAQ — K. Boudt and J. Cornelissen. Tools for the analysis of trades and quotes in R, 0.2, 2012.

RTextTools — T. P. Jurka, L. Collingwood, A. E. Boydstun, E. Grossman, and W. van Atteveldt. Automatic Text Classification via Supervised Learning, 1.4.1, 2013.

SnowballC — M. Bouchet-Valat. Snowball stemmers based on the C libstemmer UTF-8 library, 0.5, 2013.

snowfall — J. Knaus. Easier cluster computing (based on snow), 1.84-4, 2013.

timeDate — D. Würtz, Y. Chalabi, and M. Mächler. Chronological and Calendar Objects, 3010.98, 2013.

timeSeries — D. Würtz and Y. Chalabi. Financial Time Series Objects, 3010.97, 2013.

tm — I. Feinerer and K. Hornik. A framework for text mining applications within R, 0.5-9.1, 2013.

TTR — J. Ulrich. Functions and data to construct technical trading rules with R, 0.22-0, 2013.

XML D. T. Lang. Tools for parsing and generating XML within R and S-Plus, 3.98-11, 2013.

xts J. A. Ryan and J. M. Ulrich. Uniform handling of R's different time-based data classes, 0.9-7, 2013.

A.2 C++

The following list reports the author(s) and the last requested library version with publication date of the used C++-libraries.

libsvm C.-C. Chang, C.-J. Lin. Library for Support Vector Machines, 2.88, 2013.

maxent Y. Tsuruoka. Library for maximum entropy classification, 3.0, 2011.

Bibliography

S. Abe. *Support vector machines for pattern classification*. Advances in pattern recognition. Springer, London, 2nd edition, 2010. (Cited on page 92.)

C. C. Aggarwal and C. Zhai. A Survey of Text Classification Algorithms. In C. C. Aggarwal and C. Zhai, editors, *Mining text data*, pages 163–222. Springer, New York, 2012. (Cited on page 93.)

Y. Aït-Sahalia and J. Jacod. Is Brownian motion necessary to model high frequency data. *Annals of Statistics*, 38(5):3093–3128, 2010. (Cited on page 15.)

Y. Aït-Sahalia and L. Mancini. Out of sample forecasts of quadratic variation. *Journal of Econometrics*, 147(1):17–33, 2008. (Cited on page 38.)

Y. Aït-Sahalia, P. A. Mykland, and L. Zhang. How Often to Sample a Continuous-Time Process in the Presence of Market Microstructure Noise. *Review of Financial Studies*, 18(2):351–416, 2005. (Cited on page 35.)

Y. Aït-Sahalia, P. A. Mykland, L. Zhang, and F. Hall. Ultra high frequency volatility estimation with dependent microstructure noise. *Journal of Econometrics*, 160(1):160–175, 2011. (Cited on pages 31, 37, 38, and 39.)

H. Akaike. Likelihood of a model and information criteria. *Annals of Applied Econometrics*, 16(1):3–14, 1981. (Cited on page 68.)

T. G. Andersen and T. P. Bollerslev. Intraday periodicity and volatility persistence in financial markets. *Journal of Empirical Finance*, 4(2-3):115–158, 1997. (Cited on pages 42 and 43.)

T. G. Andersen, T. Bollerslev, F. X. Diebold, and P. Labys. Modeling and Forecasting Realized Volatility. *Econometrica*, 71(2):579–625, 2003. (Cited on page 34.)

T. G. Andersen, T. Bollerslev, and F. X. Diebold. Roughing it up: Including jump components in the measurement, modeling and forecasting of return volatility. *The Review of Economics and Statistics*, 89(4):701–720, 2007. (Cited on pages 40, 41, 42, and 152.)

L. Bachelier. *Théorie de la spéculation*. Gauthier-Villars, Paris, 1st edition, 1900. Translation into English by D. May: Theory of Speculation. Annales scientifiques de l'École Normale Supérieure, Sér. 3, 17 (1900), p. 21-86. (Cited on page 15.)

K. Back. Asset pricing for general processes. *Journal of Mathematical Economics*, 20(4):371–395, 1991. (Cited on page 16.)

F. M. Bandi and J. R. Russell. Microstructure noise, realized variance, and optimal sampling. *Review of Economic Studies*, 75(2):339–369, 2008. (Cited on page 34.)

A. Barazzetti, F. Cecconi, and R. Mastronardi. Financial forecasts based on analysis of textual news sources: Some empirical evidence. In S. Leitner and F. Wall, editors, *Artificial economics and self organization*, pages 133–145. Springer, Cham, 2014. (Cited on page 7.)

O. E. Barndorff-Nielsen and N. Shephard. Power and Bipower Variation with Stochastic Volatility and Jumps. *Journal of Financial Econometrics*, 2(1):1–37, 2004. (Cited on pages 41 and 42.)

O. E. Barndorff-Nielsen and N. Shephard. Econometrics of testing for jumps in financial economics using bipower variation. *Journal of Financial Econometrics*, 4(1):1–30, 2006. (Cited on page 41.)

H. Bauer. *Probability theory*, volume 23 of *De Gruyter studies in mathematics*. de Gruyter, Berlin, 1st edition, 2011 printing edition, 2011. (Cited on page 16.)

L. Bauwens, C. M. Hafner, and S. Laurent. Volatility Models. In L. Bauwens, C. M. Hafner, and S. Laurent, editors, *Handbook of Volatility Models and Their Applications*, volume 3 of *Wiley handbooks in financial engineering and econometrics*, pages 1–48. John Wiley & Sons, Hoboken, 2012. (Cited on pages 12 and 13.)

C. H. Beck. *Aktuelle Wirtschaftsgesetze*. Beck'sche Textausgaben. Beck, München, 15th edition, 2014. (Cited on page 76.)

M. W. Berry and J. Kogan. *Text mining: Applications and theory*. Wiley, Chichester, 1st edition, 2010. (Cited on page 77.)

F. Black. Noise. *The Journal of Finance*, 41(3):529–543, 1986. (Cited on page 6.)

F. Black and M. Scholes. The Pricing of Options and Corporate Liabilities. *The Journal of Political Economy*, 81(3):637–654, 1973. (Cited on page 11.)

A. Bode, H.-J. Bungartz, H.-G. Hegering, and D. Kranzlmüller. The Leibniz Supercomputing Centre. München, 2012. (Cited on page 64.)

T. P. Bollerslev. Generalized autoregressive conditional heteroskedasticity. *Journal of Econometrics*, 31(3):307–327, 1986. (Cited on page 13.)

J. Boudoukh, R. Feldman, S. Kogan, and M. Richardson. Which news moves stock prices? A textual analysis. Cambridge, 2013. (Cited on page 7.)

K. Boudt and J. Zhang. Jump robust two time scale covariance estimation and realized volatility budgets. Leuven, 2010. (Cited on page 151.)

K. Boudt, C. Croux, and S. Laurent. Robust estimation of intraweek periodicity in volatility and jump detection. *Journal of Empirical Finance*, 18(2):353–367, 2011. (Cited on pages 42, 43, and 44.)

K. Boudt, J. Cornelissen, C. Croux, and S. Laurent. Nonparametric Tests for Intraday Jumps: Impact of Periodicity and Microstructure Noise. In L. Bauwens, C. M. Hafner, and S. Laurent, editors, *Handbook of Volatility Models and Their Applications*, volume 3 of *Wiley handbooks in financial engineering and econometrics*, pages 447–464. John Wiley & Sons, Hoboken, 2012. (Cited on page 42.)

Č. Božić. *Applications of intelligent systems for news analytics in finance*. PhD thesis, Karlsruher Institut für Technologie, Karlsruhe, 2013. (Cited on page 7.)

A. P. Bradley. The use of the area under the ROC curve in the evaluation of machine learning algorithms. *Pattern Recognition*, 30(7):1145–1159, 1997. (Cited on page 117.)

L. Breiman. Bagging Predictors. *Machine Learning*, 24(2):123–140, 1996. (Cited on page 91.)

L. Breiman. Arcing Classifiers. *The Annals of Statistics*, 26(3):801–849, 1998. (Cited on page 91.)

L. Breiman. Random Forests. *Machine Learning*, 45(1):5–32, 2001. (Cited on page 92.)

L. Breiman, J. H. Friedman, R. A. Olshen, and C. J. Stone. *Classification and regression trees*. Chapman & Hall, New York, 1st edition, 1993. (Cited on pages 91 and 92.)

K. P. Burnham and D. R. Anderson. *Model selection and multimodel inference: A practical information-theoretic approach*. Springer, New York, 2nd edition, 2010. (Cited on page 69.)

T. Busch, B. J. Christensen, and M. Ø. Nielsen. The role of implied volatility in forecasting future realized volatility and jumps in foreign exchange, stock, and bond markets. *Journal of Econometrics*, 160(1):48–57, 2011. (Cited on page 152.)

P. Carr and R. Lee. Volatility derivatives. *Annual Review of Financial Economics*, 1(1):319–339, 2009. (Cited on page 2.)

P. F. Christoffersen and F. X. Diebold. How relevant is volatility forecasting for financial risk management? *The Review of Economics and Statistics*, 82(1):12–22, 2000. (Cited on page 4.)

K. L. Chung and R. J. Williams. *Introduction to Stochastic Integration*. Modern Birkhäuser Classics. Springer, New York, 2nd edition, 2014. (Cited on page 17.)

L. Collingwood and J. Wilkerson. Tradeoffs in Accuracy and Efficiency in Supervised Learning Methods. *Journal of Information Technology & Politics*, 9(3): 298–318, 2012. (Cited on page 135.)

R. Cont. Empirical properties of asset returns: stylized facts and statistical issues. *Quantitative Finance*, 1(2):223–236, 2001. (Cited on page 29.)

F. Corsi, F. Audrino, and R. Renò. HAR Modeling for Realized Volatility Forecasting. In L. Bauwens, C. M. Hafner, and S. Laurent, editors, *Handbook of Volatility Models and Their Applications*, volume 3 of *Wiley handbooks in financial engineering and econometrics*, pages 363–382. John Wiley & Sons, Hoboken, 2012. (Cited on page 30.)

D. L. Davies and D. W. Bouldin. A Cluster Separation Measure. *Pattern Analysis and Machine Intelligence*, 1(2):224–227, 1979. (Cited on page 85.)

K. Demeterfi, E. Derman, M. Kamal, and J. Zou. A guide to volatility and variance swaps. *The Journal of Derivatives*, 6(4):9–32, 1999. (Cited on page 2.)

J. Demšar. Statistical comparisons of classifiers over multiple data sets. *Journal of Machine Learning Research*, 7(1):1–30, 2006. (Cited on pages 105 and 106.)

J. E. Dennis and R. B. Schnabel. *Numerical methods for unconstrained optimization and nonlinear equations*, volume 16 of *Classics in applied mathematics*. Society for Industrial and Applied Mathematics, Philadelphia, 1st edition, 1996. (Cited on page 63.)

M. Dettling and P. L. Bühlmann. Boosting for tumor classification with gene expression data. *Bioinformatics*, 19(9):1061–1069, 2003. (Cited on page 91.)

G. Dougherty. *Pattern recognition and classification: An introduction*. Springer, New York, 1st edition, 2013. (Cited on page 85.)

M. Dowideit and S. Ertinger. Maschinen haben die Börse übernommen. *Handelsblatt*, April 24th, 2013. (Cited on page 4.)

N. Duan, W. G. Manning, C. N. Morris, and J. P. Newhouse. A comparison of alternative models for the demand for medical care. *Journal of Business and Economic Statistics*, 1(2):115–126, 1983. (Cited on page 54.)

R. O. Duda, P. E. Harting, and D. G. Stork. *Pattern Classification*. Wiley, New Delhi, 2nd edition, 2006. (Cited on pages 84, 86, and 92.)

S. T. Dumais. Improving the retrieval of information from external sources. *Behavior Research Methods, Instruments, & Computers*, 23(2):229–236, 1991. (Cited on page 79.)

J. C. Dunn. A fuzzy relative of the ISODATA process and its use in detecting compact well-separated clusters. *Journal of Cybernetics*, 3(3):32–57, 1973. (Cited on page 85.)

F. Eder. Maulkorb für die Ratingagenturen: Bonität von EU-Ländern soll nur noch drei Mal im Jahr veröffentlicht werden. *Die Welt kompakt*, January 17th, 2013. (Cited on page 2.)

C. T. Ekstrøm. *The R primer*. Taylor & Francis, Boca Raton, 1st edition, 2012. (Cited on page 76.)

R. Engle. Risk and Volatility: Econometric Models and Financial Practice. *The American Economic Review*, 94(3):405–420, 2004. (Cited on page 1.)

R. F. Engle. Autoregressive Conditional Heteroscedasticity with Estimates of the Variance of United Kingdom Inflation. *Econometrica*, 50(4):987–1007, 1982. (Cited on page 13.)

R. F. Engle and A. J. Patton. What good is a volatility model? *Quantitative Finance*, 1(2):237–245, 2001. (Cited on page 30.)

D. N. Esch. Non-normality facts and fallacies. *Journal of Investment Management*, 8(1):49–61, 2010. (Cited on page 51.)

A. Escribano and R. Pascual. Asymmetries in bid and ask responses to innovations in the trading process. *Empirical Economics*, 30(4):913–946, 2005. (Cited on page 132.)

B. S. Everitt. *Cluster analysis*. Wiley series in probability and statistics. Wiley, Chichester, 5th edition, 2011. (Cited on page 85.)

B. S. Everitt and D. J. Hand. *Finite mixture distributions*. Monographs on applied probability and statistics. Chapman and Hall, London, 1st edition, 1981. (Cited on page 55.)

T. Fawcett. An introduction to ROC analysis. *Pattern Recognition Letters*, 27(8): 861–874, 2006. (Cited on page 117.)

R. Feldman and J. Sanger. *The text mining handbook: Advanced approaches in analyzing unstructured data*. Cambridge University Press, New York, 1st edition, 2nd printing edition, 2008. (Cited on page 77.)

R. A. Fisher. The use of multiple measurements in taxonomic problems. *Annals of Eugenics*, 7(7):179–188, 1936. (Cited on pages 89 and 90.)

K. R. French, G. W. Schwert, and R. F. Stambaugh. Expected stock returns and volatility. *Journal of Financial Economics*, 19(1):3–29, 1987. (Cited on page 13.)

J. H. Friedman, T. Hastie, and R. Tibshirani. Additive logistic regression: a statistical view of boosting. *The Annals of Statistics*, 28(2):337–407, 2000. (Cited on page 91.)

W. H. Greene. *Econometric Analysis*. Prentice-Hall, New Jersey, 5th edition, 2003. (Cited on pages 67 and 73.)

U. Grenander and M. Rosenblatt. *Statistical analysis of stationary time series*. Chelsea, New York, 2nd edition, 1984. (Cited on page 32.)

J. E. Griffin and R. C. A. Oomen. Sampling returns for realized variance calculations: Tick time or transaction time? *Econometric Reviews*, 27(1-3):230–253, 2008. (Cited on pages 20 and 21.)

S. S. Groth and J. Muntermann. An intraday market risk management approach based on textual analysis. *Decision support systems*, 50(4):680–691, 2011. (Cited on page 7.)

F. E. Grubbs. Sample Criteria for Testing Outlying Observations. *The Annals of Mathematical Statistics*, 21(1):27–58, 1950. (Cited on page 24.)

F. E. Grubbs. Procedures for Detecting Outlying Observations in Samples. *Technometrics*, 11(1):1–21, 1969. (Cited on page 24.)

F. E. Grubbs and G. Beck. Extension of Sample Sizes and Percentage Points for Significance Tests of Outlying Observations. *Technometrics*, 14(4):847–854, 1972. (Cited on pages 25 and 26.)

E. Haddi, X. Liu, and Y. Shi. The Role of Text Pre-Processing in Sentiment Analysis. *Procedia Computer Science*, 17(1):26–32, 2013. (Cited on page 153.)

D. B. Hall. Zero-inflated poisson and binomial regression with random effects: A case study. *Biometrics*, 56(4):1030–1039, 2000. (Cited on page 55.)

D. J. Hand. *Construction and assessment of classification rules*. Wiley series in probability and statistics. Wiley, Chichester, 1st edition, 1997. (Cited on page 117.)

D. J. Hand and R. J. Till. A Simple Generalisation of the Area Under the ROC Curve for Multiple Class Classification Problems. *Machine Learning*, 45(2): 171–186, 2001. (Cited on page 118.)

E. J. Hannan and B. G. Quinn. The Determination of the Order of an Autoregression. *Journal of the Royal Statistical Society: Series B (Statistical Methodology)*, 41(2):190–195, 1979. (Cited on page 69.)

P. R. Hansen and A. Lunde. A realized variance for the whole day based on intermittent high-frequency data. *Journal of Financial Econometrics*, 3(4):525–554, 2005. (Cited on page 152.)

J. M. Harrison and S. R. Pliska. Martingales and Stochastic Integrals in the Theory of Continuous Trading. *Stochastic Processes and their Applications*, 11 (3):215–260, 1981. (Cited on page 19.)

J. Hasbrouck. The dynamics of discrete bid and ask quotes. *The Journal of Finance*, 54(6):2109–2142, 1999. (Cited on page 132.)

T. Hastie, R. Tibshirani, and J. H. Friedman. *The Elements of Statistical Learning*. Springer Series in Statistics. Springer, Dordrecht, 2nd edition, 5th printing edition, 2011. (Cited on pages 88, 89, 90, and 91.)

Y. Hochberg. A sharper Bonferroni procedure for multiple tests of significance. *Biometrika*, 75(4):800–802, 1988. (Cited on page 26.)

Y. Hochberg and A. C. Tamhane. *Multiple comparison procedures*. Wiley series in probability and mathematical statistics: Applied probability and statistics. Wiley, New York, 1st edition, 1987. (Cited on page 26.)

S. Holm. A simple sequentially rejective multiple test procedure. *Scandinavian journal of statistics*, 6(2):65–70, 1979. (Cited on page 26.)

C. M. Hurvich and C.-L. Tsai. Regression and Time Series Model Selection in Small Samples. *Biometrica*, 76(2):297–307, 1989. (Cited on page 69.)

S. M. Iacus. *Simulation and Inference for Stochastic Differential Equations: With R Examples*. Springer Series in Statistics. Springer, New York, 1st edition, 2008. (Cited on page 15.)

S. M. Iacus. *Option pricing and estimation of financial models with R*. Wiley, Chichester, 1st edition, 2011. (Cited on pages 15 and 17.)

J. E. Jackson. *A user's guide to principal components*. Wiley, New York, 1st edition, 3rd printing edition, 2005. (Cited on page 92.)

N. Japkowicz and M. Shah. *Evaluating learning algorithms: A classification perspective*. Cambridge Univ. Press, Cambridge, 1st edition, 2011. (Cited on pages 99, 110, and 112.)

K. S. Jones. A statistical interpretation of term specificity and its application in retrieval. *Journal of Documentation*, 28(1):11–21, 1972. (Cited on page 79.)

B. Jørgensen. Exponential Dispersion Models. *Journal of the Royal Statistical Society: Series B (Statistical Methodology)*, 49(2):127–162, 1987. (Cited on page 54.)

T. Jurka. maxent: An R Package for Low-memory Multinomial Logistic Regression with Support for Semi-automated Text Classification. *The R Journal*, 4(1): 56–59, 2012. (Cited on page 88.)

A. T. Kalai and R. A. Servedio. Boosting in the presence of noise. *Journal of Computer and System Sciences*, 71(3):266–290, 2005. (Cited on page 91.)

P. S. Kalev, W.-M. Liu, P. K. Pham, and E. Jarnecic. Public information arrival and volatility of intraday stock returns. *Journal of Banking & Finance*, 28(6): 1441–1467, 2004. (Cited on page 124.)

I. Karatzas and S. E. Shreve. *Brownian motion and stochastic calculus*, volume 113 of *Graduate texts in mathematics*. Springer, New York, 2nd edition, 2007. (Cited on page 19.)

W. J. Kennedy and J. E. Gentle. *Statistical computing*, volume 33 of *Statistics*. Dekker, New York, 1st edition, 1980. (Cited on page 64.)

H. Kömm and U. Küsters. Forecasting zero-inflated price changes with a Markov switching mixture model for autoregressive and heteroscedastic time series. *International Journal of Forecasting*, 31(3):598–608, 2015. (Cited on pages 6, 8, 47, 53, 55, 56, 58, 59, 61, 63, 72, and 147.)

U. Kruger and L. Xie. *Statistical monitoring of complex multivariate processes: With applications in industrial process control*. Statistics in practice. Wiley, Chichester, 1st edition, 2012. (Cited on page 123.)

U. Küsters. *Hierarchische Mittelwert- und Kovarianzstrukturmodelle mit nichtmetrischen endogenen Variablen*, volume 31 of *Arbeiten zur angewandten Statistik*. Physica, Heidelberg, 1987. (Cited on page 62.)

U. Küsters, J. Thyson, and C. Becker. Monitoring von Prognoseverfahren. In P. Mertens and S. Rässler, editors, *Prognoserechnung*, pages 383–422. Physica-Verlag, Heidelberg, 2012. (Cited on page 123.)

D. Lambert. Zero-inflated poisson regression, with an application to defects in manufacturing. *Technometrics*, 34(1):1–14, 1992. (Cited on page 55.)

J. Läuter. *Stabile multivariate Verfahren: Diskriminanzanalyse, Regressionsanalyse, Faktoranalyse*, volume 81 of *Mathematische Lehrbücher und Monographien. II. Abteilung, Mathematische Monographien*. Akademie Verlag, Berlin, 1st edition, 1992. (Cited on page 90.)

J. Läuter, E. Glimm, and S. Kropf. Multivariate tests based on left spherically distributed linear scores. *The Annals of Statistics*, 26(5):1972–1988, 1998. (Cited on pages 89 and 90.)

N. Lavesson. *Evaluation and analysis of supervised learning algorithms and classifiers*. Blekinge Institute of Technology licentiate dissertation series. Blekinge Institute of Technology, Karlskrona, 1st edition, 2006. (Cited on page 100.)

P. M. Long and R. A. Servedio. Random classification noise defeats all convex potential boosters. *Machine Learning*, 78(3):287–304, 2010. (Cited on page 91.)

L. Loss, T. Paredes, and J. Seligman. *Fundamentals of securities regulation*. Wolters Kluwer Law & Business, Austin, 5th edition, 2011. (Cited on page 22.)

C. D. Manning and H. Schütze. *Foundations of statistical natural language processing*. MIT Press, Cambridge, 6th edition, 2003. (Cited on page 75.)

Y. Mansour. Boosting Using Branching Programs. *Journal of Computer and System Sciences*, 64(1):103–112, 2002. (Cited on page 91.)

A. Marazzi and V. J. Yohai. Adaptively truncated maximum likelihood regression with asymmetric errors. *Journal of Statistical Planning and Inference*, 122 (1–2):271–291, 2004. (Cited on page 44.)

R. Martin and R. Zamar. Bias robust estimation of scale. *The Annals of Statistics*, 21(2):991–1017, 1993. (Cited on page 44.)

M. McAleer and M. C. Medeiros. Realized Volatility: A Review. *Econometric Reviews*, 27(1):10–45, 2008. (Cited on page 32.)

P. McCullagh. Regression models for ordinal data. *Journal of the Royal Statistical Society: Series B (Statistical Methodology)*, 42(2):109–142, 1980. (Cited on page 54.)

G. J. McLachlan and D. Peel. *Finite Mixture Models*. Wiley series in probability and statistics. Wiley, New York, 1st edition, 2000. (Cited on pages 53 and 55.)

G. J. McLachlan, K.-A. Do, and C. Ambroise. *Analyzing microarray gene expression data*. Wiley, Hoboken, 1st edition, 2004. (Cited on page 100.)

R. C. Merton. Option pricing when underlying stock returns are discontinuous. *Journal of Financial Economics*, 3(1-2):125–144, 1976. (Cited on page 40.)

R. C. Merton. On estimating the expected return on the market: An exploratory investigation. *Journal of Financial Economics*, 8(4):323–361, 1980. (Cited on page 14.)

V. Milea. *News analytics for financial decision support*. PhD thesis, Erasmus Research Institute of Management, Rotterdam, 2013. (Cited on page 7.)

Y. Min and A. Agresti. Modeling Nonnegative Data with Clumping at Zero: A Survey. *Journal of the Iranian Statistical Society*, 1(1-2):7–33, 2002. (Cited on page 53.)

M. A. Mittermayer and G. F. Knolmayer. Text Mining Systems for Predicting Market Response to News. Lisbon, 2007. (Cited on page 6.)

M. Mohri, A. Rostamizadeh, and A. Talwalkar. *Foundations of machine learning*. Adaptive computation and machine learning. MIT Press, Cambridge, 1st edition, 2012. (Cited on pages 99, 100, and 101.)

J. Mullahy. Specification and testing of some modified count data models. *Journal of Econometrics*, 33(3):341–365, 1986. (Cited on page 54.)

J. Muntermann and A. Guettler. Intraday stock price effects of ad hoc disclosures: The German case. *Journal of International Financial Markets, Institutions & Money*, 17(1):1–24, 2007. (Cited on pages 124 and 125.)

P. Nakov, E. Valchanova, and G. Angelova. Towards deeper understanding of the LSA performance. In N. Nicolov, editor, *Recent advances in natural language processing III*, volume 260 of *Amsterdam studies in the theory and history of linguistic science Series IV*, pages 297–306. Benjamins, Amsterdam, 2004. (Cited on page 82.)

R. C. A. Oomen. Properties of bias-corrected realized variance under alternative sampling schemes. *Journal of Financial Econometrics*, 3(4):555–577, 2005. (Cited on page 20.)

R. C. A. Oomen. Properties of realized variance under alternative sampling schemes. *Journal of Business and Economic Statistics*, 24(2):219–237, 2006. (Cited on pages 20 and 21.)

A. J. Patton. Volatility forecast comparison using imperfect volatility proxies: Realized Volatility. *Journal of Econometrics*, 160(1):246–256, 2011. (Cited on page 20.)

J. Petring and T. Bayer. Deutsche Börse hofiert Algo-Trader: Neues Angebot erleichtert vollautomatischen Computerhandel mit Staatsanleihen. *Financial Times Deutschland*, September 9th, 2011. (Cited on pages 2 and 50.)

M. J. Pieper. *Advanced text mining methods for the financial markets and forecasting of intraday volatility*. PhD thesis, Karlsruher Institut für Technologie, Karlsruhe, 2011. (Cited on page 7.)

M. F. Porter. An algorithm for suffix stripping. *Program*, 14(3):130–137, 1980. (Cited on page 77.)

P. E. Protter. *Stochastic Integration and Differential Equations*, volume 21 of *Stochastic Modelling and Applied Probability*. Springer, Berlin, 2nd edition, 3rd printing edition, 2005. (Cited on pages 16, 33, and 38.)

M. Rosenblatt and R. A. Davis. *Selected works of Murray Rosenblatt*. Selected works in probability and statistics. Springer, New York, 1st edition, 2011. (Cited on page 32.)

P. Rousseeuw and A. Leroy. A robust scale estimator based on the shortest half. *Statistica Neerlandica*, 42(2):103–116, 1988. (Cited on page 44.)

R. E. Schapire. The strength of weak learnability. *Machine Learning*, 5(2):197–227, 1990. (Cited on page 90.)

G. Schwarz. Estimating the Dimension of a Model. *The Annals of Statistics*, 6(2): 461–464, 1978. (Cited on page 69.)

R. J. Serfling. *Approximation theorems of mathematical statistics*. Wiley series in probability and statistics. Wiley, New York, 1st edition, 1980. (Cited on page 62.)

D. J. Sheskin. *Handbook of parametric and nonparametric statistical procedures*. CRC Press, Boca Raton, 2nd edition, 2000. (Cited on pages 105, 106, 107, and 108.)

W. Stefansky. Rejecting Outliers by Maximum Normed Residual. *Technometrics*, 14(2):469–479, 1972. (Cited on page 25.)

S. J. Taylor. Financial returns modelled by the product of two stochastic processes: A study of daily sugar prices, 1961-79. In O. D. Anderson, editor, *Time series analysis*, volume 1, pages 203–226. North-Holland, Amsterdam, 1982. (Cited on pages 12 and 13.)

S. J. Taylor and X. Xu. The incremental volatility information in one million foreign exchange quotations. *Journal of Empirical Finance*, 4(4):317–340, 1997. (Cited on pages 42 and 43.)

J. Tobin. Estimation of relationships for limited dependent variables. *Econometrica*, 26(1):24–36, 1958. (Cited on pages 53 and 54.)

C. J. van Rijsbergen. *Information retrieval*. Butterworths, London, 2nd edition, 1979. (Cited on pages 112 and 114.)

W. N. Venables and B. D. Ripley. *Modern applied statistics with S*. Statistics and computing. Springer, New York, 4th edition, 5th printing edition, 2004. (Cited on pages 89 and 155.)

J. E. Walsh. Some non-parametric tests of whether the largest observations of a set are too large or to small. *The Annals of Mathematical Statistics*, 21(4): 583–592, 1950. (Cited on pages 23 and 26.)

J. E. Walsh. Correction to "Some non-parametric tests of whether the largest observations of a set are too large or too small". *The Annals of Mathematical Statistics*, 24(1):134–135, 1953. (Cited on page 23.)

J. E. Walsh. Large sample nonparametric rejection of outlying observations. *Annals of the Institute of Statistical Mathematics*, 10(3):223–232, 1959. (Cited on page 27.)

A. R. Webb and K. D. Copsey. *Statistical pattern recognition*. Wiley, Hoboken, 3rd edition, 2011. (Cited on page 83.)

S. M. Weiss, N. Indurkhya, and T. Zhang. *Fundamentals of predictive text mining*. Texts in computer science. Springer, London, 1st edition, 2010. (Cited on pages 76 and 115.)

F. Wilcoxon. Individual comparisons by ranking methods. *Biometrics Bulletin*, 1 (6):80–83, 1945. (Cited on page 106.)

P. Willett. The Porter stemming algorithm: then and now. *Program*, 40(3):219–223, 2006. (Cited on page 78.)

R. Winkelmann. *Econometric analysis of count data*. Springer, Berlin, 5th edition, 2008. (Cited on page 54.)

J. Wu. *Advances in K-means Clustering: A Data Mining Thinking*. Springer Theses, Recognizing Outstanding Ph.D. Research. Springer, Berlin, 1st edition, 2012. (Cited on page 92.)

J. Zhang. *Visualization for information retrieval*. The information retrieval series. Springer, Berlin, 1st edition, 2008. (Cited on page 137.)

L. Zhang. Efficient estimation of stochastic volatility using noisy observations: A multi-scale approach. *Bernoulli*, 12(6):1019–1043, 2006. (Cited on page 39.)

L. Zhang, P. A. Mykland, and Y. Aït-Sahalia. A tale of two time scales. *Journal of the American Statistical Association*, 100(472):1394–1411, 2005. (Cited on pages 35, 36, 37, and 38.)

M. Y. Zhang, J. R. Russell, and R. S. Tsay. Determinants of bid and ask quotes and implications for the cost of trading. *Journal of Empirical Finance*, 15(4): 656–678, 2008. (Cited on page 132.)

Z.-H. Zhou. *Ensemble methods: Foundations and algorithms*. Chapman & Hall/CRC machine learning & pattern recognition series. CRC Press, Boca Raton, 1st edition, 2012. (Cited on page 90.)

MIX
Papier aus verantwortungsvollen Quellen
Paper from responsible sources
FSC® C105338

If you have any concerns about our products,
you can contact us on
ProductSafety@springernature.com

In case Publisher is established outside the EU,
the EU authorized representative is:
Springer Nature Customer Service Center GmbH
Europaplatz 3, 69115 Heidelberg, Germany

Printed by Libri Plureos GmbH
in Hamburg, Germany